CONFIDENT
IDENTITY

CONFIDENT IDENTITY

Christian Strategies to Forget Who You Aren't and Discover Who You Really Are

MATT PAVLIK MA, LPCC-S

BRINGING YOUR POTENTIAL TO LIGHT

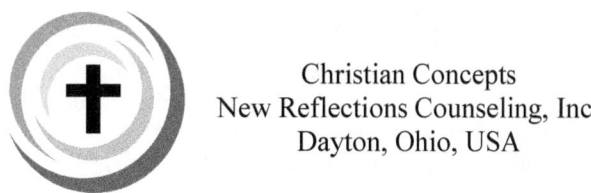

Christian Concepts
New Reflections Counseling, Inc.
Dayton, Ohio, USA

CONFIDENT IDENTITY
Copyright © 2017 by Matt Pavlik

2017 07 26 --- First Edition (print)
2017 12 31 --- Cover Redesign
2018 08 01 --- Updated Life Experiences Exercise
2019 06 01 --- Minor adjustments

All rights reserved. No part of this publication may be reproduced, stored in a retrieval system, or transmitted, in any form or by any means, electronic, mechanical, photocopying, recording, or otherwise, without the written permission of the author.

Published in the United States of America by Christian Concepts (christianconcepts.com), an imprint of New Reflections Counseling, Inc. (newreflectionscounseling.com).

The author offers Internet addresses as suggested resources but does not guarantee the validity of the content. Because of the dynamic nature of the Internet, any links may have changed since publication and may no longer be valid.

Some of the examples are composites from several situations. Details and names have been changed to protect anonymity. Any resemblance to persons alive or dead is purely coincidental.

This book is not intended to be a replacement for professional counseling.

Unless otherwise indicated, all Scripture quotations are from the ESV® Bible (The Holy Bible, English Standard Version®), copyright © 2001 by Crossway, a publishing ministry of Good News Publishers. Used by permission. All rights reserved.

Scripture quotations taken from the Holy Bible, NEW INTERNATIONAL VERSION®. Copyright © 1973, 1978, 1984 by Biblica, Inc. All rights reserved worldwide. Used by permission.

Pavlik, Matthew Edward, 1971-
Confident Identity: Christian Strategies to Forget Who You Aren't and Discover Who You Really Are / Matt Pavlik.
    ISBN-10: 0-9863831-5-5 (softcover)
    ISBN-13: 978-0-9863831-5-1 (softcover)
1. Identity (Psychology) —Religious aspects—Christianity
2. Confidence—Religious aspects—Christianity
3. Personality—Religious aspects—Christianity
4. Shame—Religious aspects—Christianity
5. Hope—Religious aspects—Christianity
6. Purpose—Religious aspects—Christianity
7. Self-esteem—Religious aspects—Christianity

BV4509.5 P38 2017   248.4—dc23

Self-perception, Truth, Healing, Stress, Work, Emotions, Counseling, Change, Growth, Brain, Anxiety, Encouragement, Self-acceptance, Burnout, Meaning (Philosophy), Codependency, Addiction, Vocation, Developmental psychology, Rejection (Psychology), Femininity, Masculinity, Perfectionism, Spiritual Gifting, Self-deception, Authority, Gender identity, Object relations (Psychoanalysis), Intelligence, Compulsive eating

Dedication

To my children, Abby, Christy, Daniel, and Luke:

May God always grant you a Confident Identity.

CONTENTS

Foreword ix
Preface xi
Acknowledgments xiii
Introduction 1

Part I — Understanding Your Identity 5

    1. Ashamed or Confident 7
    2. Fearful or Secure 19
    3. Doubtful or Hopeful 27
    4. Rejected or Accepted 37
    5. Isolated and Desolate 49
    6. Connected and Fruitful 59

Part II — Discovering Your Identity 73

    7. Digging for Identity Clues 75
    8. Your Physical Identity 87
    9. Your Gender Identity 93
    10. Your Cognitive and Emotional Identity 105
    11. Your General Spiritual Identity 115
    12. Your Specific Spiritual Identity 125
    13. Your Personality 135
    14. Your Strengths at Work 149
    15. Assembling Your Identity Clues 157

Part III — Using Your Identity 161

    16. Vision: How Far I Can Go 163
    17. Consecration: Be Prepared to Go 175
    18. Mission: Go Make a Difference 183

Supplemental Material 193

Closing Thoughts 195
Appendix A — You 2.0 Prayer 197
Appendix B — Movie and Music List 199
Appendix C — Spiritual Identity Scriptures 201
Appendix D — Values Cutouts 203
Appendix E — Discover More Interests 205
Appendix F — Example Statements 207
Selected Bibliography 209
Index of Scriptures 211

Foreword

Have you ever read a book that leaves you in a thoughtful place of contemplation long after the last page has been turned and the book is closed?

Confident Identity is that kind of book.

Days after reading its final pages, I found myself deliberately and intentionally processing the content of this book. Thinking through my personality, pondering my gifts, and praying through my God-given and life-shaped identity, I couldn't shake the significance of its words. I felt a sense of purpose after reading its words — a driving challenge to explore, expand, and exercise my identity for not only myself but also for the edification of those around me and for the glorification of my Heavenly Father.

Confident Identity is a conversation-starter, a thought-generator, and a game-changer.

Combining Scripture, clinical theories, and practical tools, Matt has thoughtfully crafted a beautiful resource for not only those seeking to better understand and strengthen their identity but also for those who work in both lay and professional settings. The book is filled with an abundance of insightful questions, constructive ideas, easy-to-read charts, and meaningful activities and tests which allow an individual to thoroughly explore and contemplate their identity.

This resource does a wonderful job of providing the reader with mini therapeutic sessions that can be done in the confines of a home, over a cup of coffee with a trusted friend, in a church community group, or even in the safety of a therapist's office. As a therapist myself, this will be in a quick-to-reach spot in my office, as I see this book being a helpful clinical resource when thinking through treatment plans and case conceptualization for those who are struggling in understanding, defining, and forming their identity.

Every follower of Christ could benefit from reading and engaging with the content of this book; I know I have.

Jessica Buczek MS, LPC
June 2017

Preface

I've always wanted my life to have meaning. I spent my teenage years trying to make sense of life. What is the meaning of life? Until I became a Christian at 20 years old, I couldn't find an answer.

I'm still working on my answer today, but I have a much better one than I did 30 years ago. I don't stumble around in the dark as much. I spend more time figuring out the best way to make use of my time — and actually using it.

This book is, in a sense, my story of a search for an identity. I believe it's your story, too, because it's everyone's story.

Who you think you are has more power to determine the course of your life than anything else. I can think of only four possible answers to "Who am I?"

1. Are you a randomly assembled group of cells — a culmination of billions of years of evolution? Nothing more than an animal with a brief 100 years to live and then you'll cease to exist?
2. Are you a species planted by an extraterrestrial life form — the descendants of a people who didn't care to explain where you come from and why you're on this planet?
3. Were you created by a distant and indifferent god who delights in seeing you suffer and is too lazy or too selfish to mount a rescue mission?
4. Or, instead, are you the intentional and specific creation of a God who loves and cares about you so much that He did rescue you out of a sick world?

Life is really hard because you don't live in Paradise. If you don't have an identity or don't know God's love, then all that remains is attempting to extract the most pleasure from every moment you have. What happens when life doesn't go the way you want it to? There's only more despair now and/or more later when you face death.

But life isn't that bleak. You don't live in a meaningless vacuum, and this makes all the difference. Hope exists for today in the life you have here because of the reality you have beyond this life.

Who you are changes the course of the world because of all God has done to set you free and empower you with His Holy Spirit. God has defeated and disarmed your primary obstacles (death, sin, and the curse), thereby opening a path before you.

Be on a journey of discovery. Look beyond your obstacles, be they rejection, failure, or fear. The enemy makes use of these to block your vision of a glorious hope.

Seek to know and understand the God who created you. Jesus said to love your neighbor as yourself. To truly love someone, you need to know them warts, wonder, and all. You have a backstage pass to your own life. You and the Holy Spirit get to witness the internal workings of God's creation: you. The more you fully understand your identity in relation to Jesus, the more you can understand and love others.

Too often, people ignore themselves as they seek to love others. But you can't possibly love others until you're intimately aware of all that God has placed in you. Then you can experience love for God and yourself and, finally, genuine affection for others. So pursue your Confident Identity; don't shy away from investing in discovering God's amazing creation.

I've struggled to understand my significance over the years. I've felt lost and adrift on a great, empty ocean. This book will give you a major boost forward in life. It's not a shortcut, because you'll need to do the work for yourself, but it should keep you from wandering aimlessly in shark-infested waters and point you toward a safe haven called *home*. You can be at home with yourself because Jesus is your Immanuel — God with you.

Acknowledgments

Thanks to God, who loves me, works to ensure I have a Confident Identity, and empowers me to complete His work.

Thanks to my parents for their dedication to pray as I follow God's calling.

Thanks to my clients, who teach me every day how to be a better counselor.

Thanks to Will Alejandro, who helped me talk through what I wanted to say.

Thanks to the following test readers who provided feedback that made this a better book:

> Jessica Buczek, Ingrid DeDecker, Tim Hill, Abby Pavlik, Christy Pavlik, Ed Pavlik, Georgette Pavlik, Sophia Sparks, Renette Steele, and Crisinda Tackett

Introduction

I created this book to help you accelerate your growth and understanding of who you are. As you will see, knowing yourself is a shortcut to enjoying life and the best way to find peace and satisfaction. You can maximize your God-given potential as you live out the six steps to confident living:

1. **Be:** Simply exist and receive love.
2. **Identity:** Develop the sense of who you are.
3. **Do:** Practice and grow in skills.
4. **Mission:** Fulfill your purpose.
5. **Live:** Enjoy the time you have.
6. **Sacrifice:** Invest your time in others.

You start life with little knowledge of who you are. The dashed lines represent a lack of definition. You mature (grow in definition) as you learn and follow the six steps.

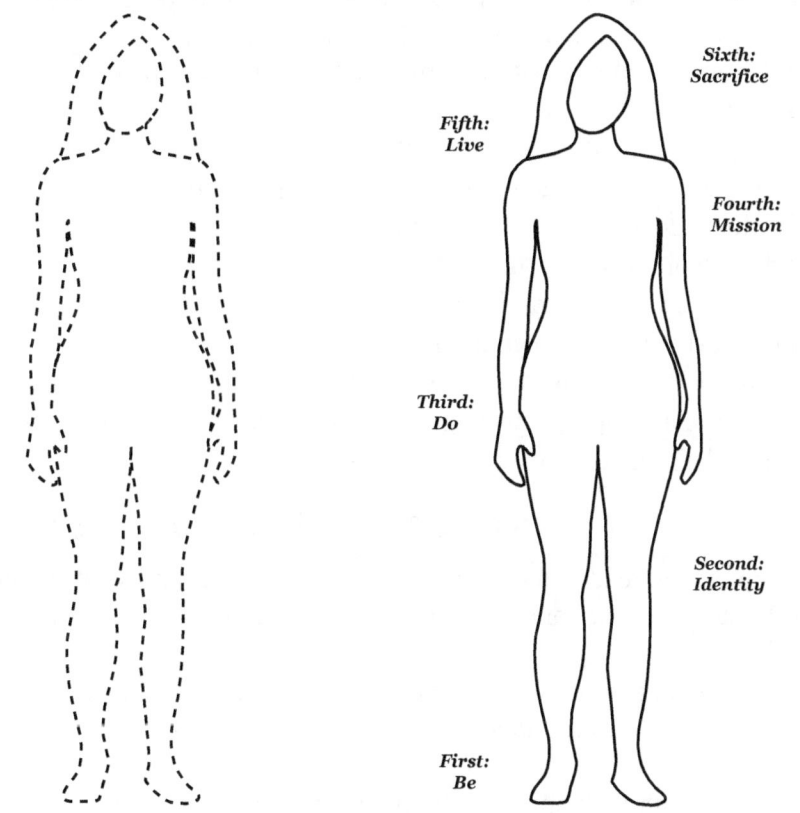

By wisdom a house is built, and by understanding it is established;
by knowledge the rooms are filled with all precious and pleasant riches.
—Proverbs 24:3–4

Unless the LORD builds the house, those who build it labor in vain.
—Psalm 127:1a

The Lord, with wisdom and understanding, establishes your identity —
like a house filled with precious and pleasant riches.

What I Believe about Identity

Beyond God Himself, your identity is the most important and powerful gift God has given you. You wouldn't exist without your identity. Here is what I believe to be true:

- Every human is created in God's image.
- You have an identity that exists only in the context of your relationship with God.
- If you want to enjoy life and make the most of it, you must understand exactly who you are. This includes a spiritual and a practical understanding of why God made you the way He did.
- Every Christian has a general spiritual identity. This book covers this identity and so much more. You need to understand your personality and your uniqueness.

Who Will Benefit from This Book

You can be alive and understand some things about yourself but still be far away from God's intentions for your life. I wrote this book while thinking about an identity crisis — an opportunity for growth. Everyone has to face a crisis of identity. I'm convinced it's part of God's plan in a fallen world to shape and mature us into who He made us to be.

Both men and women struggle with identity, often in different ways, but both will benefit from this book. This book is especially for you if you:

- Are struggling with how to make your life work
- Like to understand how things work — how each part functions in relation to the whole
- Want to learn the details of God's design
- Like to reflect in order to gain understanding
- Want a full-brain learning experience
- Appreciate visual diagrams to gain understanding
- Learn best by seeing principles and ideas in their simplest form
- Want to apply the appropriate principles and ideas to bring about positive change
- Want to make the most of your time in counseling

How to Get the Most out of This Book

- As you complete the readings and exercises, I suggest sharing your insights and questions with your trusted friends, fiancé(e), partner, and/or counselor. You can even use this book in group discussions.
- Read the chapters in the order presented. If you haven't already done so, read the Preface. Although some chapters can stand alone, most chapters build upon previously developed ideas.
- Move slowly through the book by fully digesting a chapter before moving on to the next one.
- Expect further insights with each chapter you read.
- Have fun with this! You're about to embark on a full-scale learning experience.
- Use the checkboxes (□) in the Next Steps sections to mark when you've completed the exercises at the end of each chapter.
- For the movie exercises, be sure to use the questions in Appendix B and review the comments and cautions (some movies are rated R).
- Journal your thoughts and feelings while reading each chapter.
- Draw images that represent your learning experiences; this will engage more of your brain.

- Use the Blueprint Space to journal and draw.
- Share your insights with your partner or others with whom you share a close relationship; ask them questions about what you're reading.
- Seek counseling to address those topics that identify one of your tender spots.
- Use this book as part of your counseling.
- When making tough, life-changing decisions, allow one or more trusted advisors or counselors the opportunity to offer their perspective (Proverbs 15:22). I've made every effort to be clear and accurate, but even the inerrant truth of the Bible can be applied incorrectly.
- As you work through the material, it will stretch you, and some of your emotional baggage will surface. You may feel encouraged but also uncomfortable. This is by design. Pursue the material at a pace you can manage, but don't give up. Those who push through will benefit the most.

Editorial Notes

- See the copyright page for disclaimers.
- When referring to singular nouns where the gender is unimportant or unknown, I often use the plural pronouns "they" or "their" instead of the more awkward "he or she" or "his or her."
- I alternate between "he" and "she" except where the example naturally calls for one gender over the other. Although each gender has its own strengths and weaknesses, either gender can, at some point, struggle with just about any problem. The use of a particular gender in an example doesn't mean I'm excluding the other.
- Unless otherwise noted, when I speak of identity, I'm assuming the reader is a Christian. If you're not a Christian yet, you'll benefit from the book, but some of the attributes of a Christian identity (for example, spiritual gifts) won't apply to you. This is because the Holy Spirit provides the gift, and only Christians gain the Holy Spirit.

How This Book Is Structured to Help You

If you were going on a geological excavation, you would first need to have a clear picture of what you were looking for. Then you'd use the appropriate tools to investigate. After you found something, you'd assimilate your discovery into your working knowledge. That is exactly what you'll be doing with your identity in this book.

Part I	**Chapters 1–6**	**Understanding God's Design of Your Identity**
Part II	**Chapters 7–15**	**Discovering God's Design of Your Identity**
Part III	**Chapters 16–18**	**Using God's Design of Your Identity**

Part I — Understanding Your Identity

Chapter 1   **Ashamed or Confident**

Chapter 2   **Fearful or Secure**

Chapter 3   **Doubtful or Hopeful**

Chapter 4   **Rejected or Accepted**

Chapter 5   **Isolated and Desolate**

Chapter 6   **Connected and Fruitful**

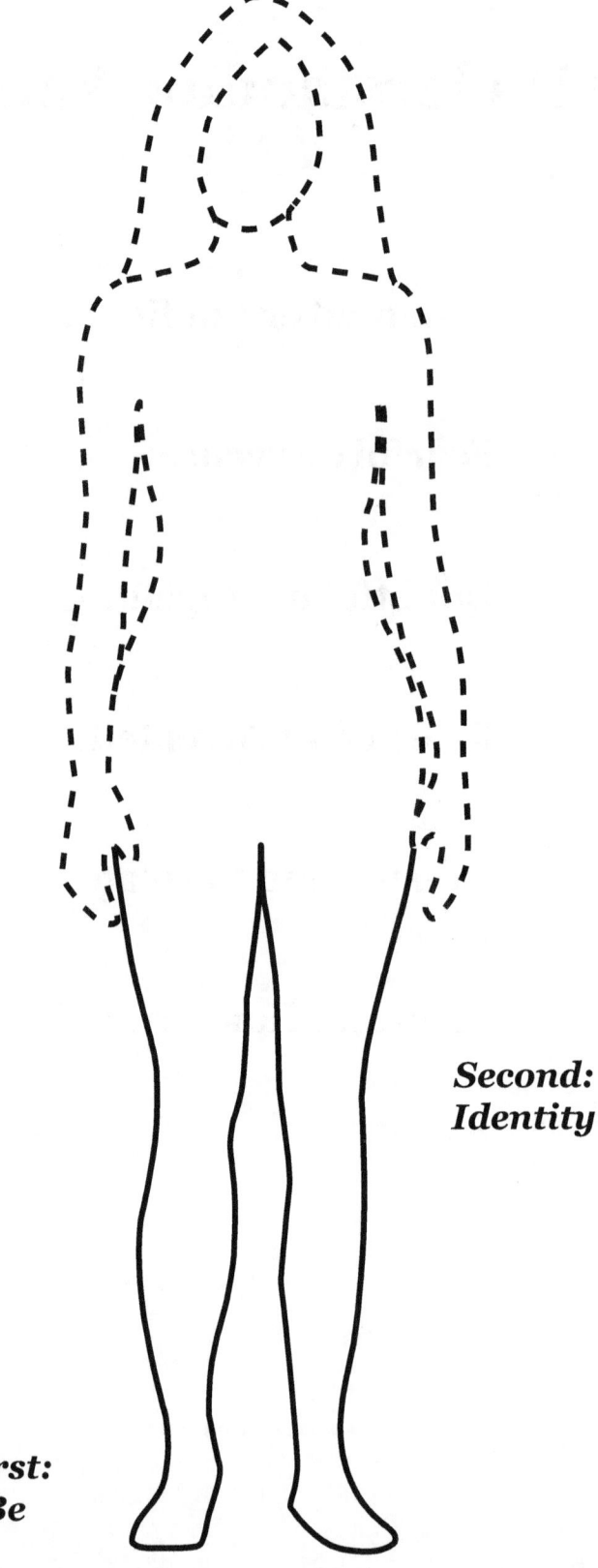

Understanding (God's Design of Your Identity)

Chapter 1

Ashamed or Confident

Amy wipes away her tears and steps outside. The door clicks behind her. As she walks toward her car, she pushes down intrusive feelings of rejection and forces herself to focus on her communications class.

At least now I'll have more time to make progress on my final project.

As she nears her car, the left side of her face twitches. She stops abruptly. Then her face betrays her again. She counts each twitch.

Three . . . Ack!

She retrieves her keys and unlocks the door.

Four . . . What's going on with me? Stop it! People are staring. Keep going. Don't look.

As she gets in her car, she throws down her purse. Her breathing quickens and a wave of nausea sweeps over her. She touches her face, but it doesn't feel like it's hers.

Five . . . Six . . . Why is this happening? I'm freaking out!

She grips her steering wheel with both hands. The tighter she grips, the more she believes she can make the twitching stop.

Seven . . . Eight . . . I'm okay. I'm okay. I'm okay. No, I'm not okay. I'm such a loser. I'll never be able to find the right man. I don't know who to be. Being me isn't working.

Nine . . . Ten . . . This isn't funny, God. I can't handle this!

She starts the car and drives away.

I hope I never feel this humiliated again.

Shamed into Who You Aren't

Shame is the deep-down sense that who you are is defective and worthless and therefore, you aren't needed or wanted by anyone. Shame is a problem of epidemic proportions. All who struggle with it become isolated from the cause and the cure: relationship. Relationships have the potential to affirm or to reject who you are.

Going without acceptance is not an option. In terms of basic needs, affirmation of who you are is second only to water, food, and shelter. Without acceptance, you'll be tempted to try to be someone else. But this *never* produces a Confident Identity. At best, under extreme psychological trauma, it prevents more serious harm — but even then, avoiding your identity is only a temporary solution. To return to health, you'll have to reconcile with your identity later in life.

This isn't the first time Amy has felt the sting of rejection. Each time she loses a relationship, she suffers devastating loss because she emotionally overinvests in the men in her life.

Amy is faced with a seemingly lose-lose situation. She can have the pain of staying in a dysfunctional relationship, or she can have the pain of being alone. She knows all too well that loneliness can be as painful as a going-nowhere relationship. There has to be another option for her. What is going to help her move toward health?

Amy is experiencing a classic identity crisis. Identity crises come in different flavors, but the root of the problem is always an insufficient amount of internal resources to meet the demands of life. Amy doesn't want to remain as she is; however, her current emotional resources aren't sophisticated enough to resolve her problem in a way that's good for her.

A weak identity can result in a whole host of problems. Instead of a losing a relationship, she could have been stuck in a going-nowhere job or, even worse, a going-nowhere life. When a challenge pops up in her life, she faces uncertainty. Does she have enough within her to meet life's demands? Is she willing to put in the effort to move past the obstacles?

How deep Amy goes to address her problems will determine whether this pattern will continue. Has she experienced enough pain to motivate her to put in the effort to move forward? Or will she try again in much the same way, unwilling to face her pain, passively wishing for a new and better path to present itself?

Amy's identity crisis reveals her vulnerability. Some finite number of negative experiences (such as her failed relationships) result in pervasive, negative, and overwhelming beliefs.

What Is Identity?

Who am I? Doesn't everyone long to know the answer to this question? Yes and no. Yes, we want to know the positives. We have a built-in desire to be recognized and to be significant. No, we fear making contact with the parts we're ashamed of. Instead, we hide those parts so we don't have to feel shame.

You can't make up your identity as you go. Instead, you discover the identity God has already planned and created. You live in the context of a story greater than yourself. God wants you to dig, as if for a treasure, to uncover your part in His story. Seek and you shall find, He says; knock and the door will be opened. To understand yourself completely, you need both a deep internal understanding of yourself and an extensive understanding of God and the rest of creation.

Your *self-image* is how positive or negative you see yourself. Your *self-worth* or *self-esteem* is how much you value yourself.

God makes each person in His image. Each person is one-of-a-kind: sufficiently intricate to be recognizably distinct from every other person. Given a complicated enough task, everyone will approach the same task differently in some way.

These four dictionary definitions[1] capture the essence of identity. Identity is:
1. "Who you are." This definition encapsulates what I mean by *identity*.
2. "The set of characteristics by which you are definitively recognizable." This definition clarifies that we can use *identity* to distinguish you from others.
3. "Your unique characteristics held by no other person." This definition clarifies that *having an identity* means you have something that no one else will ever have.

---

[1] Compiled from yourdictionary.com/identity and dictionary.com/browse/identity.

4. "What remains the same, constant, persisting over time, under varying circumstances." This definition provides the insight that identity must be permanently yours, or else it really isn't part of you.

Unfortunately, what you understand as your identity includes both accurate and inaccurate information mixed together. These true and false parts — some of which you know, and some of which you don't know about yourself — make up your Earthly Identity.

Imagine your Earthly Identity as a passenger balloon. The balloon ride won't be pleasant if the basket never completely leaves the ground. Dragging along the ground would rattle you to your core as you bumped into boulders, hillsides, trees . . . The sandbags represent what is false because they weigh you down and keep you from your True Identity. The balloon and the basket represent what is true. The balloon provides lift, and the basket contains and carries you where you need to go.

God designed you to fly at a certain height. Your False Identity keeps you from attaining the optimal altitude. However, sometimes God allows you a False Identity to keep your pride in check — so you don't think too highly of yourself (2 Corinthians 12:7). A weakness like this helps you see your need for God.

Your Earthly Identity is based on present day reality. I've divided Earthly Identity into three overlapping parts or perspectives to help you better understand identity: True (Potential plus

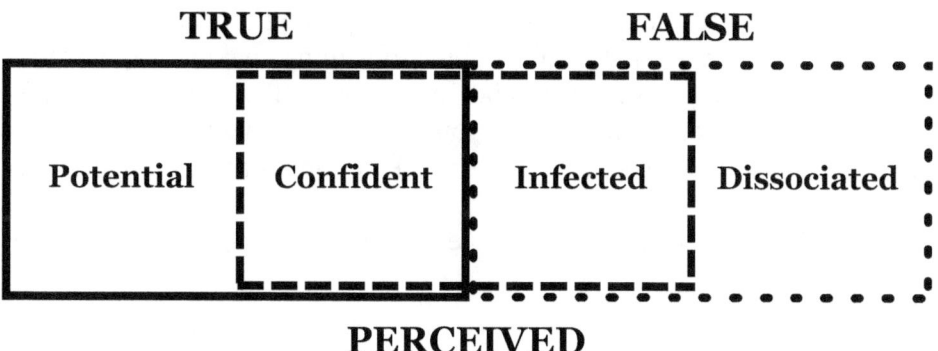

Confident Identity), False (Infected plus Dissociated Identity), and Perceived (Confident plus Infected Identity). In heaven, only your True Identity will be present.

True Identity

Your True Identity is God's original design for you, intentionally planned before you were born (Ephesians 2:10). Imagine yourself in heaven standing next to Jesus, complete, confident, and fully aware of who you are (1 Corinthians 13:12). Your True Identity will no longer be partially hidden from you.

Although you haven't yet fully realized your True Identity, it is permanent and complete (in God's mind). Identity cannot be permanently lost, but we frequently lose sight of it. You know some of it, and some of it you don't. Your True Identity represents your new self and includes the positive aspects of your strengths and weaknesses (Ephesians 4:22–24).

True Identity can be divided into Potential Identity and Confident Identity.

Potential Identity

Only God knows everything about you. Your Potential Identity is the part God knows but you have yet to discover (or have discovered but forgotten). It's the part of your True Identity that you aren't in touch with or that hasn't yet emerged.

Confident Identity

Identity is what something *is,* as distinguishable from everything else. *Confidence* is the assurance of something. To have a Confident Identity means you're living with the assurance of knowing who you are. You know yourself and aren't ashamed. Your identity is not nearly as relevant when it is hidden, nor when it's discovered but not appreciated, embraced, and put into play. You function with your Confident Identity as you achieve awareness and acceptance of your True Identity, resulting in a unique set of actions that ultimately further God's kingdom.

False Identity

Your False Identity is the opposite of your True identity. Whatever is outside of God's intentional design is false. Your False Identity develops because of negative life experiences, some of which you're aware of, some of which you aren't.

Your False Identity includes the negative self-concepts resulting from negative experiences wrongly attributed as defining your identity. These false beliefs, or lies, actively feed your self-image, creating interference during your battle for a Confident Identity.

Your False Identity is like cancer in some ways and a cloak in others. Cancer is otherwise healthy cells gone bad because of defective instructions.[2] The cancerous part of your identity includes the aspects of yourself that are diseased (or in spiritual terms, sinful; see Romans 8:1–11). These parts need to be removed. A cloak can hide something, making it appear to be something that it isn't. You can deceive yourself into believing you're well when you aren't. You can bury negative beliefs, preventing you from realizing you're sick. Also, you can cover in shame what is good but vulnerable and hurting. These parts need redemption, or to be brought out of hiding and healed.

Together, your Infected Identity and Dissociated Identity make up your False Identity.

---

[2] For an intriguing description, see cancercenter.com/discussions/blog/cancer-when-good-cells-go-bad.

Infected Identity

Your Infected Identity is who you falsely believe you are. When you buy into a lie about yourself, you're infected. The cure involves separating out and removing the infection without destroying the true but hurting parts of yourself. What can be especially debilitating is brooding over the lie — punishing yourself with how true you think the lie must be. This is like exposing an infected wound to more germs. For example, Amy, who struggles with her face twitching, has conscious thoughts that she is a loser. At an emotional level, she really believes she is a loser.

Dissociated Identity

Your Dissociated Identity is a false, subconscious idea that impacts your self-image. When an event is too painful to dwell on, one option is to disconnect from the memory of it. On the surface, this can save you from the event's distress (and the resulting shame), but it also prevents you from healing the wound. For example, Amy lacks insight into exactly why her face is twitching. Therefore, her reason for being stuck in a negative cycle likely has something to do with a part of her she isn't quite ready to be in touch with.

The only way to heal the part of you that is dissociated is to first become aware of it. In counseling terms, this step is called *integration, re-association,* or even *remembering.* Integration is like stitching your broken pieces back together; awareness effectively converts those pieces to Infected (see the preceding section) so you can continue the healing process.

Perceived Identity

Your Perceived Identity (depicted as the middle dashed rectangle in the Earthly Identity figure earlier in this chapter) is the identity you're conscious of — the image of who you believe you are at any given moment. Only part of your Perceived Identity is your True Identity; the other part includes your False Identity, or what feels true but isn't. The true part of your Perceived Identity is your Confident Identity. The false part is your Infected identity.

The ABCs of a Confident Identity

God is the ultimate powerful weapon against evil. You, being made in God's image, have an identity that is also powerful. If God has secret weapons, your identity is one of them. Not knowing your identity is like being a superhero who isn't aware of their superpowers.

Your identity is a gift from God, possessing both power and permanence. When you have a Confident Identity, you approach life head-on instead of running away. Moving toward your God-given identity increases your capacity for His power to be active in your life, whereas moving away decreases your potential.

To successfully find a lost person, a bloodhound must first learn the target's scent. For you to find your true self, you first need to learn the essential characteristics of your true self. Here are the ABCs (and more) of a Confident Identity: You want to be Aware of your significance, Belonging in your place, Convinced of your design, Devoted to God, Established by God, and a Formidable weapon.

At the end of each section, I've included a list of words that represent each characteristic. Reflect on each word; then select the word you feel best captures the meaning of your identity, or write in a word you feel is a better fit. This will help you create a personalized definition of a Confident Identity.

Aware of Your Significance

If you're a Christian, then you're the salt and light Jesus mentions in Matthew 5. Jesus teaches about two aspects of identity: One, you're like salt, an invaluable mineral that has multiple, unique purposes. Two, you're like light, meant to illuminate God and His truth to others. God intends that you become aware of who you are for the benefit of others.

> *You are the salt of the earth. But if the salt loses its savor, how can it be made salty again? It is no longer good for anything, except to be thrown out and trampled by men.*
>
> *You are the light of the world. A city on a hill cannot be hidden. Neither do people light a lamp and put it under a basket. Instead, they set it on a lampstand, and it gives light to everyone in the house. In the same way, let your light shine before men, that they may see your good deeds and glorify your Father in heaven.*
> —Matthew 5:13–16

A salt identity is potent, powerful, valuable, and useful. A salt-without-savor identity would be bland, dull, worthless, and useless. Jesus says you're savory!

A bright identity is helpful, beautiful, and worshipful. It illuminates, is meant to be on display, and glorifies God. A shamefully hidden identity serves no purpose. Jesus says you're bright!

Fear and shame block you from knowing your identity. You can't discard the shame-covered parts. You can hide from yourself, but you can't hide from God. Because God created you, you're better off experiencing God examining you so He can lead you into greater awareness and understanding.

> *My frame was not hidden from you*
> *when I was made in the secret place,*
> *when I was woven together*
> *in the depths of the earth.*
>
> *Search me, God, and know my heart;*
> *test me and know my anxious thoughts.*
> *See if there is any offensive way in me,*
> *and lead me in the way everlasting.*
> —Psalm 139:15, 23–24 (NIV)

You're significant because of your existence — the way God made you — not because of what you do. Your first responsibility is to simply be; then be who you were made to be. Are you willing to know yourself more deeply?

Select the word or words which best fit with your identity as Aware of Your Significance:

- ☐ Wise to
- ☐ Alive
- ☐ Curious
- ☐ Seeking
- ☐ Cognizant
- ☐ Expanding
- ☐ Growing
- ☐ Other:

Belonging in Your Place

When you belong, you're in your proper place (not lost, not an outcast). You're in relationship with others, not in isolation. In order to belong, you need to be able to share who you are. Are you willing to spend time with others and share your understanding of your identity? Can you spend time being the light and allowing others to be the light to you?

Select the word or words which best fit with your identity as Belonging in Your Place:

- ☐ Fit in
- ☐ Connected
- ☐ Valued
- ☐ Contributing
- ☐ Revealing
- ☐ Accepted
- ☐ Involved
- ☐ Other:

Convinced of Your Design

A person with a Confident Identity pursues God's design — their True Identity. To achieve a Confident Identity, you need to increase your perception of your potential and decrease your beliefs in your false perceptions.

All Christians have a spiritual identity. Your spiritual identity consists of these primary truths:

1. You were created/designed/made in God's image (Genesis 1:27).
2. You're a child of God (Galatians 4:3–7).
3. You're loved by God (Romans 8:35–39).
4. You're predestined and chosen by God (Ephesians 1:11, 2:10).
5. You're a place for God's power/glory (2 Corinthians 1:22, Ephesians 3:16).
6. You're a part of the Body of Christ (1 Corinthians 12).
7. You're salt and light (Matthew 5:13–16).

Some of these truths you might not completely understand, and that's okay for now. Chapter 11 explains them in more detail.

Your belief in your design will be tested. Going through trials strengthens your belief in your identity. You don't doubt God created you. The more you're confident of your spiritual identity, the more you can be salt and light to those around you.

Select the word or words which best fit with your identity as Convinced of Your Design:

- ☐ Proven
- ☐ Tested
- ☐ Unwavering
- ☐ Bold
- ☐ Solid
- ☐ Sound
- ☐ Confident
- ☐ Other:

Devoted to God

You want to know God. You recognize when your relationship with God becomes polluted or diluted. You relentlessly weed out whatever blocks your connection to God. You're addicted to God and not anything else.

Select the word or words which best fit with your identity as Devoted to God:

- ☐ Dependent on God
- ☐ Hope is in God
- ☐ Enthusiastic
- ☐ Attached
- ☐ Loyal to God
- ☐ Integrity (you're not double-minded)
- ☐ Sincere
- ☐ Other:

Established by God

You, as a trusting child, are able to look to God. You've experienced God's affirmation (you're not orphaned). You accept God as Father and allow Him to be Father to you as He was Father to the returning prodigal son. You understand that you can't be confident in yourself without being confident in God.

Select the word or words which best fit with your identity as Established by God:

- ☐ Affirmed
- ☐ Vouched for
- ☐ Secure
- ☐ Protected
- ☐ Authoritative
- ☐ Rooted
- ☐ Positive
- ☐ Other:

Formidable Weapon

The first five ABCs are all about growing and establishing your identity. As God is strengthening your identity, He is defining your purpose. The natural next step is acting upon what you know. You're ready and willing to act (you're not passive). You resist and rebuke evil like Jesus did.

> *For we are his workmanship, created in Christ Jesus for good works, which God prepared beforehand, that we should walk in them.*
> —Ephesians 2:10

Select the word or words which best fit with your identity as a Formidable Weapon:

- ☐ Fearless
- ☐ Potent
- ☐ Significant
- ☐ Powerful
- ☐ In force
- ☐ Irrefutable
- ☐ Unwavering
- ☐ Other:

Moving Beyond an Identity Crisis

While facing an identity crisis, you'll ask questions like these: *Who am I? What's the purpose of my existence? What's the meaning of life?* And most conclusively, *Can I face the challenges of life?*

Passage through an identity crisis is a necessary step toward (and only way to) freedom and maturity. An identity crisis can be an internal conflict between settling for the status quo and taking the risk to become something more. Successfully resolving the conflict requires that you expand your capabilities in some way. Anything less than this leaves you unchanged and likely discouraged.

An identity crisis could also be called the challenge of growing pains. Your available responses to an identity crisis are limited by how willing you are to confront the challenge. Consider the following four options, presented in order from least to greatest effort required: Drifting, Conforming, Transforming, and Achieving.[3] The four options correspond to the attitudes of the two sons in the Parable of the Prodigal Son (Luke 15:11–32).

---

[3] See the flowchart at the end of the chapter for more detail.

Drifting

Remain dependent on others. Be immature and unwilling to care or act.

This person could be described as a capricious drifter who lacks responsibility. The younger son demanded his inheritance. He lacked respect for both his father and the wealth. He squandered the inheritance with careless living (v. 11–13).

Conforming

Ignore the identity conflict. Be willing to act responsibly by conforming to others' ideas but not enough to invest the energy to develop your own ideas.

The older son worked dutifully for his father. He also lacked respect for his father and the wealth. His heart was closed to his father; he didn't experience his father's generosity. He didn't dare to risk pursuing his own life; he resented working for his father (v. 25–32).

Transforming

Honestly pursue and search for your own answers. Be willing to invest in developing your ideas but not yet willing to embrace God's ideas.

The younger son dared to leave behind the default security of his father's house. He squandered the money he had but eventually moved toward responsibility by accepting whatever job he could find. When his attempts at responsibility failed, he considered returning to his father but without the status of son (v. 14–19).

Achieving

Confidently embrace God's answers. Be willing to invest in discovering and then accepting who God made you to be.

This is not conforming; this is integrating and reconciling your identity with God's identity. Success means an honest appraisal that results in an identity with integrity. The father loved his son and didn't accept his son's diminished self-image. The son accepted his father's love and celebrated with him (v. 20–24).

Choose a Level of RISC

The younger son took the greater risk and lost his wealth. However, his newfound appreciation of his father's love was worth it. The older son didn't consider risk as an option, so he had resentment instead of appreciation.

When you're faced with an identity crisis, choose a level of investment and therefore RISC:

1. Remain immature.
2. Ignore the challenge.
3. Search for answers.
4. Come together with God.

Each successive option requires greater investment, awareness, and confrontation, but results in a stronger identity. What level of RISC are you willing to take?

Having an identity crisis is like becoming lost in the woods. Believing God doesn't have anything for you and that you'll be okay if you work hard is an easy trap to step on. But while the threat of becoming painfully and permanently lost is ever-present, there are multiple ways out, no matter what problem you are experiencing or how long you've been stuck. These paths will lead you out of the woods and back to civilization, where healthy relationships can be formed.

God can speak to you about your direction, making a shortcut through dense woods. God can help you find a lake and tell you where to fish (John 21). He knows the best direction because He knows the destination — the end goal. You can become confused by too many options, but God can lead you home. Then you can focus your energies on being true to yourself and your values in the midst of your day-to-day life. Achieving a Confident Identity demands your willingness to take the greatest RISC.

What Is Ahead

By reading and applying this book, you'll significantly increase your awareness of who you are. You'll grow in your Confident Identity and live a fruitful life. You have a unique combination of characteristics that point to a purpose only you can fulfill. You can step further into all that God made you to be.

The remainder of Part I will help you further understand identity so you can increase your Confident Identity and decrease your sense of False Identity.

Part II of this book focuses on helping you discover your uniqueness by looking at specific aspects of your identity: physical, gender, cognitive, emotional, spiritual, personality, strengths, and abilities.

Part III will help you pull all these ideas and discoveries together and motivate you to be strong in the battle for your Confident Identity. You'll define a vision and a mission for your identity.

For Reflection

1. Do you believe you are salt and light? Because Jesus said you are, being salt and light is part of your True Identity.
2. An identity crisis is actually an opportunity for you because the struggle can produce growth. Unfortunately, the crisis is usually forced into your awareness by something negative (failure, rejection, low self-worth, loss, trauma). What negative circumstances reinforce this struggle for you? Whether you succeed or fail, God is cheering you on!
3. Imagine going through life without ever making the effort to search for your identity. Then imagine learning who you are on each step along the way.
4. To what degree are you willing to make an investment to see your potential come to light?
5. Non-Christians and Christians alike can achieve an identity, each having a strong sense of who they are. But the core of their identities will be in opposition, like darkness and light (see Matthew 13:24–30, 2 Corinthians 6:14, John 8:39–47).

Next Steps

- ☐ Review the words you selected that best fit your identity (see the section "The ABCs of a Confident Identity"). Thank God if you already feel these words are true about you. Ask God to help you experience these words so you can grow into your Confident Identity.
- ☐ Follow the flowchart at the end of this chapter. Where are you? Realize that reversing course by choosing maturity and moving toward God is possible at any time.
- ☐ Media for Further Learning (see Appendix B for more questions)
    - ☐ Movie: *The Lion King*. How does Simba learn from the past and accept his identity?
    - ☐ Music: *I'll Lead You Home* by Michael W. Smith
- ☐ Write out your definition of Confident Identity and Infected Identity in your Blueprint Space. Then describe these parts of your identity as you know them by being as specific as possible.

- ☐ Ask God to increase your awareness of your Potential and Dissociated Identities and to decrease your belief in your Infected Identity.
- ☐ What identity crisis are you facing that blocks you from moving forward? Describe your "wall" in your Blueprint Space. Journal about how stuck or trapped you feel. Are you able to see how growing your Confident Identity can move you up and over the wall? Return to this question as you complete each part of this book to see how much better you're becoming at scaling these walls.

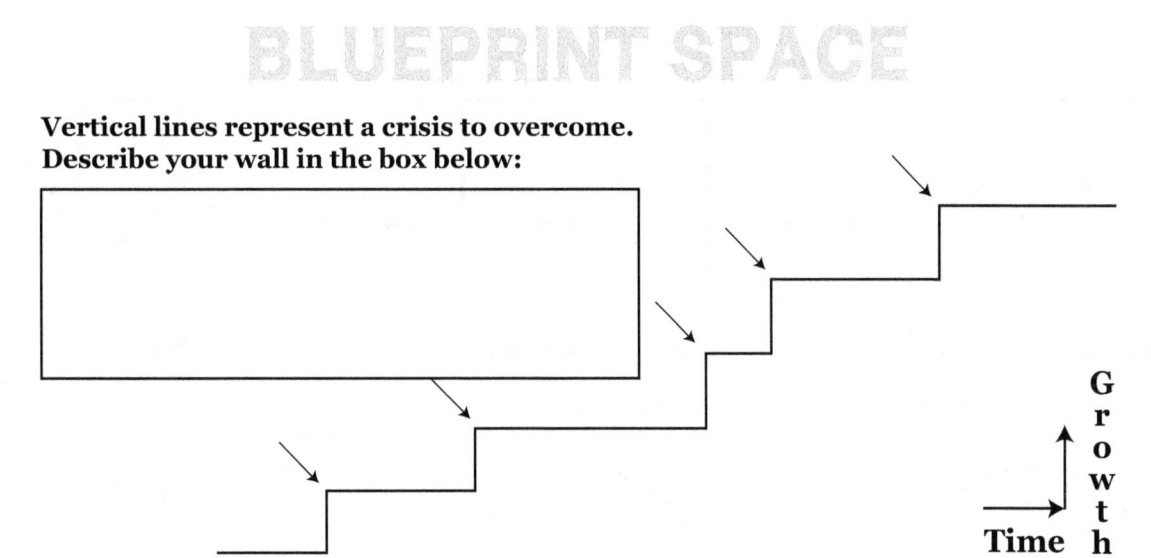

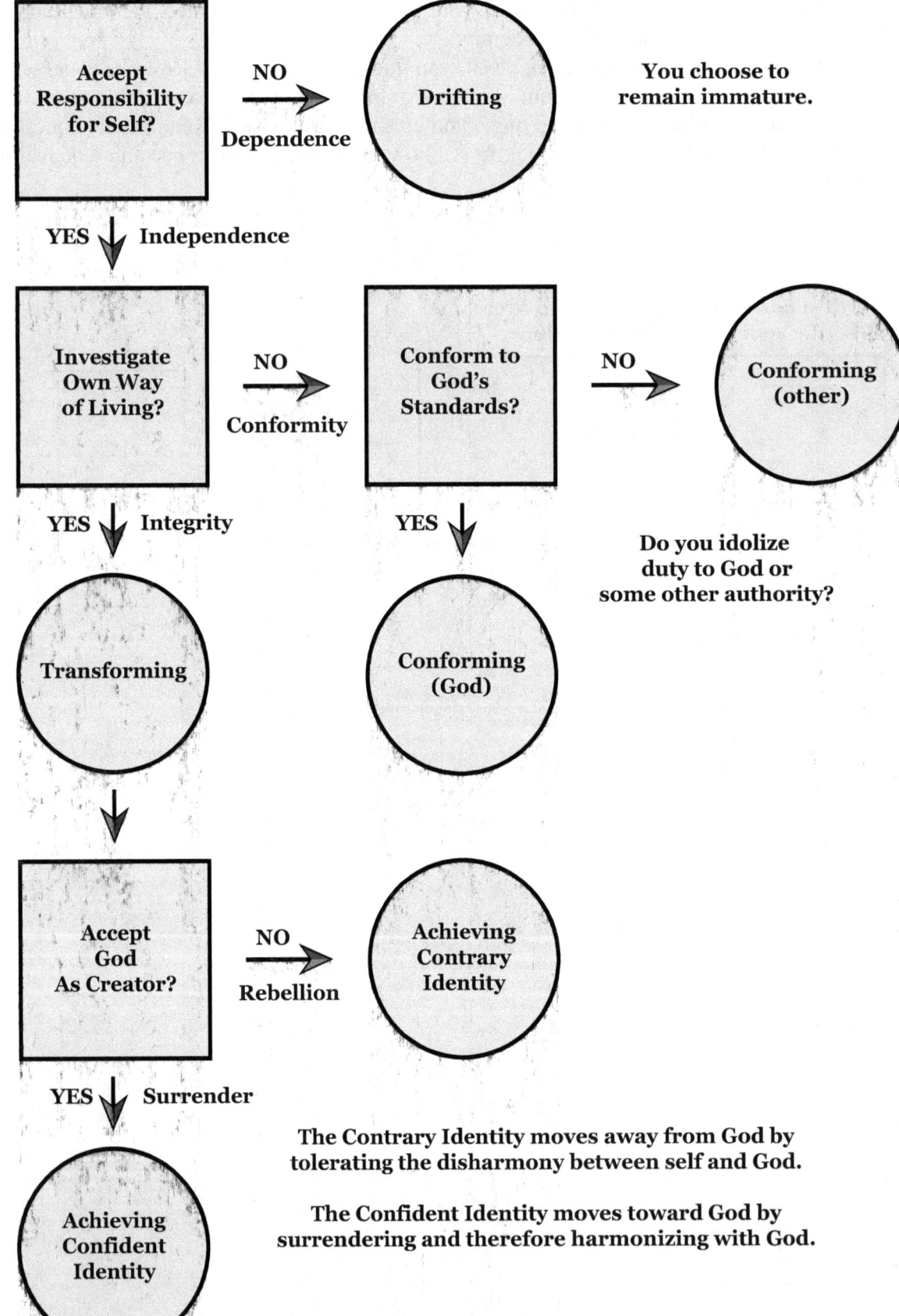

Chapter 2

Fearful or Secure

After a difficult breakup a few months ago, Amy struggles to pull herself together. If you could be like God and know Amy's thoughts even before she does, you'd hear this:

I can't make it on my own. I'm not enough. I'm just a replaceable nobody. I can't handle being alone. I can't survive the embarrassment of constant rejection. Something's deeply wrong with me. I need help to change something.

But Amy doesn't ever consciously think these thoughts because she isn't that self-aware. Instead, she decides to find another man to fill the hole in her heart. Her efforts pay off, and soon she finds herself engaged. She glows with excitement at the prospect of marriage.

I know I've found the best partner for me this time, she thinks. *We're only two months away from our wedding and honeymoon to the Bahamas!*

Then, only a few months later, she tells her husband good news with a gleam in her eye: "I'm pregnant!"

Her husband hugs her and says, "Wow, that didn't take long."

Amy says, "I'm so happy God's given me a child to love, nurture, and grow. I wonder who's growing inside me — a boy or a girl? We know the baby is human, made in the image of God, and made from our DNA. But that's all we know."

Her husband says, "I want to name him Max."

Amy says, "But what if it's a girl?"

Rest in God's Intentional Design

You were a complete mystery to your parents as you grew in your mother's womb. But you weren't a mystery to God. God chose your parents as well as the specific time in history for you to be born (Acts 17:26). Your identity exists apart from your awareness of it. Even when you don't know who you are, God does. Not only did God know you before you were conceived, He knows everything you'll ever do. In Psalm 139, God lets you know that He made you intentionally and perfectly.

For you created my inmost being; you knit me together in my mother's womb. I praise you because I am fearfully and wonderfully made; your works are wonderful, I know that full well. My frame was not hidden from you when I was made in the secret place, when I was woven together in the depths of the

earth. Your eyes saw my unformed body; all the days ordained for me were written in your book before one of them came to be.
—Psalm 139:13–16

Only God knows your complete (True) identity, whether you're 50 seconds old or 50 years old. Even the oldest human is still like a baby compared to God, who has always existed.

I could describe myself as a 45-year-old male with brown hair and brown eyes. That's what you'd find on my ID card. While that's a description, it only scratches the surface of my identity. But what if I knew the answers to questions like these?

- Why was I created?
- Who am I?
- Who will I become?
- Who cares?
- What am I supposed to do with my life?

I imagine the answers would be quite valuable to me. How about you? How would knowing the answers improve the quality of your life? Without answers, the best you can do is haphazardly fumble through life, always wondering if what you do has any significance.

If you could ask only one question, what would it be? How about this: *What was God thinking when He created me?*

Knowing you were intentionally made unique is as important as knowing you're unconditionally loved. These two ideas can't be separated without diminishing your self-worth. Together, they mean you're loved for being the you that no one else can be. Without this kind of love, you'd be highly likely to do some stupid, crazy, exhausting, outlandish, inefficient, reckless things to feel even a drop of worth. Trading what you have for something better is the number one trap of all time, first experienced by Adam and Eve as they sought something more than the sufficiency of what God had already provided (Genesis 3:1–7).

Trying to be someone other than who God made you to be is the greatest compromise of your values you can make. To have self-esteem means that you value and like yourself the way God made you.

Don't Fear: God Can't Make a Mistake

Everything God does, He does intentionally. Your biggest mistake is to believe you're a mistake. God wants you to live in confidence, and He wants you to faithfully trust He indeed made you with purpose. He also wants you to do all you can to discover your Potential Identity.

I propose that your dream, like mine, is to be cherished and valued as you act naturally — totally as yourself. Imagine being praised for your natural talent. You didn't have to work for it — you just are who you are. God did the work of creating you, and you enjoy the fruits of His labor.

Don't Fear: You Are Beautifully Unique

You're unique, and no one else can compete. This doesn't mean you'll passively waste away because your life is boring. God leaves you responsible for the excitement and challenges of discovering and developing your natural abilities and then figuring out the best ways to make use of them.

If no one seems to appreciate who you are, don't give up on yourself; instead, step further toward all that God made you to be. The more you move closer to what God intends for you, the more you'll appreciate His handiwork.

What do you see in this snowflake? How many different shapes can you find?

There is beauty in how God masterfully formed you and me — in how one part relates to another. Sometimes beauty can be found in the smallest detail, and other times, it's in the whole snowflake. Keep looking for the beauty of who you are.

Rest in God's Personal Design

Amy and her husband named their first child Max. Amy graduated college when Max was 2. Then, when he turned 3, they had a second son and named him Sam. Despite the boys' age difference, Max and Sam grew up together playing all kinds of sports. Max especially liked baseball.

One summer afternoon, when Sam was 11, Sam pitched a baseball hoping to make Max swing and miss. Even though the ball was outside the strike zone, the ball floated within Max's reach and he blasted it over Sam's head.

Sam missed the plate with his pitch, but he didn't miss when he threw his glove at Max. The glove hit Max at the same time Sam's choice words hit Max's ears. "How am I supposed to win against you? This isn't any fun!" Neither Sam nor Max had fun that day.

Max wasn't hurt, but he did tell his father what had happened. Later, Sam and his father talked for a couple of hours about Sam's frustration. Sam brought up questions he'd asked before: "Why did God make me this way? Why am I terrible at sports, while Max is the star player on his team?"

Sam's father tried to help him see that he couldn't be talented in everything. "I know you're smart because math comes so easily for you," he said. "You're also younger than Max. Max has had three more years to develop his abilities."

"Well," Sam said, "I don't think I'll ever be as talented as Max."

"Maybe not with baseball," his father said, "but we'll find and develop the talents God has given you. Give yourself time to understand all God made you to be."

Don't Fear: God Designed You Perfectly

God is in control of all things, and this includes you. Creator God chooses your special abilities, and this also means He chooses what abilities you won't have. He has it all planned out — *exactly* who He wants you to be. To form something is to separate what it *is* from what it *isn't*.

I saw the angel in the marble and carved until I set him free.
—Attributed to Michelangelo

Even if God chose to consult you regarding your design, He couldn't consult you before He made you. Furthermore, you can't change God's design. As Creator, He has a higher understanding of your purpose. Possessing eternal life guarantees God made you for special purposes.[4]

One of you will say to me: "Then why does God still blame us? For who is able to resist his will?" But who are you, a human being, to talk back to God? "Shall what is formed say to the one who formed it, 'Why did you make me like this?'" Does not the potter have the right to make out of the same lump of clay some pottery for special purposes and some for common use?
—Romans 9:19–21

Only through your relationship with God can you reach your full potential. You aren't able to fully conceive of all He has planned for you (1 Corinthians 2:9). Only He can completely bring forth the intentions of His design. God's touch brings forth the life within you. He resurrects and redeems you from death and the clutches of evil.

You're less than God but capable of doing greater works than Jesus, because you can access the power of the Holy Spirit through prayer.[5]

$$(YOU)^{GOD}$$

Truly, truly, I say to you, whoever believes in me will also do the works that I do; and greater works than these will he do, because I am going to the Father. Whatever you ask in my name, this I will do, that the Father may be glorified in the Son. If you ask anything in my name, I will do it.
—John 14:12–14

Don't Fear: You Are Perfectly Limited

By definition and by God's design, your identity has serious limitations. To be unique is to be limited but no less perfect. He designed you with limitations so that you would need Him. He made you so that you'll fit together with Him. You have access to God's power, but you're not all-powerful. God's power is made perfect in your weakness (2 Corinthians 12:9).

Knowing your limitations goes hand-in-hand with knowing your identity. Knowing who you *aren't* is as important as knowing who you *are*. Some limitations are God-imposed. These

---

[4] See "Meyer's NT Commentary" at biblehub.com/commentaries/romans/9-21.htm.
[5] For a more detailed explanation, see desiringgod.org/messages/doing-the-works-of-jesus-and-greater-works.

constructive limitations provide shape, distinction, and value. Other limitations are destructive because they're self-imposed or other-imposed. These exist because of false beliefs and misunderstandings about identity.

To increase your Confident Identity, work toward accepting the constructive limits, which I address in the following sections, and reject the destructive limits, which I cover in Chapters 4 and 5. Your constructive limits are spiritual, physical, mental and emotional, and personal and natural ability related.

Spiritual Limits

Everyone is born once through a physical delivery — think of this person as You 1.0. But not everyone is born again (You 2.0) through a spiritual delivery (John 3:1–16). Before being reborn, you have a spiritually dead, broken identity. From the moment of conception, you're spiritually dead because man's condition changed with Adam's sin. Spiritual death means you're cut off from a life-giving connection to God.

You need God to recreate or upgrade you so you'll have a connection with Him. When you become a believer, you cross over from spiritual death to life. From the moment of spiritual conception, you're spiritually alive because man's condition changed with Jesus's perfect sacrifice. As part of your spiritual rebirth (You 2.0), you gain God the Holy Spirit as a deposit, securing your identity for eternity (what will eventually be You 3.0).

You Version	Description
You 1.0	Born with a broken identity because of Adam and Eve.
You 2.0	Reborn with a new spiritual life, but You 1.0 is still present.
You 3.0	Promised upgrade when you reach heaven (version 2.0 required to upgrade; version 1.0 no longer present or supported).

Although You 2.0 is spiritually alive, you're limited in the sense that you must still contend with You 1.0. In this life, even after rebirth, you must contend with sin, evil, and the curse. In the afterlife, you won't need further major upgrades because you'll be fully compatible with God — He will completely and finally remove all that is incompatible with Him.

. . . Sin came into the world through one man, and death through sin, and so death spread to all men because all sinned . . .

For if many died through one man's trespass, much more have the grace of God and the free gift by the grace of that one man Jesus Christ abounded for many.

We know that the Law is spiritual; but I am unspiritual, sold as a slave to sin. I do not understand what I do. For what I want to do, I do not do. But what I hate, I do. And if I do what I do not desire, I admit that the Law is good. In that case, it is no longer I who do it, but it is sin living in me that does it.

Now the law came in to increase the trespass, but where sin increased, grace abounded all the more, so that, as sin reigned in death, grace also might reign through righteousness leading to eternal life through Jesus Christ our Lord.
—Romans 5:12, 15, 20–21, 7:14–17

See Appendix A for a prayer you can pray to move from 1.0 to 2.0.

Physical Limits

You're completely dependent upon God. He holds together everything physical by His power (Colossians 1:16–17). Jesus is the vine (the source), and you're a branch (John 15:1–11). God can be everywhere, but you can't. You can't create something out of nothing. Your body is wearing out, and you'll eventually die. You need air to breathe, water to drink, and food to eat.

Mental and Emotional Limits

God is perfect (complete) in knowledge and understanding. You have limited knowledge and awareness. You have only so much time to learn everything God knows. God will always know more than you do. When He wants you to know something, He will reveal only as much as needed and no more, as Paul experienced on multiple occasions (Acts 9:17–18, 2 Corinthians 12:1–10).

God limits your understanding while you're here on earth. A persistent fog blocks you from completely understanding who you are. You must live with two limits while you're here on earth:
1. Some truths won't be revealed until heaven.
2. Some distortions will remain until heaven.

When I was a child, I talked like a child, I thought like a child, I reasoned like a child. When I became a man, I put the ways of childhood behind me. For now we see only a reflection as in a mirror; then we shall see face to face. Now I know in part; then I shall know fully, even as I am fully known.
—1 Corinthians 13:11–12

If you don't know yourself or God completely, how can you know what is real and not real in your everyday life? God is more trustworthy than your self-image or life experiences. Even though you can't see God clearly, the Bible says God is perfect. That's enough to know you can trust and depend on God, the only absolute, self-sustaining being, even when life experiences don't match what the Bible teaches.

Personal and Natural Ability Limits

God is a person; He has a personality. I see God as unique primarily because of His heart — the depth of His love. No one can out-love God. He is praiseworthy because of His unlimited goodness and mercy. He is limited only in the sense that He can't be evil. In human terms, this could be "He's so busy being good that He doesn't have time to be bad." God maxes out on all abilities. For example, no one is more intelligent than God.

Sam learned that he has limits. God made him better at math than Max but not as good at baseball. Compared to others, you also have your strengths and weaknesses.

Compared to God, you're in a whole other category. You can't be God. You can't be everything to everybody. Your limitations mean you aren't self-sustaining but depend upon God for your life and well-being.

God invented the diversity of personalities and abilities and spread them out to billions of people. You're whole, but you're a fraction of God's creation. You are part of a community of believers. Only as a community of believers, the Bride of Christ, are we a suitable match to all that God is in Jesus Christ.

Facing the reality of these limitations might seem discouraging. However, these restrictions mean that you're responsible only for what's within your control and that God is responsible for the rest. Your responsibility ends where your identity ends. You are free to focus on all you are — and free from worrying about all you aren't.

Rest in the Security of God's Love

God's love for you is personal and attentive — more than enough to keep your sense of worth high. You are unique and therefore indispensable. When God dwells in you, He activates your potential to full capacity to accomplish amazing work (Ephesians 2:10).

God is love . . . Love is patient and kind; love does not envy or boast; it is not arrogant or rude. It does not insist on its own way; it is not irritable or resentful; it does not rejoice at wrongdoing, but rejoices with the truth. Love bears all things, believes all things, hopes all things, endures all things. Love never ends.
—1 John 4:8, 1 Corinthians 13:4–8

For Reflection

1. How easy or hard is it for you to rest in God's love?
2. Be born only once, and you'll end up dying twice. But be born twice, and you'll have an unending loving relationship with God.
3. *What was God thinking when He created me?* How do you read this — as a straight question or as a tongue-in-cheek question at your own expense?
4. In what way are your limitations good? Bad? In what ways, if any, are you frustrated with your limitations?
5. What would life be like without limitations?
6. Describe what life would be like if you were unique, needed, and consequently without competition.

Next Steps

- Create your own unique snowflake at blog.inventables.com/2014/11/snowflake-generator.html.
- Media for Further Learning (see Appendix B for more questions)
  - Movie: *Evan Almighty*. How does God show love to Evan?
  - Movie: *Toy Story*. How does Buzz Lightyear struggle with his identity?
  - Music: *You Are I Am* by MercyMe
- Fearful people-pleasing is the opposite of having a Confident Identity. Do you ever experience rejection and end up in the trenches of fear and anxiety? Would you like to be at peace instead of worrying about things out of your control? All of us need acceptance. We must find it from the right people at the right time. Read Psalm 118, focusing especially on applying verse 6, "The Lord is on my side; I will not fear. What can man do to me?"
- In your Blueprint Space, list your abilities and your limitations. How do they work together to shape your identity?
- Read about God's sovereignty at theopedia.com/sovereignty-of-god. How does the concept of sovereignty help define your identity?
- Are there any limitations you can mitigate? What roles do God and others play in this? How can you reduce any unnecessary vulnerabilities?
- Read John 14:12–14. Ask God for the power to do greater works in His name and in His will.

BLUEPRINT SPACE

Chapter 3

Doubtful or Hopeful

After Amy's positive start to marriage, the next fourteen years are average. She enjoys raising her sons, but her husband makes subtle and sometimes not-so-subtle comments about her gaining weight. She copes by focusing on her children and staying numb to her husband's hurtful words.

One day, Amy's husband speaks words to her that signal her marriage is over: "I love you, but I'm not in love with you." Within a year, she is divorced and all alone. Her world is shattered, and the shock of being abandoned again plunges her into despair.

I am overwhelmed by piercing silence.
What did I do to deserve this?
Death, come quickly to end my misery.

Why did You make me so unattractive?
I hate who I am.
God, where are You that I might hope?

I should have taken better care of myself.
I am in distress because of my failure.
Yet I haven't completely forgotten about You.

You are faithful, strong, and protective.
I am embarrassed around others.
God, You are so far out of my reach.

I am weak and exhausted.
I feel worthless, like trash headed to the dump.
May I never throw You out of my life!

Have Hope: God Is in Control

At some point in time, discouragement will come knocking at your door. Whether you let it in or it busts open the door, you'll have to contend with it. Discouragement may infiltrate your thoughts, but as a Christian, you have eviction power.

The Matrix, a popular movie from 1999, contrasts two approaches to life. One is real, and the other is a fake alternate reality. Real life is raw, messy, and difficult. The fake life isn't completely believable, but it is simple and pleasant.

Neo, the main character, starts out living in the fake reality. While living in the Matrix, Neo is woefully missing his full potential. As he realizes his life isn't making sense, he experiences a total identity crisis. He must come to terms with deciding which reality he is going to trust: the only reality he's ever known, as one-dimensional as it is, or a richer reality he hopes and suspects must exist.

If you aren't careful, you can be lulled into believing that what you see is all there really is. Neo doubted his significance — he doubted he was "The One." If the devil already has you believing you aren't significant, then he'll move on to someone else. That might make your life easier but only because you've removed yourself from reality.

You're in a battle for your identity. The devil wants you to either fear him, believing you can lose everything, or doubt your significance, believing you have nothing worth losing. The belief system you accept defines your reality. The battle is real, but your part in the battle is already won when you accept your True Identity as your reality. God wants you to fully participate in His reality, but whether each battle is won or lost is up to God. Embracing this means accepting that you'll lose some battles while evil wins. Fortunately, God has already won the war. God accepts responsibility for making it all work out in the end (Romans 8:28).

Your perception is your reality, but it's not always God's reality.

God appoints you to manage your thoughts. Once you form a conviction inside your head, no one can take that away from you. You can be confident in a profound spiritual truth or a meaningful experience. No one can prevent you from aligning with the truth. With God's truth, you have power to destroy spiritual strongholds (2 Corinthians 10:4–5).

God has given you an identity to manage. You're responsible for knowing yourself and living out your identity. You might not be able to do anything about your life circumstances.

Life will not always go in your favor. This doesn't necessarily mean you've done something wrong. You're responsible for being true to who you are and then faithful in your actions. God is responsible for the outcomes. Though your sour life experiences can be difficult to understand, God doesn't want you to worry about them — they aren't your responsibility.

God's in control, and He's your defender. As a way of life, trust Him to be in control of the results. How much do you trust God with the results? Trust can free you from excessive control and worry if you let it.

When I am afraid, I put my trust in you.
In God, whose word I praise, in God I trust; I shall not be afraid.
What can flesh do to me?
—Psalm 56:3–4

Life experiences influence what you believe. But what you acknowledge as truth determines how much you'll let experiences influence you. One of these ideas will trump the other. You're the major deciding factor in how that happens.

If you start with the philosophy "I deserve to be happy!" you'll be more likely to jump at the next gratifying opportunity, even if you must adjust your values away from God's truth. However, if you first appreciate that "God is a solid, unchanging reality!" you'll use that idea to make sense of your life experiences. Your life will be so much better aligned to God.

You can't win the battle for your identity without hope. If your primary reason for living is to secure your happiness, you need only wishful thinking, not real hope.

Have Hope: Your Struggle Is Temporary

Real hope means really living because you understand your future is secure. You're free to invest in eternity instead of focusing on being comfortable now. The reason for your hope must transcend your existence.

Socrates said the unexamined life is not worth living. Is your life worth living? Jesus said if you try to find your life, you will lose it, but if you lose your life for His sake, you will find it (Matthew 16:25). Jesus isn't making an anti-examination statement. He is saying that, in order to find your identity, you need to look beyond your earthly life.

You need a deeply rooted reason to go on living. Without one, you leave yourself in a precarious position. *Jesus's return cannot come soon enough*, you may think. *I'm better off dead than alive. Nobody would miss me if I had never been born.*

When you're without a solid foundation, a small crisis or a humongous inconvenience can uproot your life and leave you begging for death to come quickly. I'm not trying to be overly dramatic. I'm thinking of a plant with shallow roots. Such a plant is susceptible to the erosive effects of many small raindrops and equally as vulnerable to an average thunderstorm. Even if you aren't experiencing a great storm, without a foundation, you'll be in danger.

> *Everyone who comes to me and hears my words and does them, I will show you what he is like: he is like a man building a house, who dug deep and laid the foundation on the rock. And when a flood arose, the stream broke against that house and could not shake it, because it had been well built. But the one who hears and does not do them is like a man who built a house on the ground without a foundation. When the stream broke against it, immediately it fell, and the ruin of that house was great.*
> —Luke 6:47–49

If being sent to a corrupt prison doesn't provide ripe conditions for testing a shaky foundation, then nothing will. The movie *The Shawshank Redemption* demonstrates four responses to prison life that correspond to the four responses to an identity crisis as described in Chapter 1.

1. Andy Dufresne is a type of Christ; he has reached the Achieving response to an identity crisis. He is sent to prison for a crime he didn't commit, but he remains hopeful. Despite the injustice, he keeps his integrity and influences others for good. He lives for something beyond what seems possible given his immediate circumstances. He waits patiently for his time.
2. Red is like a disciple; he is a seeker, much like the Transforming response. He is guilty but doesn't lose complete touch with what it feels like to hope.
3. Brooks, in much the same situation as Red, allows prison to drain all semblance of hope from his life. He has a Conforming response to his crisis.
4. The other prisoners are near-sighted. They are unaware of a deeper reality, much like the Drifting response to an identity crisis.

Red isn't like the others. He becomes a "believer," catches hold of what Andy demonstrates, and chooses to take action upon it instead of dying a victim of his circumstances. He confronts his dim perspective. Red is teachable; he dares to hope.

You can't live without hope. When you have hope, you have some reason to go on living.

> *And not only the creation, but we ourselves, who have the firstfruits of the Spirit, groan inwardly as we wait eagerly for adoption as sons, the redemption of our bodies. For in this hope we were saved. Now hope that is seen is not hope. For who hopes for what he sees? But if we hope for what we do not see, we wait for it with patience.*
> —Romans 8:23–25

Brooks is released from prison after serving a near life sentence. He can't handle life outside of prison. He became too accustomed to the walls, which provided a false sense of security for him. Because he was a Conformer, his life crumples without the prison structure to keep him molded in shape. Too many decisions were made for him on the inside, and he doesn't know how to adjust to being a free man. He loses motivation to go on living.

An identity crisis, depending upon what you do with it, can resolve for better or for worse. What you refuse to confront becomes your limit. Brooks doesn't confront prison life like Andy. Instead, he allows it to shape him. Anything that you become accustomed to can be like a prison that keeps you from a thriving, healthy life.

Mark Petticord draws parallels between prison life and everyday life:

> Institutionalization isn't limited to the penitentiary. Many become tolerant, dependent and accustomed to the false security promised by the walls of their personal prisons. It could be the wrong career or job that's going nowhere, a toxic relationship or circumstance that seems out of their control. They become hopeless victims, accept their lot in life and just give up hope.[6]

The Israelites in Egypt faced the same problem when God freed them. They didn't know how to think like free people. They failed to keep up hope while enslaved. When God set them free, they continued to act like helpless slaves. They hated being slaves, but they hated trusting God with uncertainty even more. They lacked the spirit and faith to take the land God gave them, so God let them die in the wilderness.

Being a slave or imprisoned doesn't always have to be through a literal prison. Sometimes it can be allowing even the smallest untrue thoughts about yourself to take root in your life. God's promises apply to you as much as they apply to me. He says if you will lift up your hands, He will part the sea. You will pass through untouched while your enemies will be vanquished. Goodness and mercy will follow you all the days of your life (Exodus 14:16, Psalm 23:6).

If you let Him lead, He will free you from your bondage to this world into a fuller existence. Even in the wilderness, you can enjoy His Holy Spirit as your daily provider, healer, and deliverer.

Have Hope: Invest in Eternity

Through this book, I help you get busy living *and* get busy dying: You need to die to clinging to this life and pursuing its pleasures as an end. Living for the temporary provides a false sense of security. Living this way leaves nothing saved or stored up for the future; everything is spent. If you invest everything in the present moment, eventually you'll lose everything. But if you invest in eternity, you'll have treasure in heaven. Investing only in immediate pleasure is foolish; investing in eternity brings hope.

To grow in your Confident Identity, you'll have to believe life holds something more than you already have. Abundant life awaits you — but you won't fully experience it until the next life.

> *The thief comes only to steal and kill and destroy.*
> *I came that they may have life and have it abundantly.*
> —John 10:10

Paul faced intense persecution and was smart enough to figure out the afterlife would be a better place. He also knew his Confident Identity and how important it was for him to be present to communicate spiritual truth. Convinced of his significance, he remained. You are also significant.

---

[6] successmentor.com/get-busy-living-or-get-busy-dying

> *For to me to live is Christ, and to die is gain. If I am to live in the flesh, that means fruitful labor for me. Yet which I shall choose I cannot tell. I am hard pressed between the two. My desire is to depart and be with Christ, for that is far better. But to remain in the flesh is more necessary on your account. Convinced of this, I know that I will remain and continue with you all, for your progress and joy in the faith, so that in me you may have ample cause to glory in Christ Jesus, because of my coming to you again.*
> —Philippians 1:21–26

Paul had two positive options to choose from. This is different from thoughts of suicide. Suicidal thoughts are caused by the hopelessness of immediate circumstances: Death seems like the only solution to a situation misunderstood as hopeless. But when you're in touch with your Confident Identity, you possess a reason to live.

Life circumstances can steal the passion to live. You can become comfortable with the false sense of security. Your prison might be a career you didn't choose or a painful relationship you don't want anymore. As a Christian, you don't necessarily need to quit your job to experience freedom, but you do need to quit your self-imposed mental prison cell. When you lack hope, you're out of touch with who you really are.

To achieve true hope and freedom, you must stay true to God's values and the identity God gave you. Invest in what will last. Take the risk to bring your potential to light and pursue your life vision and dreams. Get busy living your True Identity and get busy dying to a False Identity.

A Shaky Foundation Produces Doubt

A person with a predominantly Confident Identity knows their true self and therefore lives by faith and trusts God with life's varied outcomes. But a person with a predominantly Infected Identity struggles to find joy and settles for a less authentic life. If you're more invested in your Infected Identity, or if you're trusting in other things beyond God's design, then you've built your house on sandy, shaky ground. When the storms of life come, you might find yourself suffering great loss (Luke 6:47–49).

Everyone has aspects of both the Confident and the Infected Identity. But, don't think of yourself as half all good and half all bad — as in, if you could throw out the bad, you'd be perfect. You're a whole person with some false beliefs that taint your identity. Instead of abandoning your whole self, know that you need Jesus to purify your beliefs and self-understanding so you can see yourself correctly.

Use these two contrasting lists to evaluate how healthy you are. Then you'll see the areas of your life needing improvement.

Confident Identity	Infected Identity
Has hope — trusts God	Has doubt — controls outcomes
Establishes being before doing	Establishes doing without being
Freedom mindset — true security	Slave mindset — false security
Genuine and vulnerable	Masked and guarded
Focused living	Distracted living
Healthy attachment to roles	Overinvests in roles

Invests in what is eternal	Invests in what is temporary
Sees potential in self	Sees self as worthless

You can confuse all sorts of things with your identity. A lack of a clear understanding of identity can lead you to reach for whatever is available for a sense of identity. Clinging to a pseudo-identity is better than knowing no identity at all. This situation is common in dysfunctional families where a True Identity is not modeled or allowed. You can eliminate confusion and do better by realizing that wealth, behavior, and responsibility aren't part of your identity.

Identity Isn't Wealth

Wealth and possessions are often substituted for identity, but anyone who prioritizes wealth knows that it doesn't bring lasting fulfillment. Hopefully, there will never come a day where you find your security in your earthly treasures like the rich farmer in the Gospel of Luke.

> *And he said to them, "Take care, and be on your guard against all covetousness, for one's life does not consist in the abundance of his possessions." And he told them a parable, saying, "The land of a rich man produced plentifully, and he thought to himself, 'What shall I do, for I have nowhere to store my crops?' And he said, 'I will do this: I will tear down my barns and build larger ones, and there I will store all my grain and my goods. And I will say to my soul, "Soul, you have ample goods laid up for many years; relax, eat, drink, be merry."' But God said to him, 'Fool! This night your soul is required of you, and the things you have prepared, whose will they be?' So is the one who lays up treasure for himself and is not rich toward God."*
> —Luke 12:15–21

Identity Isn't Behavior

Identity isn't action or behavior. Identity, or who you think you are, drives behaviors. Actions produce specific results and help you discover your identity, but they don't allow you to create your identity. For example, if you favor being analytical, that's part of your identity. You might like to work logic puzzles for mental stimulation, but God made you analytical before you ever worked a puzzle. Working puzzles can result in the self-knowledge that you excel at being analytical.

Identity Isn't Responsibility

Identity isn't fulfilling a particular role or responsibility. Roles are close to identity, but they aren't equal to identity. Roles can change; your identity cannot change. Examples of responsibility roles include mother, father, husband, wife, employee, and boss. As you can see, these are connected to and influence your self-image, but they aren't meant to define you permanently. Who you are supports and determines the style of your fulfillment of these roles, but you're much more than any one role.

Amy found this out the hard way:

Why is this happening to me?
Am I a loser?
Is there a way off this misery-go-round?

God, why did You create me?
Men want nothing to do with me.
No one misses my presence.

I wake up and go to bed lonely.
At least I still have my children.
They won't abandon me.

Even roles as parents are temporary, so having a child (or not having one) cannot be part of identity. Otherwise, an infertile person might conclude they're defective and live with the lie that something is personally wrong with them or that God is punishing them. Or a parent who has lost a child may develop the false belief that, "I am less of a person now that my child is gone. What will I do with the rest of my life?" Nor do parents lose their identities as kids grow up and move away. Moms give birth to helpless babies, but from the time the umbilical cord is cut, the goal is to raise a child who will eventually be independent.

Parenting a child is a privilege and a role, not an identity. Your identity is in the God-given ability to attach, nurture and love. A parent doesn't lose their identity or stop living just because the child is no longer there. If a parent loses a child, the grief is life-changing. The pain will never completely go away, but a hopeful path forward exists, even in the worst of circumstances.

Overinvesting in a role is not only possible but actually quite common. Roles can be adaptive because they provide some immediate sense of worth that might be desperately needed. Unfortunately, the more desperate the need, the more intense the clinging, and then the more intense the disillusionment and depression when the role fails to fulfill expectations of self-worth. This is because the expectations are unrealistic.

A role can also develop into a False Identity. This happens when the role becomes inflated and then larger than the whole sense of identity. Examples of such roles include: class clown, perfectionist, dutiful helper, and troublemaker/black sheep. These exaggerated roles, even though they can reveal part of a person's identity, are really only placeholders until developing a True Identity becomes safe.

A Firm Foundation Produces Hope

God determines your True Identity; therefore, it cannot be lost or taken from you. God's design of your identity is permanently protected. Your very existence depends upon God. He created you with great potential and holds you (body, mind, and spirit) together by His power and will. He designed you as a unique being with a unique purpose. He holds the only key to understanding the meaning of your life.

Identity Is Being

As a human being (not a human doing), your True Identity consists of the raw talents and abilities that God wired into your DNA. You can't be anything you want to be. If you're born with light skin, you can't have dark skin. A flower cannot turn into a horse. Without the talent to play basketball, you can't be a Michael Jordan. There's nothing wrong with playing basketball regardless of your raw talent, but you'll be better off if you develop your greatest potential abilities instead of trying to be a Jordan when that is an unrealistic goal.

What if you're short and you want to play basketball? Your height is a superficial limitation compared to the ability and desire God placed inside you. You must ultimately follow your heart as God lives inside you and directs your steps. God looks at the heart, particularly a heart tuned to

Him, not external appearances. In *Star Wars*, Han Solo says, "Never tell me the odds." If you focus on what seems improbable, you limit God's design and power.

Even when your potential for something is present from birth, the ability often requires practice and experimentation. Early on in life, you don't know what gifts and abilities God designed in you. If you don't experiment with many different possibilities, you might miss your calling! You'll doubt you have significance. If you never pick up a pencil and give drawing an honest try, you'll never become an artist. Even when you know you have potential, you have a choice to embrace your God-given gifts or reject them.

Because God created you, He knows exactly what your experimentation will produce. This doesn't eliminate your free will. God knows everything, but from our perspective, we must search, discover, and make choices. He wants you to have assurance and to hope in the future-you that He is sculpting before your eyes.

> *Now faith is the assurance of things hoped for,*
> *the conviction of things not seen.*
> —Hebrews 11:6

Identity is not determined by anything temporary. If something is going to end at some point, then it cannot be part of your identity. Examples include your job, your health, and your relationships. When what you rely on as your identity ceases to exist, this can result in a world of hurt and create a deep sense of being lost. You'll be better off if you don't put your identity into anything that you can lose.

Who you are at your core has more to do with your raw characteristics and abilities (your God-given superpowers) rather than either the roles and responsibilities you take on in life (your super suit) or what you do (your fight against evil). Your power is in your identity, not in your costume.

In the following figure, the farther away the concentric circles are from the center, the greater the distance from your True Identity. If you don't understand who you are at your core, you might slip into a panic when you lose the outer layers.

Internalized Sense of Identity

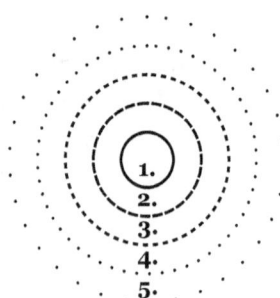

Statement	Scope	Duration	
1. "I have aesthetic and spacial abilitities"	Ability	Eternal	More General and Permanent
2. "I am an artist"	Role	Lifetime	
3. "I am an art educator"	Career	Decades	
4. "I am a high school art teacher"	Job	Years	More Specific and Short-lived
5. "I am painting a picture of a farm"	Project	Months	

Raw talents and abilities are permanent and generalize well. You'll be better off building your self-image on these instead of on specific and narrow skills. Seeing yourself as having one specific ability narrows your options. Instead of saying, "I paint pictures of farms well," you can broaden your self-image by realizing, "I have aesthetic and spatial abilities." Equating your identity with the former comes with great risk if, for example, you can no longer find people interested in farm paintings. You'll feel worthless because your self-image is defined the wrong way.

A stable lifetime career can result in an unhealthy sense of loss (in what you perceive to be your identity) if you associate your identity with the tasks at hand rather than the abilities you bring. The abilities can transfer and apply to other careers, but a specific role or job at your company is probably gone forever.

Make the effort to base your identity on eternal abilities rather than external realities or temporary assignments. Of course, beyond these practical considerations, all Christians have a spiritual identity based on their relationship with God (which we explore in later chapters).

For Reflection

1. "God didn't call me to be successful; he called me to be faithful." —Mother Teresa
2. An identity crisis is an opportunity for growth and the acceptance of responsibility.
3. Consider the following phrases. What do they mean? Why are they thought or spoken?
    - "You aren't yourself today."
    - "I don't know who I am anymore."
    - "I wish I knew God's will for my life."
    - "I came to my senses and remembered who I was."
    - "Why was I ever born?"
    - "What if I never get married?"
4. Are you aware of anything that you're relying upon too heavily? If you lost it, would you suffer more than grief? Would you suffer an identity crisis?
5. What roles are a part of your life? How healthy is your investment in each?
    - Mother/father
    - Husband/wife
    - Provider/caregiver
    - Daughter/son
    - Brother/sister
    - Employee/employer
6. In what ways are you like a prisoner? If you were a bird in a cage and the cage door became unlocked, would you have any desire to choose freedom?
7. Read about the rich man and Lazarus in Luke 16:19–31. What does this passage teach about identity and comfort? How can you be content in this moment rather than happy only when a future event occurs?

Next Steps

- ☐ Has your understanding of Confident Identity changed since you started reading this book? What have you learned about yourself? Record any insights in your Blueprint Space. Do you believe you're significant? Set a goal to believe this by the time you finish this book.
- ☐ Consider the main project you have going right now. What abilities do you use every day that are not specific to the project? (For example, an architect has spatial and creative design abilities that might also be used in a career as an athletic shoe designer.)
- ☐ Media for Further Learning (see Appendix B for more questions)
    - ☐ Movie: *The Shawshank Redemption.* Read more about Shawshank at successmentor.com/get-busy-living-or-get-busy-dying.

☐ Movie: *The Matrix.* Read about the Christian themes in *The Matrix* at awesomehouse.com/parallels.html.
☐ Music: *I Have This Hope* by Tenth Avenue North

BLUEPRINT SPACE

Chapter 4

Rejected or Accepted

Amy, now divorced for a year and in her 30s, arrives home after a long day at work.

Being a single mom is exhausting, but at least I'm moving on with my life and I have a steady boyfriend. I'm looking forward to seeing him at Max's game this weekend.

The next day her phone rings, and she answers. "Hi, Amy," her boyfriend says. "How are you doing? Hey, listen, I'm not going to be able to go to Max's game on Saturday. Actually, I've been thinking, I need some time to myself. I don't think we should be dating exclusively. . ."

He keeps talking, but his words fade into the background as heartache hijacks Amy's chest. Feeling dizzy, she sits down hard.

Rejected and alone again. This is too much for me. I can't take this anymore. Why did you let this happen, God? Where are you?

A few more weeks go by without Amy hearing from her boyfriend. While getting ready for work, she looks into her mirror and winces. Cutting words from the past echo in her head: "You've put on some weight since the wedding. I'm not attracted to you anymore. I found someone else."

Why do I keep choosing men who end up leaving me? Now I'm older and single again. I need to lose some weight, or no man will be interested in me.

Amy turns away from the mirror.

Ugh. Not attractive!

As she looks into the mirror again, she feels anxious and confused.

How am I ever going to move past this when I have this mirror to remind me?

Awareness of Emotional Health

Amy is lost and needs to know which direction will lead to being found the fastest. But before she starts moving, she first needs to know where she is; otherwise, she might make matters worse. She could end up heading in a random direction and become more lost.

How did Amy end up adrift in such painful circumstances? Her overall emotional health is bound up in two factors: her self-image and her life experiences. Her emotional health can be no better than what she sees through these two distorted lenses. Self-image is vulnerable to negative influences. When she incorrectly interprets her life experiences, her self-image suffers. Being able to sort out truth from fiction is essential for emotional health.

Self-Image

Self-image (the more common term for Perceived Identity) is your internal view of yourself — your understanding of who you are. Looking in the mirror is uncomfortable for Amy because of her negative, internalized self-image. She is having a hard time feeling attractive given the evidence she has to the contrary. The mirror is neutral because it only reflects what's in front of it, but it's enough to dredge up past painful conversations (experiences).

Current self-image is the sum of the impact of all previous life experiences. It represents current ability to interpret life experiences and neutralize the negative ones.

Amy rates her self-image at 70 percent negative. Where do you estimate your self-image to be? First determine whether your self-image is positive or negative; then choose its strength as a percentage between 0 and 100 percent.

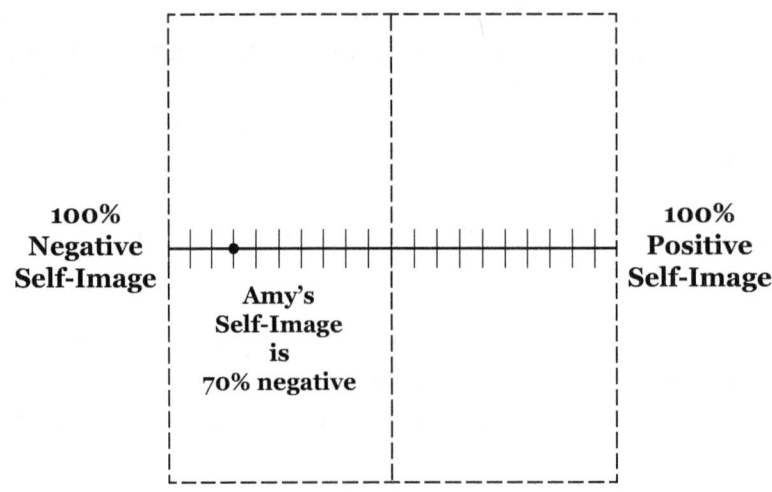

Life Experience

Life experience is everything that happens to you as you look to people — including God — and things. To be alive is to be confronted with a constant flow of experiences. As you interact with your environment, you can make observations and receive feedback.

For better or for worse, experiences are a strong factor in changing self-image. Experiences can be positive, as in an encouraging word from your friend or the Holy Spirit speaking truth into your heart as you read the Bible. Or they can be negative as in verbal or physical abuse by a bully at school. Your interpretation of your experiences makes all the difference because when your heart is negative, even a positive experience can be perceived as negative.

Current environment is what you are experiencing in your life right now. For example, consider the quality of your relationships with friends, family, and God. Then include the quality of your activities, such as hobbies, church community, work, and so on. A positive environment is supportive and life-building. You need an environment where you can grow.

Do not be deceived: "Bad company ruins good morals."
—1 Corinthians 15:33

*Make no friendship with a man given to anger, nor go with a wrathful man,
lest you learn his ways and entangle yourself in a snare.*
—Proverbs 22:24–25

Amy has had too many negative experiences with men. Because of her breakup, Amy's current environment is 40 percent negative. Where do you estimate your current environment to be? First determine whether your current environment is positive or negative; then choose its strength as a percentage between 0 and 100 percent.

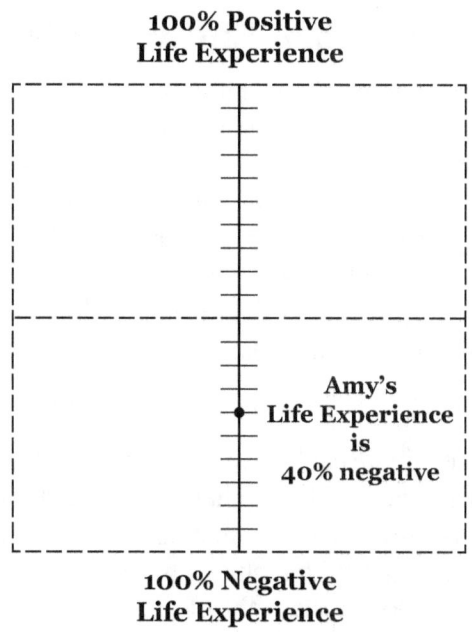

Emotional Health

How positive or negative your self-image and life experiences are in relation to each other determines the current state of your emotional health. By evaluating self-image and life experience, Amy becomes more aware of her emotional health. Both are negative, but her self-image is more negative than her life experience. This means she won't become significantly worse.

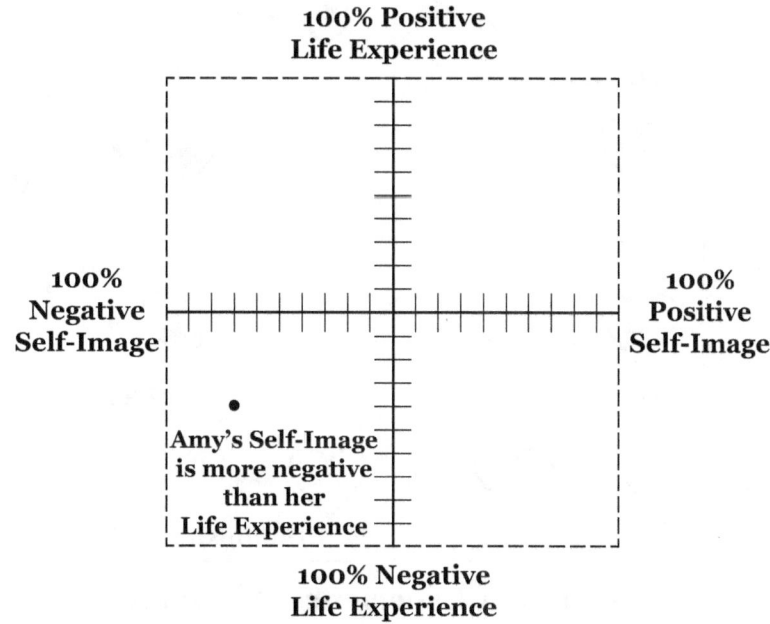

Amy is staying focused on the men in her life instead of feeling the pain of her own need. Deep down, she desires attention so she'll feel worthwhile. Her environment is still negative but likely won't cause her to feel much worse than she already does. This knowledge will help her determine what kind of positive experiences she needs in order to move her self-image into positive territory.

Awareness of Life Momentum

Life momentum is a measure of how fast your self-image is improving or worsening. When you're aware of your momentum, you'll better understand yourself and can proactively make positive changes in your environment.

If a new experience is more negative than your current self-image, then the change in self-image will be negative. Similarly, if your new experience is more positive than your current self-image, this leads to a positive change in self-image. If you aren't experiencing anything new and significant, then your life can't improve and might become worse by default!

This formula defines how self-image changes:

Current Self-Image + New Experience = Potential Change in Self-Image

You can use this formula to evaluate each new experience. Estimate your current self-image as already described in the "Self-Image" section. Then, estimate the impact of the new experience (whether positive or negative). Adding the two elements yields an estimate of your new self-image.

In the following diagram, each heart with a plus or minus symbol inside represents current self-image, and the plus or minus symbol to the right of each heart represents life experience. If we compare the relative size of positive or negative self-image with life experience, we get eight life momentum zones.

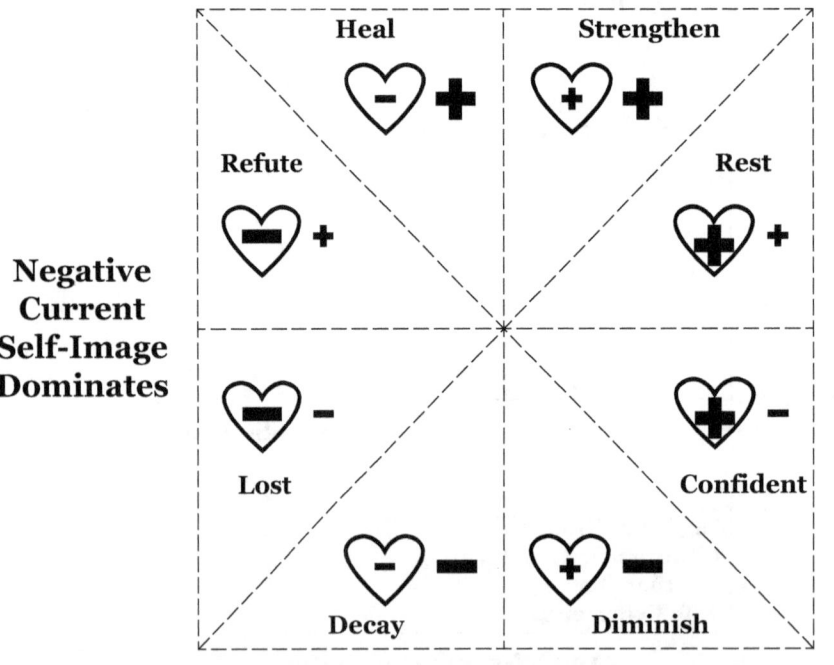

When the symbol outside the heart is larger, this indicates that the experience is enough to make significant changes to self-image. For example, in the Heal Zone, the large plus sign indicates that a positive life experience is enough to dominate and change the negative self-image. Here's how the zones compare, based on whether the life experience or self-image dominates:

- **The two bottom zones:** Negative life experience dominates self-image.
- **The two top zones:** Positive life experience dominates self-image.
- **The two left zones:** Negative self-image dominates life experience.
- **The two right zones:** Positive self-image dominates life experience.

Finding your zone will help you begin to quantify several things, giving you a sense of your direction in life. Do you have positive or negative momentum? Are you stagnant? How resilient or vulnerable are you to life experiences? How big or small is the impact of what you're going through? How buried are you in your past experiences?

Movement between zones happens as your environment becomes more positive or more negative. Environments usually change gradually. For example, even if Amy were to change her environment and meet a Godly man, her negative self-image would likely continue to dominate for a while (Refute Zone). More than likely though, she'd first choose a man who is only slightly less negative (Lost Zone). Even if you have a strong negative self-image, as you choose an increasingly stronger positive environment, you can move from the Decay Zone to the Strengthen Zone (Decay to Lost to Refute to Heal to Strengthen).

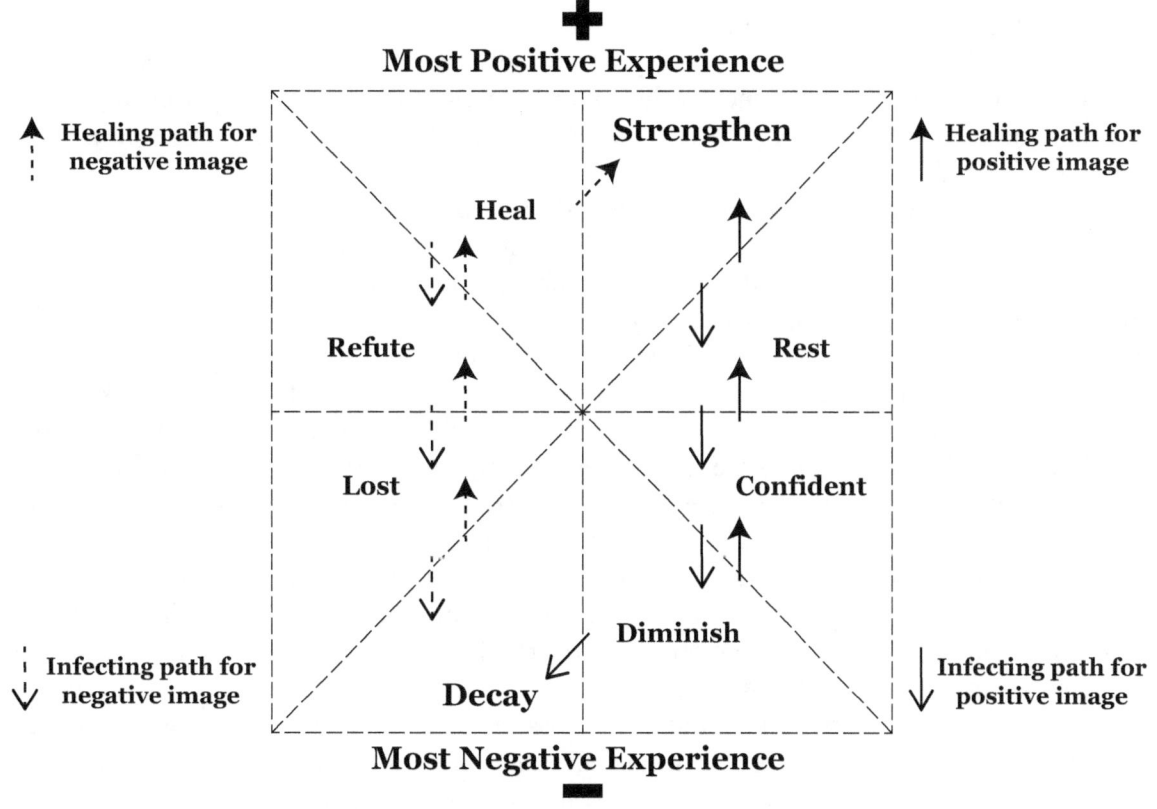

Healing doesn't happen overnight. As you're moving in the right direction, you'll still feel pain while you recover. Think of Decay as being in the emergency room, Lost as intensive care, Refute as rehabilitation, Heal as home recovery, and Strengthen as fully recovered.

Relational support helps move you toward Strengthen, whereas relational wounds move you toward Decay. Receiving support from others is positive and is often enough to outweigh the negatives. Sometimes God supports you directly, and at other times He supports you through others. If you know you are loved, even an extremely difficult situation becomes bearable. I didn't say *easy* or *fun!* The positive experiences build up resistance to negative experiences, and the support you receive makes you more resilient.

Unfortunately, the opposite is true, too. Going through a negative experience without support can double the pain. This happens all too often when children are abused and don't have a parent who protects and validates them.

For the remainder of the chapter, as I explore each of the eight zones, I continue to use Amy as an example, as if she was living in each zone.

Two Dominant Negative Experience Zones

These zones are found at the bottom with a large negative to the right of each heart. If you find yourself in either of the negative experience zones, this means you're facing a negative life situation that is overwhelming your self-image. You're losing the battle for achieving a Confident Identity because you're vulnerable to believing lies resulting from negative experiences. You're actively moving away from the truth.

Sometimes life experiences are beyond your control (bad things happen to good people). At other times, you choose the experience or the circumstances that lead to the experience (you make a mistake and suffer the consequences). Whether you choose the experience or not, your environment is crushingly negative.

Don't forget that your True Identity — God's design for you — is always positive. Identity is *not* having something done to you that is out-of-line with the truth, such as: name-calling, neglect, abuse, or rape. These experiences, if you're vulnerable to them, can only result in a False Identity.

Because of the pain involved, denying negative experiences (employing poor coping strategies) is tempting. In our example, Amy looks in her mirror. Before she has a chance to register what she sees, she distorts the image. She does this because she sees a reality that she doesn't like or can't accept. She allows her fear of rejection to interfere with reality and thus overrides the truth of the mirror. She sees what she wants to see. She copes by denying the truth, or she's confused at best.

If Amy doesn't like how her accurate mirror stirs up uncomfortable feelings, she could choose a different mirror. She might not want to face the deeper pain of rejection, so she could surround herself with people who tell her, "You don't need to lose weight." No one likes being uncomfortable. Often, we pick mirrors that tell us we are acceptable so we don't have to face our need to grow. However, denying experiences never results in an improved self-image. Instead, it only takes the healing option off the table.

In extreme situations, dissociation might be necessary to survive. *Dissociation* is disconnection from experiences that are too overwhelmingly negative. Memories don't heal on their own. To heal, you'll need to revisit the memories when you're in a more positive environment.

Decay Zone

The Decay Zone is the worst place you can be because your negative self-image is actively becoming worse. Either you're hitting bottom, or you will soon.

In grade school, Amy was bullied by several kids who called her names like "fatso." She was too weak to defend herself, so she developed a negative self-image. As a teenager, Amy received ongoing negative feedback: "You're always going to be fat and ugly." She agreed with the abusive comments.

Nobody cares. God made me ugly for a reason. I'll show them I can lose weight. I'll never be fat again. I'll be so skinny that I'll steal the attention away from those who called me fat.

Or, Amy might move to a place where she considers ending her life.

I'm unlovable. My situation is hopeless. I'm better off dead.

Desperate for control amidst devastating negatives, she might adopt an overcompensating strategy that numbs the pain but doesn't provide any healing. She could reject what is considered normal and end up exaggerating reality. She makes up her own reality and turns a blind eye to the negative consequences of her behavior. She might not like how overweight she is, so she decides that being ultra-skinny is the way to go. This severe coping numbs and isolates Amy from outside help; it blocks the pain but allows the wound to continue to fester and deepen.

Diminish Zone

In the Diminish Zone, you experience overwhelmingly negative events that move you further away from the truth you know.

Amy might receive negative feedback similar to what she received in the Decay Zone but react to it differently. Her husband shames her for being overweight. He acts selfishly as a way to maintain control. Hearing negative words while she has some positive self-worth is more shocking and therefore more painful. She knows her husband to be otherwise a nice guy, but she starts to collapse under his negative words.

I don't look good enough for my husband. I must be fat since he says I am. I look average and I exercise a little every day. Maybe God is speaking to me through my husband — telling me to lose weight. I'm an awful person for eating so much. I better lose weight or else I'll really be unacceptable.

To avoid her fear of being rejected, Amy can choose a denial strategy that overlooks her problem. Instead of healing the infection, she denies it and will end up losing any sense of a positive self-image.

She can't accept that she's overweight, so she chooses an internal reality to defend herself against her negative self-image: *I'm fine. I don't need to change anything.* She might employ a strategy to deny that her husband ever said such horrible things. She thinks, *That didn't happen.* Or alternatively, if there is any truth to what her husband said, she rationalizes, *My friend Sarah weighs as much as I do. My weight isn't a problem.*

Two Dominant Positive Experience Zones

Heal ♡− ✚   ♡+ ✚ Strengthen

These zones are found at the top, with a large positive sign to the right of each heart. Here, your positive experiences dominate your negative beliefs, resulting in strong growth. Here, you're most open to the truth and invest in personal growth, usually at the expense of some stability (a risk worth taking).

This is a spiritually healthy place to be. You're positioning yourself to be able to encounter life-changing truths. This requires being intentional by regularly investing in the potential to gain positive life experiences. This might mean matching a hunger for growth with going on a spiritual retreat, attending a life group at church, going to counseling, or meeting with a good friend.

The Holy Spirit is responsible for illuminating our minds and guiding us into truth (John 16:13). The Holy Spirit, being a person, provides an external view of reality; however, living within you, He also has direct access to your internal view of reality. Sometimes God works through others to provide this enlightenment.

When Amy is in one of these positive-experience zones, her view of reality becomes clearer. She is better able to discern what is true so she won't take in the wrong messages. She puts herself in a positive position by reading her Bible, taking to heart her pastor's sermon, or accepting encouragement from a friend or her counselor.

Heal Zone

In the Heal Zone, you experience truths that are stronger than your internalized negative beliefs. This is the best zone for recovery from negative life events. Your True Identity is growing because your Infected Identity is shrinking.

You can use your improving self-image to reinterpret past experiences. If you're already healthy enough, this will happen automatically. If you aren't, your past is buried deep enough that you have to go looking for it so you can introduce it to your new positive experiences.

I know I'm loved, Amy thinks, *but I don't feel it all the way yet. I know the truth; I can see what is false. I know those lies don't apply to me but I don't quite feel it in my heart.*

Amy tentatively accepts some positive experiences but remains skeptical at other times.

Strengthen Zone

The Strengthen Zone is the best place to be. In this zone, you experience truths that are stronger than your already internalized positive beliefs. You'll want to be in this zone for areas where you have already made progress but want to become stronger. Your Potential Identity is shrinking because your Confident Identity is growing.

Staying in a place of consistent growth requires high energy and focus. You must be intentional about staying on top of all that life throws at you. This can be an uncomfortable zone because growth happens as God stretches you beyond familiar territory in order to increase your capacity and allow you to hold more positive experiences.

I'm loved. In fact, I sense God loving me right now. I feel good about myself and God is blessing me with more positive experiences from Him.

Amy wholeheartedly accepts positive experiences and welcomes growth opportunities.

Two Dominant Negative Self-Image Zones

These zones are found at the left, with the large negative sign inside each heart. Here, your negative self-image has taken root so deeply that your life experiences are too weak to make a significant difference. Thoughts of change and hope are replaced with depression that comes with feeling stuck and trapped. Your environment is stagnant and weak.

You've developed a hardened heart such that it blocks the truth from penetrating. Your negative self-worth refutes or is ignorant of biblical truth. You've become so hopelessly indifferent that you don't seek out stronger experiences to bring change into your life.

The negatives you believe have the potential to become super-distorted. When you're this negative, you move beyond accepting the negative. Instead, you reject what is positive. For example, Amy might be slightly overweight, but believe she is extremely fat. She might not be able to trust the reality provided by a mirror.

Refute Zone

In the Refute Zone, you're so invested in your negative self-image that you discount positive experiences. Rejecting a compliment is one way this might happen.

Amy could be in a positive environment, but her heart may be too hard. Her dad says, "You look beautiful!" reflecting a genuinely positive image, but her self-image is so negative that she can't accept the compliment. She could feel a vague sense of hope but swiftly reject it. She might even become angry because of the internal conflict between the two realities.

I'll never be beautiful. I'm different. That will never be me. Dad, stop! I know what people have told me. Leave me alone already! I'm ugly. You can't accept it. I'll never change. In fact, I don't need to change. I'm fat and proud of it. People who try to compliment me are so arrogant.

Amy is overinvested in a negative image. The darkness of Amy's mind is enough to block out the image of the glorious creation she is. Even with the truth in front of her, she can't accept words of blessing from the very one who made her.

Lost Zone

In the Lost Zone, you're so invested in your negative self-image that you're numb to negative experiences. You might actually feel worse than you would in the Decay Zone, but at least here you aren't getting much worse. You can feel a heavy sense of defeat, and becoming perpetually depressed is easy.

In negative situations, Amy simply agrees with the lies. When a man points out that she's overweight, she responds with, "Yes, I know I'm ugly," and holds onto the negative belief, *I'm unwanted.* Without much positive in her life, she feels stuck going nowhere. This can lead to a fear of being rejected, then to a fear of being unattractive, and finally to anxiety about being overweight. To manage these fears apart from a strong enough positive experience, she will likely activate a coping strategy.

Without the desire or ability to seek truth as a standard to ground Amy, she is left to wander in the dark, unable to pursue growth or healing. She's free to make up her own reality and choose her own method to evaluate reality.

I'm worthless. I'm doomed to be fat forever. Where are you, God? Why was I ever born? I'm not good at anything. I'm too fat. No man is going to want me. Nothing is ever going to change. I'm already hopelessly overweight, so I might as well eat all I want.

Amy accepts defeat and resigns herself to her negative self-image. She continues to eat and put on weight because her situation feels hopeless.

Two Dominant Positive Self-Image Zones

These zones are found at the right of the diagram with the large positive signs inside each heart. You gain stability at the cost of some growth. These are the zones where you're most stable because of your positive self-image. You're definitely not losing ground, but you aren't exactly gaining, either. This a good place to rest and recognize how far you've come.

No one sees reality perfectly all the time (except God; see Hebrews 4:13). But in this life, there is such a thing as *good enough*.

There is the opportunity for rest, but also the possibility for complacency to take hold. You could feel like you're doing all right and you're tired of working so hard to improve yourself. A lack of strong, positive experiences could be the first step toward further decline into the negative experience zones.

Rest Zone

In the Rest Zone, you experience reminders of what you've already come to know as your Confident Identity. The strength of your positive experiences can deteriorate over time, but having your identity affirmed keeps it from deteriorating.

---

*When a man's ways please the LORD,
he makes even his enemies to be at peace with him.*
—Proverbs 16:7

Amy isn't bothered by negative experiences, so she can focus her energy on receiving God's love for her. She might also be experiencing less interest in growth experiences, which could eventually create problems for her. She could become complacent and not pursue God with her whole heart.

God is so good to me. I'm finally at peace — loving life and having fun.

Confident Zone

In the Confident Zone, you're able to defend your mind against negative events. You're strong enough to not be phased by them. Your Confident Identity is put to the test and found to be firmly rooted. You reject negative experiences and thoughts.

You have confidence enough to help others, but at the same time, you must be careful to not let the negative experiences accumulate and get the best of you. This isn't the time to be prideful.

Whether Amy steps on the scale and finds she has put on weight, or a man tells her she looks fat, she doesn't become overly concerned. She can accept her condition without forming the negative conclusion, *I am ugly.* She is able to look to God for approval, instead of to false idols (her weight, men, etc.).

I want to look good for the important people in my life. I have some work to do, but nothing's going to keep me from God's love. I'm beautiful even if I weigh too much right now.

For Reflection

1. Which of the zones do you find yourself in most often? Where are you today?
2. Don't let your struggle become your identity.
3. Can you see how distorted self-image and negative life experiences explain how two people can miscommunicate?
4. Read each scenario and consider how your self-image would change if you had that experience.
   - Your parents consistently favor a sibling over you.
   - You father sticks up for you when you're picked on by a teammate.
   - Your parents work multiple jobs.
   - Your husband/wife regularly makes time to spend with you at your favorite activity.
   - Your parents consistently address you angrily.

- Your mom disciplines you fairly and always in love.
- You dad abandoned your family when you were 3 years old.
- You are welcomed into a small group at church.
- Your mom clung to you for support when you were 8 years old.
- Your son forgives you for past mistakes and invites you to more family activities.

5. Review the strategies in the "Coping in the Zones" diagram. What patterns do you see? Use this figure to help diagnose and improve your responses to life experiences.

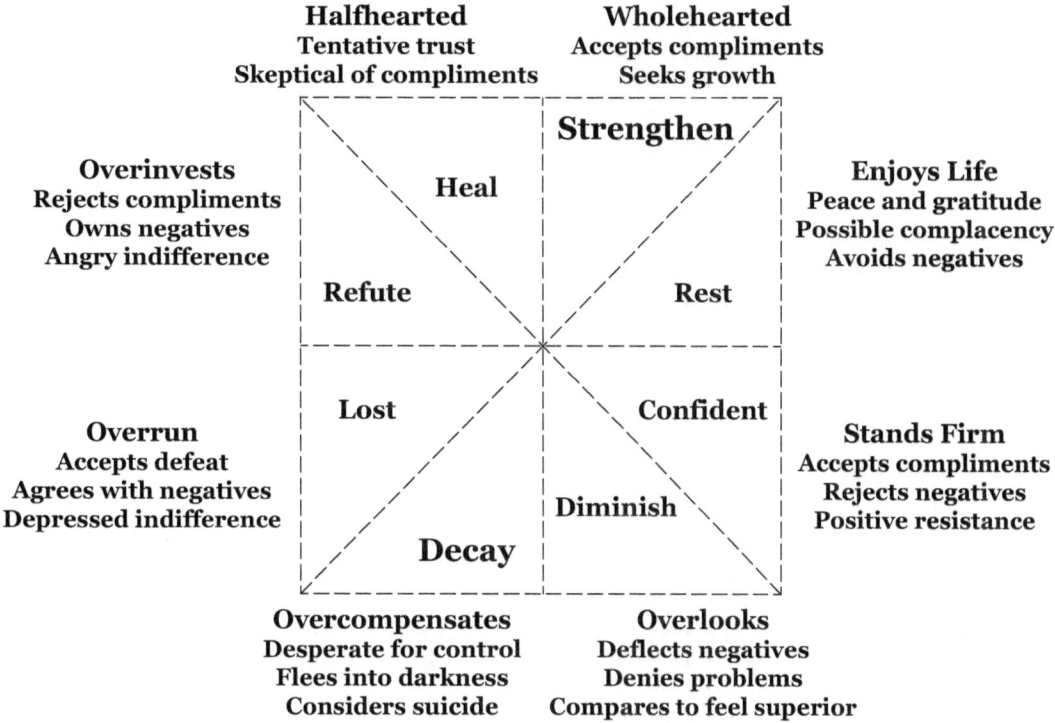

Next Steps

☐ Use crayons to color a beautiful picture. Fill the entire area but avoid using very dark colors. Then completely cover the picture using a black crayon. The colorful picture represents your True Identity. The black covering represents your False Identity — the cumulative effect of negative life experiences. Use a coin or other object to scrape away some of the black crayon. This represents your Confident Identity shining through into your awareness.

☐ Media for Further Learning (see Appendix B for more questions)
  ☐ Movie: *The Truman Show*. How does Truman cope with his circumstances?
  ☐ Movie: *The King's Speech*. How does the king overcome his issue?
  ☐ Music: *Hard Love* by Needtobreathe

☐ When was the happiest time of your life? The most discouraging time of your life? Graph out the highs and lows of your life history, labeling the most significant times. What do you notice about your life? How have you survived through the difficult times?

- Keep in mind the relationship between self-image and life-experience. Always evaluate your environment to determine if it is toxic (life-stealing) or nourishing (live-giving). Work toward becoming strong so you can be the "big plus" in someone else's otherwise negative existence.

BLUEPRINT SPACE

Chapter 5

Isolated and Desolate

Amy continues to feel lost, and her situation appears to be becoming worse.

I'm worthless. I'm doomed to be fat forever. Where are you God? Nothing is ever going to change. I'm already hopelessly overweight, so I might as well eat all I want.

Amy accepts defeat and resigns herself to her negative self-image. Her longings seem hopeless, so she continues to eat too much and put on weight.

I'm not good at anything. I'm too fat. No man is ever going to want me. Why was I ever born?

After more months of weight gain, Amy feels crushed to the point of desperation. But hitting bottom helps her attempt to turn her life around. She joins a weight-loss program. While the people in her program aren't believers, they hold her accountable to her goals. She stops gaining weight and starts to lose some weight. Yet, even with all her efforts, she still feels lonely and confused.

Life can be so unfair. I've been trying so hard for years. Will I ever find a good companion in this life?

Suffering Consequences from the Curse and Sin

Whenever you experience emotional pain, the consequence of sin and the curse are involved. When you're in pain, you have a choice: Trust God or your own way. If you neglect to trust God, you become vulnerable to the forces of evil and ultimately make matters worse. More suffering presents another opportunity to choose God's way or to dig deeper into your own solution.

Identity is an interesting concept because to comprehensively define it requires considering your relationship to God, others, and your environment. You can't make sense of your identity unless you consider the world in which you live. God doesn't make us with a desire for something (such as food) without also providing a way to fulfill the desire. God supplies all you need to develop your True Identity, but you still must contend with your False Identity.

To understand the state of your False Identity, consider it in the context of the curse, hurtful experiences, and fruitless activities. The curse leads to wounding relationships (negative experiences), which lead to a False Identity, which results in fruitless labor:

1. **The curse:** Because of sin, which separates us from God, God cursed creation. The curse makes negative experiences possible.
2. **Wounding relationship:** A wounding relationship is any negative life experience resulting in a more distant connection to God.
3. **False Identity:** This is a negative distorted self-image. Negative experiences can cover up your True Identity if you let them.
4. **Fruitless labor:** Fruitless labor is effort spent in striving for what is a False Identity, which results in false security. You cope with negatives instead of facing the truth and pursuing healing.

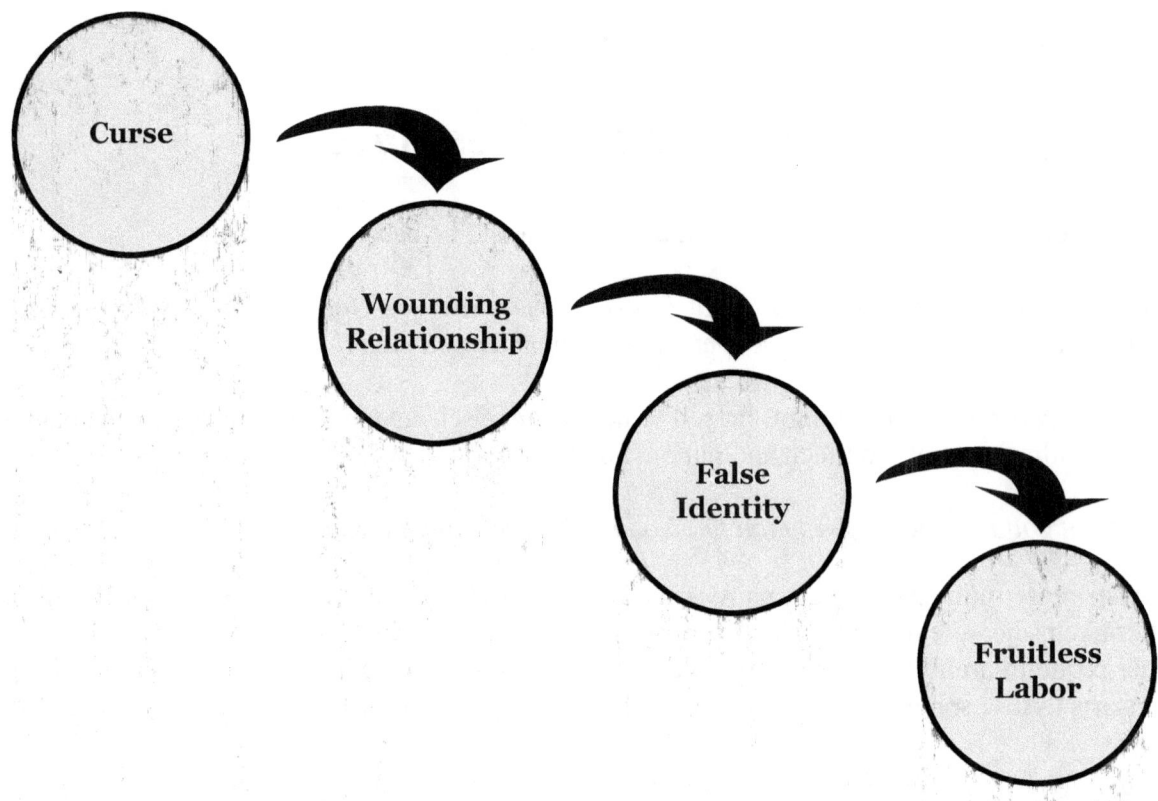

Whenever you choose your own way, you'll likely end up creating more problems and consequences that you'll have to deal with later. Usually, you won't be able to get yourself out of your own mess. The same thing happened to Adam and Eve.

Enter This World Cursed

Adam and Eve entered this world in a near perfect condition. God wired them for loving, intimate relationship with Him and each other. And that's exactly what they experienced, until Satan entered the picture. He exploited their vulnerability, and the world hasn't been the same since.

After Adam and Eve ate the forbidden fruit, doing what God commanded them not to do, they experienced a huge shock as more consequences came into their lives. They no longer had the innocence to go straight to God with their problems. Feeling shame, they attempted to hide and find their own way out of the mess they had got themselves into (Genesis 3:8).

Adam and Eve experienced the pain of being lost as they were ejected from their home, the Garden of Eden (Genesis 3:14–24). As you read about Adam and Eve, notice the layers of pain that came from the curse. Adam and Eve suffered in ways specific to their genders and also generally as they were expelled from the garden. They lost their identities in ways we'll never completely understand.

The Lord God said to the serpent, "Because you have done this, cursed are you above all livestock and above all beasts of the field; on your belly you shall go, and dust you shall eat all the days of your life. I will put enmity between you and the woman, and between your offspring and her offspring; he shall bruise your head, and you shall bruise his heel."

> *To the woman he said, "I will surely multiply your pain in childbearing; in pain you shall bring forth children. Your desire shall be contrary to your husband, but he shall rule over you."*
>
> *And to Adam he said,*
> *"Because you have listened to the voice of your wife and have eaten of the tree of which I commanded you, 'You shall not eat of it,' cursed is the ground because of you; in pain you shall eat of it all the days of your life; thorns and thistles it shall bring forth for you; and you shall eat the plants of the field. By the sweat of your face you shall eat bread, till you return to the ground, for out of it you were taken; for you are dust, and to dust you shall return."*
>
> *The man called his wife's name Eve, because she was the mother of all living. And the Lord God made for Adam and for his wife garments of skins and clothed them.*
>
> *Then the Lord God said, "Behold, the man has become like one of us in knowing good and evil. Now, lest he reach out his hand and take also of the tree of life and eat, and live forever—" therefore the Lord God sent him out from the garden of Eden to work the ground from which he was taken. He drove out the man, and at the east of the garden of Eden he placed the cherubim and a flaming sword that turned every way to guard the way to the tree of life.*
> —Genesis 3:14–24

God created you with the perfect you in mind, just like He created Adam and Eve. But you're different, because from birth you've experienced a cursed world without the ability to overcome it on your own. Because of sin and the curse, you start spiritually dead — separated from God.

The world is cursed to work against you — ready to produce negative experiences. You even begin life with a body that is wired to work against you — ready to interpret negative experiences in the worst way possible. Because there will be negative experiences, your brain must be able to handle negative emotions (anger, fear, sadness) that weren't necessary before the fall. From day one, you start accumulating a self-image deficit. You're guaranteed to have negative experiences, so there will always be a deficit to overcome.

Yet even while you're in this condition, the stronger negatives can drive you back to God with more urgency.

Suffer Loss of Relationship

Negative experiences come about because of the curse and everyone's sin. They include the consequences of others' direct or indirect actions. All emotional pain is relational pain at some point. If someone betrays you, this is clearly relational. When you lose a loved one to health problems too early in life, you can blame it on the curse. There is only the *appearance* of God's indirect betrayal.

God is the catch-all. Whenever you're hurt, you're crying out to Him, even if you don't realize He's there. When you can't see God, taking your anger out on fellow humans who failed to love you is tempting.

The evil forces' and principalities' main goal is to drive a wedge between you and God. They thrive on participating in an emotionally wounding event. If given the opportunity, they will take advantage of your every hurt. Wounds result in feelings of rejection. You'll feel alone and abandoned. Worse might be the times you're accepted but only on condition of your perfect performance. All of this will result in an anxious, incomplete connection to God.

Develop a False Identity

Like a mirror helps you connect with your physical appearance, experiences help you connect with your self-image. Although this is great for positive experiences, this unfortunately leaves you vulnerable to negative experiences.

God gives you a strong desire to reach your True Identity, but various negative life experiences can and will knock you off-course. To the degree you drift away from your potential, you develop a False Identity, obscuring your True Identity.

You can become so off-course that you forget who you really are. The further away you are from home (your True Identity), the greater your False Identity and the more you'll feel uncomfortably lost, like Adam and Eve as they were expelled from the Garden of Eden.

A False Identity forms to the degree you buy into relational lies. A *relational lie* involves an incorrect belief about God, self, or others. Relational lies are believable because they originate from real-life experiences. A False Identity builds up as you internalize negative experiences. If this happens too much for too long, you'll lose touch with who you are. Severe trauma can even cause you to become disconnected from parts of your identity.

Choose to Exclude God

Before becoming a Christian, you lack the ability to consider God's wisdom. You have no choice but to act according to your own wisdom. After you become a Christian, you can choose between the two. You can become your own enemy by neglecting God's input. Your way might bring some immediate relief, but it moves you further away from God.

In any situation in life, you can choose to move toward or away from God. So many times, moving away appears to be the best of both worlds. You might think, *I don't have to face admitting to God I messed up, and I can make the problem go away.* Unfortunately, any time you move away from God, you're only delaying the inevitable: facing the consequences of your actions.

You can't embrace the truth and move away from God. You must embrace a lie over the truth. When you decide to shut out God, you're saying "no" to the only help available.

Moving away from God doesn't move you toward healing. Emotional pain demands your attention. Having rejected God, your only choice is to disconnect from the pain. This is like disarming a smoke alarm because it sounds so irritating. At first you have peace and quiet, but this only invites greater danger. Eventually, a fire will start somewhere in your life.

Participate in Fruitless Labor

Fruitless labor can be anything from selfish ambition to the love of money. Saving up your money for earthly gain and security isn't going to store up any treasure in heaven — the only kind that lasts. Hurtful experiences resulting in a False Identity lead directly to missing out in the participation of God's kingdom work.

Dig Your Own Wells

When you don't accept God as an option and believe the wrong things about yourself, you'll pursue whatever you perceive will bring the most immediate relief to your painful wounds. This striving to save any semblance of your worth doesn't just fail to further God's work; it actually creates more problems that require additional investment to heal.

for my people have committed two evils:
they have forsaken me, the fountain of living waters,
and hewed out cisterns for themselves, broken cisterns that can hold no water.
—Jeremiah 2:13

Many people attribute the phrase "Everyone has a God-shaped hole in their heart that only He can fill" to Pascal. His actual words are different — less modern and concise but more eloquent:

All men seek happiness. This is without exception. . . . there was once in man a true happiness of which there now remain to him only the mark and empty trace, which he in vain tries to fill from all his surroundings. . . . But these are all inadequate, because the infinite abyss can only be filled by an infinite and immutable object, that is to say, only by God himself.
—Blaise Pascal, Pensées VII(425)

Put on a Costume

Covering up sinful behavior becomes necessary when you exclude God from the solution. The hurting part of you must be locked away somewhere out of sight, not given the opportunity to make a plea for help.

In the following diagram, the image on the left represents a person who is attempting to disguise their dysfunction. From the outside, the disguised identity appears lighter. Appearances can be deceiving. A dysfunctional person chooses the quick but fruitless route of external change.

Dysfunction Disguised   **Dysfunction Targeted**
(conforming)   **(transforming)**

The image on the right represents a person who is focusing their energies on internal change. The transforming person doesn't look as light on the outside, but a deeper internal change is transforming this person.

You could choose to define yourself based on the latest pop-culture fads, but in Romans 12, God tells you not to disguise your identity with the world's costumes. Instead, God wants you to step into your true self by faith — faith that God measured out with you in mind and deposited within you. God supplies the faith that you need to achieve your identity. Your true self is neither greater nor less than God's design.

> *Do not be conformed to this world, but be transformed by the renewal of your mind, that by testing you may discern what is the will of God, what is good and acceptable and perfect. For by the grace given to me I say to everyone among you not to think of himself more highly than he ought to think, but to think with sober judgment, each according to the measure of faith that God has assigned.*
> —Romans 12:2–3

Strong living results when you value yourself accurately by maintaining a balance of humility (a positive view of God and positive attachment to God) and confidence (a positive view of yourself). As you allow yourself to become as God intended, you'll know God's will better and you'll be able to act boldly according to the faith God has given you.

The dysfunctional person tries to cope with emotional pain by over- or undercompensating. Pride results when you place too much hope in your identity while seeking too much independence from God. You might think, *I can do it myself. I don't need God.* False humility results when you place too little hope in your identity. This also results in distance from God, because you feel too unworthy to be anything of significance to Him. You might think, *I'm too ugly to be used by God.*

You can end up investing enormous amounts of energy in keeping your hurting emotions out of play. To accomplish this, you must deeply isolate the hurting parts from your day-to-day conscious functioning. Without your emotions to help you discern what is working and what isn't, you'll be more disconnected from yourself.

This pretending is sometimes called *posing*. Posing is different from dissociation. Posing has an element of hiding sin, whereas dissociation has an element of self-preservation. But the immediate effect can be the same: Part of your identity remains hidden.

A poser must increasingly devote time and energy to maintaining a false image. Living like this is no different from living a lie. A poser is a deceiver, a hypocrite who wears a mask to conceal wrong behaviors. Life becomes an attempt to manage outward appearances rather than keeping a clean heart. Once you make "doing" your primary purpose, you're no longer "being" or growing in your identity — you're only living out of what you understand your identity to be. That means you'll have a static existence rather than a dynamic one.

Lacking integrity by living as a poser and seeing yourself as inferior or superior as you compare yourself to others are perfect examples of fruitless labor. I will say more on this in Chapter 7 and again in Chapter 16.

Embrace the Ways of the Enemy

Moving away from God is equivalent to opening a door for the enemy. Aside from the semi-permanent effects of the curse, you have a living, dynamic enemy who works continually to confuse your self-image by exploiting the curse. The enemy will not stop trying to distract you from seeing and acting upon your True Identity.

> **Warning! The consequences of leaving God out of your life only compound with time. As your False Identity grows, it will progress through deception, distortion, dysfunction, deterioration, and finally, death.**

Deception

I want to be like God. I don't need God.

Once you're convinced you can be self-sustaining like God, the idea that you don't need God is quick to follow. The enemy first used this ploy with Adam and Eve to induce the fall; every sin can be traced back to this one. Sin means finding your own way that goes against God's way. Replacing God is never a good idea.

Distortion

I'm not seeing crystal clear, but I can find my own way. I'm sure God wants me to be happy. Certainly, God doesn't want me to suffer like this.

Blindness follows deception. Not seeing clearly is like telling a lie. You won't be able to see God, yourself, or others as they are. The curse that followed the fall distances you from understanding life as God originally intended. Hurting yourself while stumbling in the dark can result in a need for further deception: *I've already dug myself into a hole; I don't know how to escape, so I might as well keep digging.*

Dysfunction

I'll use things my way to suit my needs rather than as God intends. Marriage didn't work out very well for me, so I'll just live with my girlfriend. Looking at pornography won't affect my relationship.

Dysfunction is a lack of righteousness (right-use-ness). In the midst of the new depressing state of the curse, you don't think clearly and consequently go your own way. Cain killed his brother Abel. God further banished Cain, sending him away from Adam and Eve for murder (Genesis 4:8).

Deterioration

I'll work harder instead of asking for and accepting God's help. I sure am suffering! Maybe this is all I can expect from life. I'll make the best of it while I can.

Things and relationships don't last long when used contrary to design. Because of the curse, everything requires effort to be kept in good working order. The temptation to avoid the work to grow becomes irresistible. You can either pursue pleasures or seek God's help. Without God, you can't bail a leaking boat fast enough to keep from sinking.

Death

I'll stubbornly hold onto my prideful independence even unto death.

Sin ends in death (Romans 6:23). Without faith in Jesus's effort that conquered death, we are dead spiritually and will die physically apart from God as well.

Fortunately, your struggle for a Confident Identity doesn't have to end in death. In the next chapter, I show you how to recover from a negative self-image.

For Reflection

1. Read each lie and consider how much it matches your False Identity (what you believe is true, but is really false).
   - "I'm worthless."
   - "I'm unlovable."
   - "I'm too needy."

- "I'm a failure."
- "I exist to help others."
- "I'm ugly."
- "I'm not good enough."
- "I'm stupid."
- "I'm a disappointment."
- "I'm defective" or "I have to be perfect."
- "I'm insignificant" or "I'm unimportant."
- "I can't trust anyone."
- "I'm inadequate."
- "I don't belong."

2. God supplies everything you need to grow into all He intends you to be. You aren't trapped in your False Identity.

Next Steps

☐ Focus on the person you are becoming. If you aren't sure who that is yet, ask God. Say out loud, "I am becoming all God made me to be!"

☐ Your Perceived Identity includes both true and false beliefs about yourself. Take inventory of your beliefs and determine which ones are grounded in the truth of the Bible and which ones are lies. Write down both lists in your Blueprint Space.

☐ Media for Further Learning (see Appendix B for more questions)
  ☐ Movie: *Groundhog Day*. How does Phil become trapped in a negative identity?
  ☐ Movie: *The Lord of the Rings* trilogy. How does Frodo deal with the curse of the ring?
  ☐ Music: *Remind Me Who I Am* by Jason Gray
  ☐ Music: *Who I Am* by Blanca

☐ Complete the Reinforced Wound Worksheet on the following page. After you complete the exercise, share it with a trusted friend or counselor.

The goal of the exercise is to bring disconnected parts of yourself together. This can bring strong emotions into your conscious awareness. If you struggle with a serious emotional wound or trauma, consider choosing a nonthreatening trigger for this exercise, unless you're working with a counselor who can help you if you become in touch with strong emotions.

Choose a lie you believe now. Start at the top and work your way backwards in time to identify events that reinforce the negative conclusion and painful feelings from an earlier wounding event. Start by describing the triggering memory in the first area.

- The image of the worst part (a) is a picture you have stored in your brain that represents the worst part of the memory.
- The negative belief about self (b) is a lie you believe about yourself when you recall the memory (see For Reflection Question 1 for examples).
- The emotions felt (c) is what you feel when you recall the memory.
- The body sensation (d) is where you feel all of the above in your body.

Chapter 5 — Isolated and Desolate 57

Reinforced Wound Worksheet

Start with a triggering event from the present. Choose something that is recurring, unhealthy, intrusive, or damaging to you and/or others.

For Each Memory Capture:
a) Image of Worst Part
b) Negative Belief about Self
c) Emotions Felt
d) Body Sensations

a)
b)
c)
d)

Present
- -
Past

a)
b)
c)
d)

Describe the next earlier reinforcing event which comes to mind. Then, the next. Let your brain do the work by following the association to the next memory.

a)
b)
c)
d)

a)
b)
c)
d)

Earliest Wounding Event you can remember, or continue on another page.

Can you see that present day triggers account for only a fraction of the pain you are experiencing?

BLUEPRINT SPACE

Chapter 6

Connected and Fruitful

I'm not good at anything. I'm too fat. No man is ever going to love me. Why was I ever born?

These thoughts plague Amy to the point of deep despair. But hitting bottom helps her find God again.

I know what the Bible says about You, but I'm not experiencing You that way. I have to be missing something. What am I missing, God? I don't know if I'll ever feel any different, but I need to try something. God, you're my only hope.

God doesn't let Amy suffer forever. All within a week, she has several life-changing encounters. A friend goes out of her way to thank Amy for being so upbeat during a season of doubt and sadness, saying, "Thank you for believing in me when everyone else gave up on me."

At least I've made a difference in one person's life.

Her pastor, speaking about Psalm 139, helps her to see God's intimate and intentional involvement in creating her. Later that week, verse 16 pops into her head:

Your eyes saw my unformed body; all the days ordained for me were written in your book before one of them came to be.

God continues to confirm Amy's identity. She discovers something about herself on a spiritual gifts inventory: "The results indicate the strong possibility you have the spiritual gift of mercy." This helps her see that God cares for her and has always planned for her to be an encourager.

I must not be a random afterthought.

Her counselor notices her: "Amy, I love the way your heart is sensitive and open to relationships. Know that this isn't by accident. God has a purpose for you in this."

Wow! Another person is telling me I have worthwhile qualities.

Her counselor goes on to say, "Also, your thoughts about your weight are distorted. You can't base your worth on your weight. Focus on being healthy spiritually, emotionally, and physically. Then the weight will take care of itself. Find your identity in your relationship with God, not in your relationship with food."

I have to admit, deep down, I feel as anxious as ever. I like being in control. I can see clear results when I restrict my eating. I look better, and men notice that. What am I supposed to do with my fear?

Finding Your Way Home: Four Life Blessings

When kids play tag, they often have a home base. That's the place where you're immune to becoming *It*. Home is your point of origin — the safest place you'll ever have. Spiritually, God is your home base.

When you realize you're lost, the best thing you can do is point yourself in the right direction: toward home. When you're home, you're as close to God as possible. That wasn't Adam and Eve's first instinct. Their first instinct was to hide from God because of their guilt and shame. God had to eject them from their home, but He didn't abandon them personally.

Until Amy's failed relationships in her 30s, she wasn't ready to dig deep into her past to understand her dysfunctional mate choices. Like most of us, she had hopes life would work out on the first try. But in reality, she had wishful thinking so she could avoid feeling her pain. Now, she finally has the capacity to grasp how her controlling mother and absentee father left her longing to be taken care of. She didn't realize how much her emotional needs were unmet.

All of us have a need to connect with God and others, feel confident about who we are, and participate in important work. These four life blessings are everyone's most significant emotional needs.

1. **Spiritual rebirth:** You need a way to reverse the effects of the curse.
2. **God's affirming connection:** You need to belong. Your existence has to matter to somebody. You need security, knowing that you won't be left alone. You need to be unconditionally accepted. You need to understand you're loved for who you are, not for what you can accomplish.
3. **Confident Identity:** You need to know why you were created, who you are as a unique human being, and what gifts and abilities you possess. You need to be able to grow in awareness of who you are.

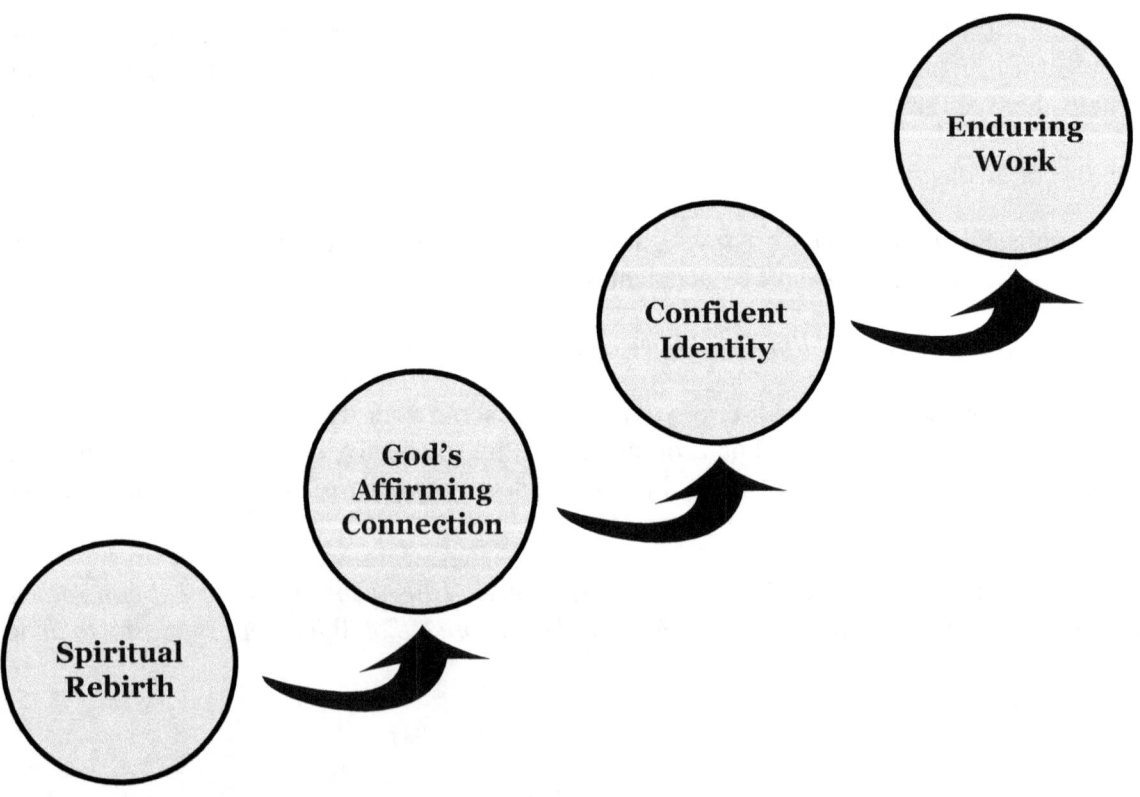

4. **Enduring work:** You need purpose. You need significant, meaningful work set aside specifically for you. You need to experience being fruitful.

These blessings sound wonderful, so why do so many people struggle to find them?

Removing Obstacles to God

Chapter 5 revealed the three primary obstacles to having a Confident Identity: the curse, your choice to sin, and resulting consequences. Whenever these things are in play, you're at risk of becoming increasingly unstable. However, as you cooperate with how God intended life to go, you'll experience progressive regeneration, not progressive deterioration.

Problems come in many different flavors, but they ultimately have the same solution. You can be aggressively angry, fearful of rejection, or addicted to pornography. You can be an emotional eater or even a chronic people pleaser. These are all symptoms of a deeper issue: insistence on immediate relief instead of taking the time to thoroughly heal. There is no such thing as a shortcut to true healing.

Sometimes life brings about legitimate suffering. Efforts to avoid legitimate suffering lead to further dysfunction. When you fail to include God in the solution, you'll usually end up making a bigger mess than if you had done nothing. Instead of avoiding suffering, bring it to God so you can confront whatever is blocking your way and causing your suffering.

I'm sure Adam and Eve wish they could have a do-over. But God isn't a God of the do-over. He's a God who works out everything for good according to His purposes (Ephesians 1:11, Romans 8:28). He wants you to keep trying until you figure out how to push through your identity crisis. Recall from Chapter 1 that an identity crisis is coming to the realization that you don't have the ability to function satisfactorily in your present life circumstances.

Realize God Is Your Only Hope

When faced with an impossible situation, you need a God who can accomplish the impossible. When you're feeling confident in God, you're able to express faith over the problems you're facing. But what if you're full of doubt and feel distant from God?

To have the motivation to work hard to remove obstacles between you and God, you need to become convinced that God is your only hope. God accomplished through Jesus Christ the work that provides you the opportunity to restore your closeness to God. Without relying on this work, you'll never realize true spiritual growth.

In Jeremiah 29:11, a popular and inspiring scripture, God promises that there is hope for you. Even though there are difficult times of not connecting with God, He never forgets those He loves.

> *This is what the Lord says: "When seventy years are completed for Babylon, I will come to you and fulfill my good promise to bring you back to this place. For I know the plans I have for you," declares the Lord, "plans to prosper you and not to harm you, plans to give you hope and a future. Then you will call on me and come and pray to me, and I will listen to you. You will seek me and find me when you seek me with all your heart. I will be found by you," declares the Lord, "and will bring you back from captivity. I will gather you from all the nations and places where I have banished you," declares the Lord, "and will bring you back to the place from which I carried you into exile."*
> —Jeremiah 29:10–14

Later in Jeremiah, God reveals more about Himself and the context of Israel's exile. As you read through Jeremiah 30:11–17, notice the paradox. God says Israel is incurable, but He also says He will provide healing. God is essentially saying, "Your situation is utterly hopeless. There is no hope for you apart from me. Only I can save you, heal you, and provide plans, hope, and a future."

> "'... I am with you and will save you,'
> declares the Lord.
> 'Though I completely destroy all the nations
> among which I scatter you,
> I will not completely destroy you.
> I will discipline you but only in due measure;
> I will not let you go entirely unpunished.'
> "This is what the Lord says:
> "'Your wound is incurable,
> your injury beyond healing.
> There is no one to plead your cause,
> no remedy for your sore,
> no healing for you.
> All your allies have forgotten you;
> they care nothing for you.
> I have struck you as an enemy would
> and punished you as would the cruel,
> because your guilt is so great
> and your sins so many.
> Why do you cry out over your wound,
> your pain that has no cure?
> Because of your great guilt and many sins
> I have done these things to you.
> "'But all who devour you will be devoured;
> all your enemies will go into exile.
> Those who plunder you will be plundered;
> all who make spoil of you I will despoil.
> But I will restore you to health
> and heal your wounds,'
> declares the Lord,
> 'because you are called an outcast,
> Zion for whom no one cares.'"
> —Jeremiah 30:11–17

After all you do to mess up your life, God desires to provide health and healing. Don't miss God's heart. God is committed to seeing you through to the end, no matter what you've done. However, even with all God has done, you still have work to do. Even when God appears to betray you, don't give up on God.

Only when you realize that God is your only hope, only then are you the most likely to put your faith in Him. This means feeling your vulnerability, lamenting and expressing your pain to Him, and entrusting the outcomes to His hands. To have a Confident Identity means your faith in God is stronger than your circumstances.

Job had a Confident Identity. Although he fully expressed his pain and feelings of betrayal, he never gave up on God.

> *Though He slay me, I will hope in Him.*
> —Job 13:15

God has a plan for you to discover who you are. He wants you to know your True Identity. You don't ever have to doubt this. This is significant because during the hardest, most discouraging times in your life, you'll be tempted to give up hope.

Being proactive is one of the best things you can do for yourself. You don't have to wait for others to get their acts together before you act. Action means something is changing. As long as anything is changing, hope is alive. Hope can't exist if nothing is going to change.

Be Repentant, Not Stubborn

Repentance removes the first roadblock: the idols in your life. An idol is anything you are depending on beyond its capacity to fulfill you. Repentance is making a commitment to God to stop using an idol. One possible idol is the role of wife or husband and another is the outward appearance of perfection. When you overinvest in a role or title, you have a long way to fall if you can no longer claim that role or title.

Amy turned to God for answers when she felt helpless. God helped her but only after she struggled for years and finally hit rock-bottom. Her sincere seeking of God came about only when she felt desperate and sensed she had no other way out of her predicament. Then she gave up on her dysfunctional solution to her problem.

Amy may no longer be married, but that doesn't mean her identity is gone. Just because she doesn't have a spouse to love and take care of, doesn't mean she's worthless. The qualities that make her a good spouse can be used for other purposes. So she's better off focusing on what will make her a healthier person overall — being reasonably secure in her identity. As a bonus, she will meet the prerequisite for a healthy marriage.

Amy found a way to choose her identity over her role as a wife. As she pursued her healing, she prayed a lot more than she used to.

My way isn't working, God. I need your help. I need to lose weight, but experiencing your love is a greater need. I long to feel loved by You. I tried a shortcut that put a man ahead of You. I surrender my need to be a wife. Being your daughter is more important.

Grieve, Don't Numb Your Pain

Lamenting removes the second roadblock: your pain. To lament, you cry out to God while you're suffering. You cast your cares onto Him (1 Peter 5:7). Laments are especially timely when God seems to be absent. Stop doing whatever you're doing to avoid facing the pain of your experiences. Take your pain to God first, before you try to understand everything. Trust that God is a parent who can hear, comfort, and soothe your hurting soul.

Psalms of lament are different from the joyous psalms of praise or thanksgiving. The purpose of a lament is to *seek God* for the resolution to difficult life circumstances. A lament is always an emotional plea, a cry for relationship, and not so much a logical argument. By the time you need to lament, focusing on logic would be like putting a Band-Aid on a broken leg (or perhaps like

breaking your other leg). A lament usually includes the following elements[7] (see Psalm 55 for an example):
- A description of the problem or crisis you are facing
- Questions addressed to God
- A declaration of trust in God despite circumstances
- A cry for God's intervention and mercy
- An acknowledgement of God's response
- Praise to God for hearing you

In contrast, to *cope* means to dull and delay emotional pain. But even when someone copes, they often reach back for control or worry about how the problem will be solved. Manipulating outcomes, while remaining disconnected from God, isn't much different from worrying. Coping treats the symptoms but doesn't heal the pain. It works well when you have no better options, but it only delays the inevitable need for true healing.

If you're in a boat with a hole in the bottom, coping is like using a bucket to bail out the water. If you're miles from land, this makes sense. Bailing is better than sinking. Once you make it back to land, it makes more sense to repair the boat than to take it out again untouched.

Some people will go to great lengths to avoid investing in deeper healing. They spend half their lives bailing because at least they feel in control and know what to expect. Bailing works as long as you have time and energy to spend emptying the boat. Also, you must continue to bail faster than the hole lets in water. Holes don't get smaller on their own; they always grow larger.

Better coping might be plugging the hole, but even that is only a temporary solution. At least in this case, the problem is acknowledged. You could always do worse by pretending the hole isn't there and ignoring the water above your ankles.

Deliverance from dysfunction (repairing the boat the right way) is superior to coping. God is the one person who can deliver you from painful consequences. Although coping has its place, healing that addresses emotional wounding is the ultimate goal.

Amy can grieve over her mistakes and lament her feeling not good enough.

Nothing is going my way. No one is ever going to like me. Have mercy on me, God. I feel alone. I'm ugly. Why did you make me this way? I feel unattractive. Not only did my marriage fail, but all my other relationships have, too. Why are men so repulsed by me? What do I need to change in order to do this the right way?

Believe God's Truth, Not Your Negative Experiences

God chose Abraham to be the father of us all (Romans 4:16–25). Even though all Abraham's experiential evidence pointed to the contrary — he had no offspring — he believed God when God told Abraham his descendants would be as numerous as the stars (Genesis 15:1–6). Not only did Abraham have to wait 25 years to experience God's promise, but God didn't make the promise until Abraham was 75 years old. Abraham could have easily become discouraged and disowned God. Instead, he chose to accept God's word to him as truth, despite his experience of being unable to have a child with his wife Sarah.

Fortunately, entrenched lies can be removed. You must refute everything contrary to God's design. Remember that circumstances don't define your identity. Don't compromise your identity for any reason. Just because the world doesn't have a need for you at a given moment, doesn't mean you're defective, unloved, or unneeded.

---

[7] crivoice.org/psalmgenre.html

The world may reject you, but Jesus has overcome the world (John 15:18–25, 16:33). Jesus didn't waste time on those who were not interested in Him. Shake the dust off your feet and continue on with God's plan for your identity (Matthew 10:14). When you experience persecution for who God made you to be, this only means your time is not yet here. God has a plan. God is treating you no differently from how He treated Jesus. Until the time is right, you're undergoing preparation.

When God wants you to wait, it's because He has other work for you to do. Find that work and focus on it. Amy was able to wait on and trust God for positive outcomes in her life.

God, I am beginning a new chapter in my life. The old way was me attempting to be my own provider instead of trusting You. My father wasn't there for me. My husband left me for another woman. All my boyfriends gave up on me. Your Word says you are trustworthy, so I need to start trusting. I'm ready. I agree with Your Word that I'm your beloved child. I believe You're for me and You won't abandon me. Take away these false beliefs that feel so real. Fill my heart with Your love.

Being Open to Affirming Connection

To understand your identity, you must consider it in the context of your connection to God and others. You can't answer the question *Who am I?* without a context. God is the context. Who is God? God is love. God is the only absolute being who doesn't depend on anything else. To survive (beyond this life), you must have a connection to Him.

God created you so that you start out not knowing who you are, and He did that for a reason. You can't grow as a person and develop your identity in isolation; you need an environment. At first, this environment is your parents, but eventually you need to see God as your parent. God gives you parents to learn how to depend on someone outside of yourself.

Attach to Others

If you want to be securely attached to God, you need to healthfully attach to others first. If you want to be emotionally healthy, you need to explore your past to assess how well you learned to attach.

God designed us to help each other grow. To grow, you require another human to be with you — to "get you" and communicate understanding. When you experience and accept someone's love, you're allowing their brain to wire (or rewire) your brain. Most mothers instinctively understand this after they give birth. They have a special attachment to their babies. While how you express the attachment changes as you mature, you never outgrow the need for it.

Being open to relationship means you're open to allowing others to change how you see life. You'll have to drop your guard and be vulnerable at some point if you hope to grow. This approach allows you to be aware of both yourself and others' impact on you. Realizing you have a choice of who to let in and who to keep out can be a healing experience in itself.

Attach to God

Your identity makes sense only in the context of your relationship with God. He created you, so your life can have meaning only to the degree you're connected to God. You can change only by bringing your whole self (healthy and broken parts) into contact with God.

Amy struggled with her identity until she experienced God affirming her through her friend, her pastor, and her counselor. The amazing week God gave her remained etched in her mind — a permanent lighthouse of truth. Until that point, her other affirming experiences were sporadic and insufficient to make a strong enough impression. God's speaking to her in multiple ways at the same time forever changed how she viewed God and therefore, how she viewed herself. He greatly strengthened her faith. God didn't change, but her view of God changed as she reinterpreted old false beliefs with new truth-filled experiences.

Thank you, God, for opening my eyes to Your truth and Your presence in my life. Now that I've tasted a deeper connection with You, I don't feel as compelled to look good on the outside at all costs. I'm beginning to feel peace. I wonder if there are more negative experiences I need to bring out in the open. Confronting my weight issues was a lot of work, but being free from that trap feels so good! Come to think of it, I bet I need to revisit those times with my dad.

Be Full, Not Empty

You can't have a Confident Identity by only removing negatives. A transformational positive experience is the only way to remove negatives. Bring in the good to displace the bad!

God made you to have an identity. A neutral identity doesn't exist. If you don't have a positive one, then you *will* have a negative one! If you feel neither negative nor positive, then you are likely numb to feelings about yourself.

Jesus presented this idea when He used an analogy of an empty house:

> *When the unclean spirit has gone out of a person, it passes through waterless places seeking rest, but finds none. Then it says, "I will return to my house from which I came." And when it comes, it finds the house empty, swept, and put in order. Then it goes and brings with it seven other spirits more evil than itself, and they enter and dwell there, and the last state of that person is worse than the first. So also will it be with this evil generation.*
> —Matthew 12:43–44

To become full, you need to do more than a quick cleaning; you need to remodel your house with positive experiences. The end goal is to be securely attached to God, experiencing that you have someone watching over you and taking care of you despite negative circumstances.

When you're faced with a negative, triggering experience, deny its false message and pray for God to displace the falsehood with truth that will take hold in your heart. Ask God for new positive experiences to put a stranglehold on the lie. As you fill yourself with God (positive experiences of God), you prevent the same negatives from returning.

Claiming a Confident Identity

Living with a Confident Identity flows naturally from being attached to God. Being attached means you're constantly able to receive God's affirmation of who you are.

Your God-created True Identity is God's design for you. Your Confident Identity is the part of your True Identity that you're aware of. Your True Identity includes your significant role in creation. You are responsible for seeking out and discovering your True Identity so that your Confident Identity increases.

God provides you with a permanent identity. Your identity cannot be taken from you (permanently or completely). Realizing this should result in security and peace. The truest version of your identity is not dependent on something that can change — you cannot lose your identity. If what you understand to be your identity can be lost, it was never a part of your identity in the first place. In reality, the false pieces were held in place only by false beliefs.

When Amy wasn't living with her Confident Identity, she was vulnerable to taking on life's problems *as* her identity. *I'm fearful about everything all day long. I'm afraid of others' disapproval. I must be an anxious person.* Amy shouldn't define herself as anxious. Instead, she should acknowledge that she feels anxious and then take appropriate corrective action.

Amy is more confident now. God's speaking directly to Amy made the difference between knowing some facts and living with her Confident Identity. Today, her faith allows her to boldly speak words of encouragement.

My identity comes from You, God. No one can take it from me! I come from You. No one can take me away from You! I belong to You.

Being made in God's image, you have all that Jesus has. Jesus is both fully human and fully God. Jesus came into the world as a baby. Years later, during His baptism, God told everyone how pleased He was with His son. Another time, Jesus stated He came only to do the work His Father showed Him to do (John 4:34, 5:19, 6:38). He spoke with authority and set out to accomplish this work while having a secure connection to His Father and confidence in His identity.

> *And when Jesus was baptized, immediately he went up from the water, and behold, the heavens were opened to him, and he saw the Spirit of God descending like a dove and coming to rest on him; and behold, a voice from heaven said, "This is my beloved Son, with whom I am well pleased."*
> —Matthew 3:16–17

Pursuing Enduring Work

To understand your identity, you must consider it in the context of the work God has planned for you.

To pursue kingdom work is no small task. Kingdom work requires preparation. God wants to invest in you so that you'll be able to invest in His work. To seek His kingdom first means to seek it first within yourself, then to seek it for others' sake (Matthew 6:33). This is always a tricky balance. I'm not saying do nothing until you're perfect. I'm saying be willing to work on yourself (which is harder) before you work on others (Matthew 7:1–5).

Knowing your identity has many benefits, but its significance is easily underestimated. Your identity is the solution to your every personal and spiritual problem. How is this possible?

For this to make sense, you have to grasp the idea that problems outside of the scope of your identity aren't your problems!

They are ultimately God's responsibility. You were designed with purpose. As long as you stay within God's intentions for your life, your God-given identity is all you need to live confidently and effectively. Consider the following examples of problems beyond the scope of your identity:
- Engaging the devil in an all-out offensive attack isn't wise. One, Jesus already defeated him. Two, only Jesus has the power to defeat him.
- You can't feed every hungry person in the world. Even Jesus, while on earth, didn't eradicate all hunger, sickness, and disease. Even though He permanently reversed the effects of the curse, we won't fully realize this until heaven.
- If you get motion sickness easily, you probably shouldn't be a pilot or an astronaut.
- If you aren't very coordinated, you probably shouldn't be a gymnast.

Your identity is a built-in priority system. You can't go wrong when you make decisions based on God's design. You can know when you're living with purpose and living without purpose. Your decisions will automatically be in line with God's will. You'll know everything you need to make life decisions. Knowing your identity means knowing what you can say "yes" to and what you can say "no" to. By knowing yourself, you'll know what to keep and what to prune from your life. No matter how difficult or ignorant other people are, you'll be able to plot your own course.

Acting upon your Confident Identity is the way to joy and success. Success doesn't necessarily mean everything is easy, but it does mean focusing only on the tasks God had in mind when He made you. Peace results when you're able to stop worrying about all that is out of your control.

What happens when you live beyond God's original intentions? When you aren't in alignment with God's design, you'll experience fatigue, burnout, depression, and/or anxiety. A screwdriver won't last long if it pounds in nails instead of turning screws. God doesn't ask us to venture beyond His purposeful design for us. You need not take on work beyond God's plan for you. You can't accomplish any more than God designed you to accomplish.

To stay within the scope of your identity and win at confidence, you must build on the foundation God has already provided. The foundation is Jesus Christ and all that He accomplished, is accomplishing, and will accomplish. You build by allowing God to mold you into the image of Jesus Christ and by helping to further God's kingdom. God gave Paul the responsibility to clearly communicate what the foundation is.

> *By the grace God has given me, I laid a foundation as a wise builder, and someone else is building on it. But each one should build with care. For no one can lay any foundation other than the one already laid, which is Jesus Christ. If anyone builds on this foundation using gold, silver, costly stones, wood, hay or straw, their work will be shown for what it is, because the Day will bring it to light. It will be revealed with fire, and the fire will test the quality of each person's work. If what has been built survives, the builder will receive a reward. If it is burned up, the builder will suffer loss but yet will be saved— even though only as one escaping through the flames.*
> —1 Corinthians 3:10–15 (NIV)

With God's support and a Confident Identity, your work will survive because it will count toward the eternal work God has planned for you (Ephesians 2:10).

Living in Freedom

The more you know God, the more you can know and accept your true self, and then the more you have freedom to let others be who they are. When you finally understand that their changing doesn't improve your identity, you no longer need others to change — although this does become more complicated when another's dysfunction appears to block your expression of your identity. Be assured that God doesn't waste a second of your life because of someone else's sin.

While you aren't responsible for what is outside your identity, you remain responsible for what is inside. You are still called to love God, yourself, and others. Without a struggle, there is no growth. Without growth, you remain dependent on others for what you could be doing yourself.

Amy continued counseling and learned more about her unique giftedness. The process of her becoming free from her unhealthy dependence upon men took a few years. During this time, she tore down the shaky foundation of depending upon her appearance for her self-worth and set in place God's foundation.

You are delivering me from my despair.
My tears are many, and I'm not yet out of trouble.
But You hear me, and You will set me on solid ground.

For everyone who can hear me speak:
Be encouraged!
Your hope in God is not in vain.

My God is with me.
I am secure in His deliverance from evil.
How can I lose in life?

I will stand against the evil that stands against You.
I will be true to what You taught me.
I will fight with your truth as my primary weapon.

Our enemy boasts of my defeat.
But the battle is Yours.
Your glory is my focus.

I have already won because You are forever on my side.
I take pleasure in doing my part.
I am hopeful as You fulfill your plans.

Eventually, Amy felt ready to be in a healthy relationship, and God brought a man into her life. During their dating and into their marriage, she felt free to look to her husband in the ways he was able to provide for her. But she also never lost the sense that she ultimately depends on God.

For Reflection

1. How can a person know their True Identity?
2. Read Matthew 17:20. In addition to praying to God about your problems, try telling the mountain you're facing about your God. How different do these approaches feel to you?
3. Why would a "screwdriver" try to be a "hammer"?
4. God is love, and without love, you're nothing.
5. Sometimes the best action is to simply rearrange or identify your priorities.
6. What problems are your problems? What problems are God's problems? What problems are neither yours nor God's?
7. What kind of problems can identity solve? What kind can't it solve?
8. How will your Confident Identity resolve your problems?
9. What do you need to do next to change your Perceived Identity so that it will look more like your True Identity?
10. What do you need to do next to build on God's foundation, Jesus Christ and all He accomplished?

Next Steps

- Divide your personal problems into those solvable by your identity and those your identity cannot solve. What is different about the lists?
- Media for Further Learning (see Appendix B for more questions)
  - Movie: *A Beautiful Mind*. How does John struggle to sort fact from fiction?
  - Movie: *Back to the Future* trilogy. How does Marty learn self-confidence?
  - Music: *No Longer Slaves* by Jonathan David Helser and Melissa Helser
- Write your own Psalm of Lament. Use Psalms 42 and 55 as examples, but don't simply paraphrase. You can also review Amy's laments. Before you begin writing, ask God to bring the right painful experience to the surface and to direct your writing. When you write, include the basic details of the event, how you felt, what you believed, and how you've reacted to the wound. Write your lament to God plainly without editing it or trying to clean it up. You can be completely honest and direct with God.
  - Read more lament Psalms: 3, 4, 5, 7, 13, 14, 17, 22, 25, 26, 27, 28, 31, 36, 39, 40:12–17, 41, 42, 43, 52, 53, 54, 55, 56, 57, 59, 61, 64, 70, 71, 77, 86, 89, 120, 139, 141, 142
  - For a deeper study of Psalms, review crivoice.org/psalmgenre.html.
  - Find someone you can trust so you can share your lament with them. Allow this to further your attachment with them and God.
  - Consider attending counseling to receive prayer to help guide you through the wound-healing process.
  - Consider attending a Formational Prayer Seminar by Healing Care Ministries (healingcare.org).
- Seek an experience of your True Identity. Consider a lie you believe and its corresponding truth. Ask God to communicate the truth in an experiential way. Close your eyes, and be open to receiving ideas, words, impressions, or feelings from God. If you experience God speaking to you, great! If you don't, that's okay. Either way, in the coming days and weeks, continue to look for other ways God will enter into your life to answer your prayer. God wants you to experience the truth!
  - Repeat this exercise as often as you like with whatever hurtful experiences you've had. God might even help you remember experiences you didn't realize you'd had.
  - Practice receiving love by sharing your hurt with others.

BLUEPRINT SPACE

BLUEPRINT SPACE

Part II – Discovering Your Identity

Chapter 7	**Digging for Identity Clues**
Chapter 8	**Your Physical Identity**
Chapter 9	**Your Gender Identity**
Chapter 10	**Your Cognitive and Emotional Identity**
Chapter 11	**Your General Spiritual Identity**
Chapter 12	**Your Specific Spiritual Identity**
Chapter 13	**Your Personality**
Chapter 14	**Your Strengths at Work**
Chapter 15	**Assembling Your Identity Clues**

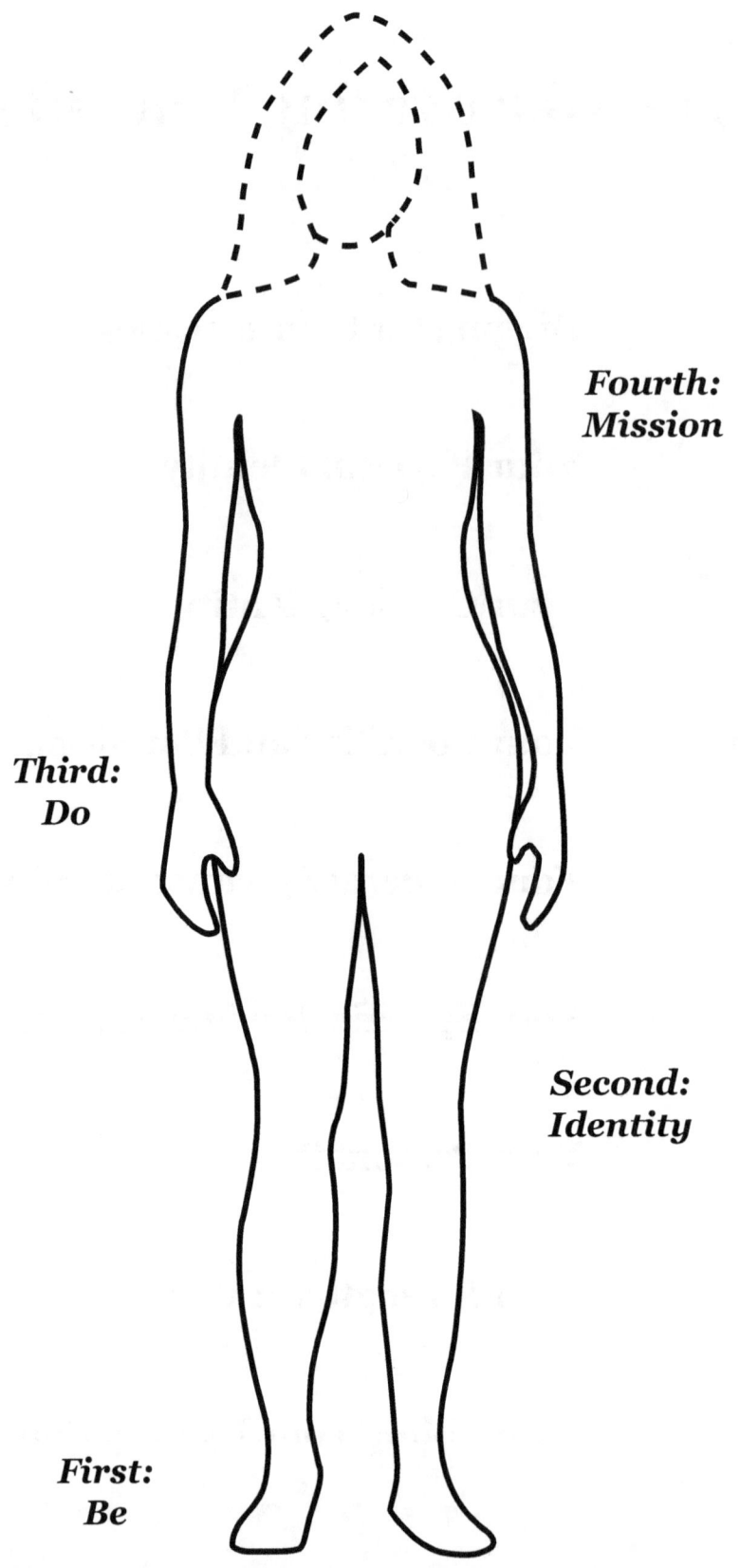

Discovering (God's Design of Your Identity)

Chapter 7

Digging for Identity Clues

Between the time John was 16 and 22 years old, he went on 12 mission trips. The people he helped always thanked him for his efforts. For the first two trips, he went because he had nothing better to do. But starting with the third trip, he acknowledged that he didn't like going. Still, he couldn't tell his parents.

One of the hardest things to do is overcome your instinct to base worth on performance. John grew up in a family that put a spiritual cover over its dysfunctional behaviors. Growing up in this family made it difficult for John to develop a healthy identity.

I feel inadequate because I'm not going into full-time ministry. I don't want to disappoint my parents, but I don't see myself as a missionary, either.

Having a family that sought approval by trading worldly competition for spiritual competition only confused matters more. When John finally left his small church community, his family and the other church members treated him like he had abandoned his Christian faith: "Hey, John! When are you going to move to Africa?" they would say. "Once you receive God's calling, there's no turning back. You're missing out on God's best plan for you."

Years later, in his 30s, John struggled with depression. His parents and sister tried to convince him that he was depressed because he had left their church family: "You're not feeling well because you aren't right with God. Come back to church with us. We miss you. Your sister married a preacher. Why aren't you pursuing your calling?"

John made half-hearted attempts to defend his decisions. Of course, this didn't change anything. He didn't know how to let go of his dysfunctional past. He didn't realize their words were emotionally abusive.

I can't disappoint my parents. I need to honor them. But I feel so angry after talking with them. I especially hate the summer family reunions when I have to be around them for days.

One summer, John had had enough. He yelled at his sister, her family, and his parents. He made a big scene that almost turned into a physical altercation, but he stormed off before that happened. His insecurity got the best of him. But fighting back was a sign his identity was starting to emerge.

John also struggled when his job became too overwhelming.

I didn't realize how much I hate working behind a desk. I'm so busy fixing problems that I never have time to talk to anyone. I hardly have time for a bathroom break. I don't dare tell my boss how I'm feeling. He probably won't do anything, anyway. Or, worse, he'll fire me.

John had a weakened sense of his identity. Because of his family's dysfunction, he lacked the confidence to completely leave behind the guilt and condemnation for his otherwise healthy desire to pursue the life he wanted.

John is an example of someone stuck in the conforming response to an identity crisis (see Chapter 1). When he was a child, his parents taught him to feel guilty unless he did what pleased them. But as an adult, he is responsible for choosing to grow instead of allowing his parents to hold him hostage.

Fortunately for John, he didn't stay stuck. After 20 years of living with obligations to his parents and failing at jobs and relationships, he talked with an older man at his new church. John finally accepted some healthy advice and found the courage to search for his own identity.

Why Dig to Find Out Who You Are?

If you want a Confident Identity, you must dig for clues to discover more of who you are. Everyone has room to grow in their understanding of their identity. This part of the book covers the more practical steps you can take to discover your identity, and this chapter introduces you to the tools that will help your search. After this chapter, you'll know why, how, and where to dig.

The remaining chapters in Part II take you deeper into knowing who you are. God created you in His image. You can better understand what this means by studying and exploring various windows into your identity. Each chapter covers a different area you can explore. This will provide practical experience in understanding how you're unique. Also, a series of evaluating questions will help you determine how well you accept your identity as given by God. Finally, in Chapter 15, you'll put it all together and write a preliminary identity statement.

The overall goal of exploring your identity is to increase the harmony between who God says you are and who you think you are (including the parts of you buried in your subconscious). How much disharmony do you feel between who you could be and how you feel because of negative life circumstances or experiences? Everyone lives with some degree of painful internal conflict, but Christ died to set you free from a False Identity.

Use Your God-Given Abilities

You'll benefit from identifying and using your abilities, but this alone won't cure a negative self-image. Your worth isn't based on which abilities God chose to give you. Remember from Part I that having a sense of *being* is a prerequisite for *doing* (using abilities).

God calls you to use your abilities for His purposes. This is abundantly clear in the Parable of the Talents (Matthew 25:14–30). In the parable, the master gives his servants talents (money) according to their ability. He is pleased with the servants who use their God-given resources. He showers them with equal praise, independent of their ability. They are good examples of a Confident Identity.

> *"Well done, good and faithful servant. You have been faithful over a little;*
> *I will set you over much. Enter into the joy of your master."*
> —Matthew 25:23

The master condemns the servant who doesn't attempt to use his ability. He lacks initiative because he focuses on his fear of failure. He lives out the lies of his Infected Identity. He is unable to perform because he doesn't feel secure in his identity.

> *But his master answered him, "You wicked and slothful servant! . . .*
> *you ought to have invested my money with the bankers,*

and at my coming I should have received what was my own with interest."
—Matthew 25:26–27

Don't leave your talents buried. There are serious consequences to not finding and using your identity. Those who completely avoid God out of fear demonstrate they don't really know Him. God wants you to trust and invest. God has given you your identity as a loving gift.

Attribute Terminology

There are so many words that can describe your attributes and aptitudes. In Parts II and III, you'll be exploring most of them, so I want you to understand how I'm using each word.

First of all, I see four different categories of attributes, which range from more focus on *being* (directly related to identity) to more focus on *doing* (indirectly related to identity):

1. **Personal:** Qualities that express your identity as a state of being
2. **Natural:** Qualities of natural ability God gave you at physical creation
3. **Spiritual:** Qualities of spiritual giftedness God gave you at spiritual rebirth
4. **Application:** Qualities that can be learned after specific training or experience or than can be prioritized after reflection on your identity

Each of the categories has its own terminology that I've adopted as follows:

Personal	Natural	Spiritual	Application
Personality type	Talents	Spiritual gifts	Skills
Personality trait	Abilities		Values
	Strengths		Passions

How to Dig

Honor God with your identity. Dig with faith, believing that God has created you as a treasure that needs to be discovered. Dig expectantly, knowing that as you learn more about yourself, you'll have more to offer others. Dig determined to discover your beauty as a unique work of art. Dig seeking God for greater understanding of His creation.

And without faith it is impossible to please him, for whoever would draw near to God must believe that he exists and that he rewards those who seek him.
—Hebrews 11:6

Use Comparison to Highlight Differences

There's a good way and a bad way to compare yourself to others. Comparison is beneficial only when you highlight God-given differences that add value to the Body of Christ. When you discover others are different from you in positive ways, this should increase their value in your eyes and cause you to praise God for their differences. For example, "I appreciate so much how you're always encouraging. I noticed you seem to know just the right thing to say to lift people's spirits."

However, you shouldn't use comparison to feel better or worse about yourself. Don't waste time going down the dark alley of comparison, trying to be someone you're not. If you're not especially gifted at encouragement, don't devalue yourself. Instead, know your gifts and pursue getting better at being you.

Evaluate Yourself with Sober Judgment

When considering your ability, be neither self-deprecating nor arrogant. Be honest. God wants you to be all you can be by using all He has given you — without trying to be everything to everybody.

For by the grace given to me I say to everyone among you not to think of himself more highly than he ought to think, but to think with sober judgment, each according to the measure of faith that God has assigned.
—Romans 12:3

You have strengths and weaknesses like everyone else. Accept your weaknesses, but don't settle for the idea that you're untalented.

Stay within God's Boundaries

God's boundaries equal God's standards and intentional design. To discover your True Identity, you don't need to explore outside the boundaries. There's plenty to discover within the boundaries. If you venture beyond God's design, you'll probably grow your False Identity.

The invisible fence is a cool invention, but I've heard stories of dogs with enough determination to run past them no matter how painful a shock they receive. Those dogs usually have a tangible reason, such as a squirrel, to endure such pain.

God's invisible fence works a bit differently — the promise of something better on the other side is only an illusion. Furthermore, once you're beyond the fence, the pain doesn't go away. There's no promised land beyond God's design. There's no alternate reality, no place beyond the fence where you can escape the pain inside the fence.

Yes, there is pain inside the fence, too.

The pain inside is different. It comes from living in a world that is bent out of shape. Healing comes only by allowing God to bend us back into the right shape, not by attempting to run out of the yard. You must believe and trust that God created you the way you are for good reason.

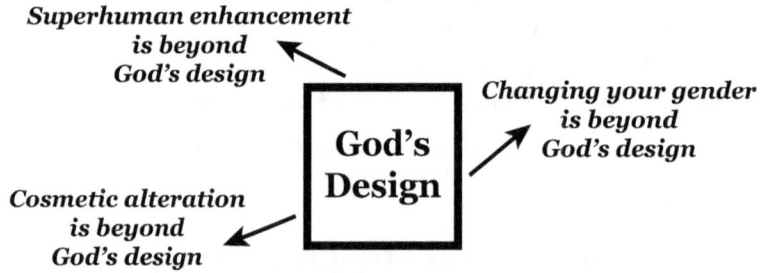

Sometimes we need to test boundaries so we can learn what we aren't. But this should last only a short time. If you find yourself outside God's safe area for an extended time, you're likely trying avoid your emotional pain instead of addressing it.

Experiment with What You Find

God made you to excel at something. As you go digging around, you'll learn both who you *are* and who you *aren't*. No person has all attributes and abilities. Just as you excel in some areas, you'll be average and even below average in others. This is by God's design. Dig earnestly and with compassion. Don't stop trying until you find what you're convinced is your True Identity. Even then, keep practicing to refine your sense of identity.

Realize You Don't Have the Full Picture

Only God knows your complete identity. Your digging can't be an exact science. What you observe might not accurately represent your identity. I don't want you to fall into the trap of focusing only on what is observable in the present moment. The observable behaviors you explore might only be *evidence* of your identity. For example, the identity of a flower isn't the fragrance you smell at one particular moment but the specific instructions within that cause a flower to develop its scent. A flower doesn't cease to be a flower when it can no longer produce a scent, but smelling the fragrance gives you a real experience of the flower's identity.

The purpose of this book is to move you closer to understanding your identity. Only in heaven will you fully know yourself and God (1 Corinthians 13:12). But there's always more insight to be gained.

The amount of information to sort through can be overwhelming, but there's also a danger of oversimplification. So stop short of putting and keeping yourself in a box. You're more intricate and complex than any one assessment or comment from a trusted loved one.

What to Dig With

To make your identity conscious, you must dig it up from your subconscious or rely on external input. You can discover your identity by looking outside yourself and by looking inward. When you look, you can choose from objective tools (based on truth) and subjective tools (which will give you more of an opinion). This makes four categories of tools for discovering your identity.

Category 1 **External and Objective** *Tool 1: Scriptures* *Tool 2: Mirrors*	Category 2 **External and Subjective** *Tool 3: Relationships*
Category 3 **Internal and Objective** *Tool 4: Holy Spirit*	Category 4 **Internal and Subjective** *Tool 5: Life Experience* *Tool 6: Self-Assessment*

When you're figuring out what to use to discover your identity, consider that you might be tempted to focus on the category that you naturally gravitate toward. An extraverted person will be likely to appreciate the external tools. Likewise, an introverted person will appreciate the internal tools. A person who prefers thinking will prefer the objective tools. Likewise, a person who prefers feeling will prefer the subjective tools.

Ideally, before you assimilate a new trait into your identity, it should be confirmed by something in each of the four categories. Coming to the wrong conclusion is easier when you don't consider something from each category. You can ask yourself, *Is this really a part of my identity? Am I seeing a trait that appears multiple times in multiple areas of my life?*

Your goal is to be confident in your identity. Sometimes you'll only need tools from one category to convince you, but often, you'll need tools from all four areas for you to feel encouraged to pursue a new direction based on your new identity.

The Bible and the Holy Spirit as Sources of Truth

I've selected six tools that you have at your disposal. Each tool is useful in its own way. I'll show you how to use these tools for greater awareness of who you are. As you use these tools, keep in mind that you can misinterpret even an objective tool and end up with a False Identity.

Before I describe each of the tools, I want to say a quick word about how the Bible and Holy Spirit work together. The combination of Scripture and the Holy Spirit can't be matched for internalizing your identity.

I believe the Bible and the Holy Spirit should be given equal weight as sources of truth. They shouldn't ever contradict each other, so you can use one to validate the understanding you receive from the other. The Bible is inspired, and therefore you need the Spirit to correctly interpret the truth. The Bible without the Spirit would not be understandable and therefore, similar to the Law, would not bring life. The Spirit without the Bible can also lead to misunderstanding because even with the Spirit whispering in your ear, without clear, definite statements, your heart is prone to wander toward what seems best to your human desires.

All Scripture is breathed out by God . . .
—2 Timothy 3:16a

The heart is deceitful above all things, and desperately sick;
who can understand it?
—Jeremiah 17:9

When the Spirit of truth comes, he will guide you into all the truth . . .
—John 16:13

Category 1: External and Objective

These tools are external to you (not a part of you) and function independent of bias. Their strength is that they are the most likely to produce accurate feedback. Their weakness is that they can provide an overwhelming amount of feedback that could be misapplied. For example, you might read a passage of Scripture and fail to understand how it applies to your situation. Applying it incorrectly might cause more harm than good.

Tool 1: Digesting Scriptural Truths

The Bible is the only written source of truth that comes directly from God. There is no better place to go to understand your identity as a Christian. As long as you read and interpret it by the Holy Spirit, who inspired its authors, you can confidently apply its truth to as the foundation of your life.

Tool 2: Looking in the Mirror

Yes, I mean actually looking in a mirror. What you observe — the shape of your body; the color of your skin, eyes, and hair; the softness or sharpness of your facial features; the flexibility of your ligaments or strength of your muscles — these are all part of your identity.

The mirror by itself is completely objective. It reflects exactly what's in front of it. However, the mirror is only as objective as the person using it. To use a mirror correctly, you also need a reasonably healthy self-image.

Don't forget to look with eyes of understanding and grace. Blemishes (whether small or large) and aging aren't meant to be descriptive of your True Identity. The blemishes should be acknowledged but not criticized or condemned.

Looking in the mirror at your face can be a lot like looking into your soul. What do you notice? Smile. What does the expression on your face tell you about your True Identity?

Category 2: External and Subjective

These tools may not always be reliable, but they're no less essential. God gives us to each other so we can relate and better understand ourselves, others, and God.

Tool 3: Evaluating Relationships

Relationships are the most important experiences and also a source of valuable feedback. Someone else can observe who you are from an outside perspective.

Your relationship-attachment quality is a measure of how positive you view relationships. It provides a big clue as to why you feel the way you do about yourself. The more others are able to meet your emotional needs, the more you'll view relationships as positive. Also, the more securely you're attached to God, the more you'll be able to complete a meaningful mission, which I discuss in more detail in Part III.

Category 3: Internal and Objective

The Holy Spirit is the only resource that can be both internal and objective.

Tool 4: Listening to the Holy Spirit

The Holy Spirit can speak to you specifically about who you are and how much God loves you. God gives us the Holy Spirit to bridge the gap between the external objectivity of Scriptures and the internal subjectivity of our hearts. The Holy Spirit provides a personally accurate interpretation of the truth — communicating and applying the truth, customized to your unique identity so you can understand it.

Category 4: Internal and Subjective

You are the resource. God gives you the ability to self-reflect and self-evaluate.

Tool 5: Remembering Life Experiences

Experiences are opportunities to learn more about who you are. Experiences alone cannot determine your identity (unless you let them), but memories contain clues to why you feel the way you do about yourself. Remembering the path you've taken is an important part of identity development.

Without awareness of what you've experienced, you're essentially flying blind in life; you'd lack insight into why you feel the way you do in the present. The past is deeply relevant to emotional healing, but by no means is it a hopelessly limiting factor if you're willing to face it and move beyond it.

Negative memories can be reinterpreted as soon as you have new information, such as new life experiences. For this reason, I recommend that you examine your life at least every five years to make sure you haven't neglected to address a negative memory or benefit from a positive memory (see the Life Experiences Exercise in Next Steps at the end of the chapter).

Tool 6: Studying Self-Assessment Instruments

Professionally designed self-assessment instruments are thought out and planned to be as accurate and comprehensive as possible. They help make the big picture personal by narrowing down where you fit amid all the possibilities. They can summarize who you are, allowing you to quickly grasp and retain a sense of your identity.

In addition to the evaluations at the end of each chapter, I'll provide references to other self-assessments. Keep in mind that you're more complex than any inventory can describe. Where an instrument may fall short, a relationship can enhance the details.

When and Where to Dig

What you've already discovered remains relatively stable. However, God might have more for you to discover beyond what you can imagine. Stay humble enough to accept that God might ask you to change directions at different seasons in your life. God wants to increase your capacity without wasting anything. I know that's part of His plan for my life. I have a computer science degree that I still use today, even though I no longer use it at a full-time job.

Unless you're exposed to some gene-altering process, chances are you'll wake up tomorrow with the same DNA. You'll still have the same eye color as you did yesterday. You'll still be the same sex as you were yesterday. But your priorities could change moment to moment, depending on what's happening. Likewise, your passions can change depending on current world or life events. For example, if you're hit by a drunk driver, you might discover you have a passion for speaking out against irresponsible drinking. Troubling times can bring out your desire to make a difference.

New experiences might create new opportunities for you to refine your Confident Identity. Some discoveries you make will be permanently etched in your mind as absolutely a part of your True Identity. At other times, you might move toward your True Identity and later need to update your understanding of who you are. This doesn't mean God's design and plan for your identity can change. This is the reason for the need to reevaluate every so often.

Because you don't know everything about yourself like God does, you can drift off target over time. You can end up imbalanced, focusing too much on some gifts and not developing others. By revisiting this book every so often, you can verify that you're looking at the correct plans and that you're moving in the right direction.

The following table shows windows into your identity (covered in the upcoming chapters) and how often to evaluate them. They vary from the more concrete and stable aspects of identity to the more volatile. All else being equal, the younger you are, the more frequently you should monitor your development. Any aspect of your identity should be evaluated immediately whenever you become aware it doesn't line up with God's design, regardless of whether it appears to be physical, mental, emotional, or spiritual.

Window into Your Identity	Degree of Volatility	Check In Every
Physical Body, Gender	Extremely Low	1 to 5 years
Cognitive, Emotional, Spiritual	Low	1 to 3 years
Spiritual Gifting	Moderate	1 to 2 years
Personality, Strengths, Abilities	Moderate	1 to 2 years
Priorities, Passions, and Interests	High	3 months

Check in with yourself every three months to quickly evaluate whether anything significant has changed. Are you spending your time according to your heartfelt priorities? Has your attitude shifted toward self, God, or others for better or worse? Do you still have the same hopes and dreams?

If everything seems well, continue as you are. However, if you sense any unrest or complacency, take it seriously by investigating further.

For Reflection

1. What is your attitude toward each of the six tools (see the section "What to Dig With")? Can you trust these "tools" to help you better understand your identity?
2. Are you aware of any buried talents?
3. John's parents created a system that produced guilt and insecurity. Every family creates some kind of dysfunctional system. What atmosphere was present in your childhood home? To what degree are you still living with its dysfunction?
4. "Everybody is a genius. But if you judge a fish by its ability to climb a tree, it will live its whole life believing that it is stupid." What do you make of this quote, which is often misattributed to Albert Einstein and possibly derived from an author in 1898 (see quoteinvestigator.com/2013/04/06/fish-climb)?

Next Steps

☐ At the end of Part II, you'll write an identity statement. Skip ahead to Chapter 15 now to review the Identity Portrait. As you read Chapters 7 to 14, fill in this sheet.
☐ Media for Further Learning (see Appendix B for more questions)
  ☐ Movie: *Ragamuffin*. How do Rich's life experiences impact his life?
  ☐ Movie: *Up*. How do Carl's life experiences affect his life?
  ☐ Music: *One Step Away* by Casting Crowns
☐ Complete the Life Experiences Exercise on the following page. This will help you with "Remembering Life Experiences" (Category 4). A comprehensive exercise like this can get you in touch with a lot of experiences you haven't felt for a long time. You might uncover family secrets that are uncomfortable. I believe this is worth the effort, but please consider what you can handle and pace yourself accordingly. This exercise can take hours or even days to complete. Try to take no longer than a month to finish it so you can gain the full benefit of the exercise.

Life Experiences Exercise

This exercise will help you discover the false negative beliefs that afflict you. You're going to look through your complete history to remember the positive and negative messages you've received about your identity. Remembering helps you make sense of your life — how you got to where you are.

Life can only be understood backward, but it must be lived forward.
—Soren Kierkegaard

How you feel about yourself, God, and others is the resulting sum of how you've interpreted all you've experienced.

To heal your emotional wounds, you need to revisit them and re-interpret them with God's help. Only God knows your true identity, so only He can speak the pure truth about who you are. Encountering God's truth will cleanse the false, negative self-image and reveal your true identity.

When a traumatic experience is too overwhelming to process as it happens, you're able to disconnect from it. You tune out and forget what has happened because it's painful.

Re-member-ing means literally piecing together again
what has become fragmented or broken.
—Margaret Silf

Take a moment before you begin this exercise to ask God to help you remember the fragments of your life and see the patterns that connect the fragments together. Chronicle your life experiences, focusing on one developmental period at a time. For each period, document *specific* memories (actual events in detail). For the first pass through, focus on writing a factual account. During the second pass, remember your *feelings* about the memory. Your feelings will lead you to the lies you believe about your identity. Record any insights you gain. If you remember more facts, add them, but continue to focus on your feelings.

Think of each episodic memory as a short story about you. For each story pay attention to your:

1. Behaviors: How did I respond to what happened? Did I accept the pain in my life or did I run from it? Did I move toward or away from God and others?
2. Body: What sensations do I feel in my body?
3. Beholdings: What did my eyes take in that produced the most significant emotion?
4. Beliefs: What did I believe about myself? What did I believe about my relationship to others, including God?

If you need help remembering, consider the homes you have lived in. Recall each home's layout and the furnishings of the various rooms. What took place in each room? How did you feel? If you're not aware of your own images, consider looking at photographs to help stimulate your memory.

Use the following eleven developmental periods and corresponding questions to document your life story.

Prior to Conception	Conception to Birth	Birth to 2 Years

- Describe the environment in which your life began. How emotionally healthy were your mother and father? Was there peace or stress? Consider the details of their lives such as their spirituality and finances as well as the big picture of their culture and world events.
- Interview family members to gain perspective on your early years. How does learning this help you understand the rest of your life?
- Were people other than your biological parents ever responsible for you for longer than a couple of weeks? Were you adopted?

2 to 5 Years	5 to 9 Years
9 to 12 Years	13 to 18 Years

- How organized or chaotic was your family? How much time did you spend together versus away from each other? How did your family recognize and respond to holidays, birthdays, and crises?
- How were you received by your parents, siblings, relatives, friends, and community? Did you feel loved and wanted, or disregarded and rejected?
- What role(s) did you play in your family? Were you invested in being a perfectionist, lightening the mood through humor, taking care of everyone, accepting the blame for the family problems, or taking care of yourself while others got all the attention? Did your role change over time? If so, how?
- What were your primary and secondary school experiences?

18 to 25 Years	25 to 40 Years
40 to 60 Years	60 Years and Beyond

- Consider your first and lasting impressions from significant events (some of these may have occurred during childhood). What were your first and follow-up experiences with school? Church? God? Work/job? College? Dating? The opposite sex? Marriage?
- How did you leave home?
- Have you lost a significant relationship through estrangement, fight, or divorce?
- If married, what was getting married like? If single, what has this been like?

Patterns and Conclusions

Ask God to help you see the impact on your identity of all the facts, feelings, and beliefs you've gathered. Write a summary impact statement for each short story (episodic memory). After you have all your impacts statements, review them for themes and patterns. Consider creating a timeline graph of the highs and lows of your life. What do you notice?

- What were your most powerful experiences? Why were they so powerful?
- What did you first believe about God? When did this occur?
- What losses have you suffered? What blessings have you experienced?
- What similarities exist between your current and past relationships?
- Are there people whose sins greatly altered your life? Are you holding onto any bitterness?
- Are there any ongoing destructive behaviors you need to stop?
- Do you have any regrets?

Can you see how the stories reinforced your false identity and helped you lose sight of your true identity? Bring each impact statement to God and ask Him to show you the truth about your identity. Ask God which wound you should focus on first. Develop a plan to address any outstanding wounds that need further healing.

The story you've written is a living story. As you uncover lies and experience God's truth, your story changes because you're more in touch with your true identity. Updating your story and adding new chapters will be healing in itself.

Write your top ten most impactful life experiences and corresponding insights in your Blueprint Space. Which experiences fit into your Confident Identity, and which ones fit into your Infected Identity?

BLUEPRINT SPACE

Chapter 8

Your Physical Identity

"Mark asked you to prom? That's awesome! Everyone thought for sure he'd ask Sarah."

"Look who's talking! You're going with Steve. I thought he wasn't your type."

"That was true before I got to know him. I'm glad I gave him a chance because I really like him now."

"Oh, please! You've only been dating for two weeks."

"Yeah, you're right. I shouldn't get so excited so quickly. What about you and Mark?"

"We're getting along pretty well. But I wonder what he sees in me. Mark's supposed to be with girls like Sarah. You know . . . cheerleader with a perfect body. Why did God make my body this shape?"

"Don't say that. You're gonna make someone a great wife someday . . . Hey, I love your hair. What did you do to make it look so full and shiny?"

"Wouldn't you like to know!"

Beauty Is Subjective

Most people would agree there are some objective qualities that define degrees of attractiveness. However, these qualities make sense only when considering general traits across a variety of people and cultures — they aren't meant to be applied personally. Unfortunately, beauty standards tend to be based on imaginary people who exist only on glossy paper because of our ability to manipulate photographs. Judging attractiveness using these unreal standards would devastate most people.

This chapter might be particularly difficult for some people, so remember that everyone can't look the same or have the same body build. Attractiveness is important, but it's only one identity attribute among many others. Basing your worth on appearance involves unhealthy, one-dimensional thinking. Your uniqueness will always be a combination of multiple attributes.

Your goal should be to use the fullness of all that God built into you (see the preceding chapter's discussion of talents). God intends for your external appearance to be in sync with your internal confidence. Invest your energy in bringing your body, mind, and spirit into harmony with each other and God's design.

If you lack internal confidence, then you might become tempted to manipulate your outward appearance to control how you feel about yourself. You don't have to alter God's design in order to be unique. If you aren't liking yourself, make peace with God regarding your identity. Finding what is most unique about you (the core of your identity) is challenging, but it's worth the effort.

Beauty is in the eye of the beholder, and whom you choose as your beholder makes all the difference in knowing and accepting your physical identity. God is your primary beholder. Don't replace Him with popular culture. Beauty is also more than skin deep. Women, your spirit makes you beautiful. Men, your spirit makes you strong.

Your goal remains to be the best you can within God's design. For example, changing your breast size or using steroids to increase your muscles alters God's design. Unless you have a clear medical reason for the change, such alterations communicate to God, "I don't think you designed me the right way. I'm not enough. I need to fix your handiwork."

You're fearfully and wonderfully made. You're perfect the way God made you. Those who reject you for lacking a specific outward (or inward) attribute aren't acting in love. You shouldn't look to them for approval. Doing so will only lead you to alter your God-given identity. Instead, find your identity in who God says you are.

Exceptional Abilities

I've selected four physical abilities that God might have given to you as an exceptional ability. They may or may not be a significant part of your identity. This list is not meant to be exhaustive; instead, it represents the diversity of physical abilities that God created.

1. Attractiveness
2. Strength
3. Agility
4. Craftsmanship

When considering a person's identity, physical *appearance* is probably one of the first things that comes to mind. Most people forget about physical *abilities*. If you're blessed with any physical ability, be sure to take the time to thank God for making you this way.

In many biblical stories, God uses the main character's abilities, uniqueness, and humanness to achieve His purposes. God used Esther's beauty and Samson's strength. God created Bezalel and Oholiab to build His ornate tabernacle. David's mighty men fought valiantly for God. All these people had in common the opportunity to use their physical identity for greater good.

Attractiveness

Although attractiveness can be physical looks, it can also include the way you carry and project yourself. Attractiveness is helpful in different ways. Physical attractiveness is valuable for news anchors and models. Charisma benefits leaders. A diplomat needs to possess the skills of persuasion and tactful communication.

If God has created you especially attractive, you should use this like anything else — to glorify God and further His plans. But external beauty is not meant to compensate for an ugly heart. Allow your inner spirit to transform your outer appearance.

---

*Like a gold ring in a pig's snout
is a beautiful woman without discretion.*
—Proverbs 11:22

> *Do not let your adorning be external—the braiding of hair and the putting on of gold jewelry, or the clothing you wear—but let your adorning be the hidden person of the heart with the imperishable beauty of a gentle and quiet spirit, which in God's sight is very precious.*
> —1 Peter 3:3–4

You are made in the image of God; therefore, you already possess what you need to be attractive. A sincere smile is attractive. A patient and understanding gesture goes a long way. A wise and humble attitude makes all the difference. Don't waste your efforts on superficial comparisons that will only lead you to become someone you aren't.

Esther: An Example of Exceptional Attractiveness

God used Esther's extraordinary beauty as a means to save His people. Her beauty attracted the king's favor, but it would have meant nothing without her willingness to risk her life to save her people. She also had poise, patience, and faith. Her respectful attitude both to Mordecai and her king stands in stark contrast to her predecessor's refusal to obey the king (Esther 1:12; 2:7–10, 20; 3:13–16; 1 Peter 3:1–6).

Strength

Similar to attractiveness, strength can have multiple meanings. It can mean physical strength or strength of character. Construction workers, utility workers, police officers, and firefighters need physical strength to build, protect, and maintain communities.

God made men with the potential for more physical strength than women. God intends men to have strong character. Men with muscle strength but without inner strength are as immature as beautiful women without inner beauty.

Samson: An Example of Exceptional Strength

Samson possessed great physical strength, but he also had a weakness that led to his premature death. He struggled with a human desire to please the women in his life, placing them above God. He resisted this temptation for a while, but once he gave in by compromising his faith, he faced severe consequences. His enemies blinded him and God didn't allow him a do-over.

Like Esther, Samson had a special gift and a desire to see God's plans triumph. He used his faith and strength to serve God by collapsing a building on God's enemies. Samson's focus on God's interests demonstrated he had learned his lesson, even though he died in the collapse, too.

Agility

Agility allows a person to move their body precisely as needed to manipulate objects or move around obstacles. Soldiers need agility to avoid dangerous situations while taking back territory from hostiles. Gymnasts, pilots, and surgeons need precision control over their bodies. Entertainers, such as clowns or magicians, must be especially coordinated.

David's Mighty Men: Examples of Exceptional Agility

During David's reign, he had 37 men in his army who fought with exceptional skill. The best of them all, Josheb-Basshebeth, killed 800 men single-handedly, all within the same battle (2 Samuel 23:8–39). All 37 men had extraordinary fighting skills, strong valor, and dedication to their work.

Craftsmanship

Craftsmanship is the ability to design attractive works of art or to manipulate material to create objects to detailed specifications. Artists, tailors, seamstresses, and architects all have a special ability to create appealing and functional things in order to make living more enjoyable and efficient.

Bezalel and Oholiab: Examples of Exceptional Craftsmanship

When God prescribes, He provides. God provides all we need to accomplish His purposes. Part of our identity is to receive God's power. God fashions and equips us to fulfill His purposes. In Old Testament times, God needed His ornate temple built. He chose Bezalel, called him by name, and provided him with:
- The Spirit of God
- Ability and intelligence
- Knowledge and craftsmanship

Notice the completeness of God's provision. God filled Bezalel with the ability to design the needed crafts, but He also gave him the ability to make the crafts. God provided *all* craftsmanship.

> *The LORD said to Moses, "See, I have called by name Bezalel the son of Uri, son of Hur, of the tribe of Judah, and I have filled him with the Spirit of God, with ability and intelligence, with knowledge and all craftsmanship, to devise artistic designs, to work in gold, silver, and bronze, in cutting stones for setting, and in carving wood, to work in every craft. And behold, I have appointed with him Oholiab, the son of Ahisamach, of the tribe of Dan. And I have given to all able men ability, that they may make all that I have commanded you*
> —Exodus 31:1–6

Body Self-Care

All of the mentioned abilities can be improved or sabotaged by how you take care of your body. Body self-care means you possess enough self-control, discipline, and maturity to properly care for your body. Your body is a temple where God's Holy Spirit dwells. The Bible teaches that because God is living within you, not caring for your body dishonors Him.

> *Flee from sexual immorality. Every other sin a person commits is outside the body, but the sexually immoral person sins against his own body. Or do you not know that your body is a temple of the Holy Spirit within you, whom you have from God? You are not your own, for you were bought with a price. So glorify God in your body.*
> —1 Corinthians 6:18–20

Proper self-care means eating nutritious foods, getting enough sleep, and receiving proper medical care. This also means you shouldn't mistreat your body when you're in any type of pain (whether emotional or physical). Here are signs you might have pain that needs to be addressed in a healthy way:
- Eating too much, too little, or too unhealthily

- Smoking or taking drugs (other than as prescribed)
- Drinking alcohol in excess
- Having sex outside of marriage
- Sleeping too much or too little

These kinds of behaviors can numb your body's sensations and messages. Your body may be telling you that something is wrong. You should never ignore these messages.

Self-care includes grooming and hygiene. Some people spend more time grooming than others. Do your grooming habits cause you to miss important events? Do you obsess about your appearance throughout the day? Or do you struggle with the opposite — letting your appearance become significantly less than its potential?

Your body image is how you view and feel about your body. A healthy body image means you accept and take care of what God has given you. However, if you have an unhealthy image, you might be preoccupied with your appearance or surrender to an unkempt appearance.

For Reflection

1. How does your appearance and body structure provide clues about your identity? When you look in a mirror, do you like what you see? Do you excel at directing your body to accomplish amazing feats?
2. Is there a part of your body you don't like? Can you associate your dislike with any particular negative experience?
3. What is your relationship with food? Do you eat less than your body needs, or do you purge when you eat more than your body needs? Do you use food to nourish your body, or do you use it like a drug?
4. Do you have a physical ability or attribute not considered in this chapter?

Next Steps

- ☐ Complete the Physical Identity Self-Assessment on the following page.
  - The purpose of the Talent section is to identify exceptional abilities. While these areas can certainly be developed, you should base your answers more on raw talent.
  - The purpose of the Self-Image section is to identify areas where you can improve your self-worth with respect to the chapter focus.

  After completing the assessment, journal and talk to God about what you're learning about yourself. What areas can you develop further? What areas are strengths? Weaknesses? What areas need emotional healing? What areas are a priority and worth your time right now to improve? What's your plan for improving?
- ☐ Media for Further Learning (see Appendix B for more questions)
  - ☐ Movie: *Beauty and the Beast* (1991). How does Belle look beyond outward appearances?
  - ☐ Music: *Beautiful* by Plumb

Physical Identity Self-Assessment

Instructions: Rate each statement as CT for Completely True, ST for Somewhat True, SF for Somewhat False, or CF for Completely False. Write in any physical talents you have that aren't listed.

Physical Talent Statement	Rating	R#
1) I'm coordinated (excellent body spatial awareness).	CT ST SF CF	
2) I'm athletic (physically fit, possessing endurance).	CT ST SF CF	
3) I have exceptional body strength.	CT ST SF CF	
4) I can easily create works of art (pottery, furniture, paintings, etc.).	CT ST SF CF	
5) I'm exceptionally beautiful or attractive.	CT ST SF CF	
6) I have fine control over my movements (hands of a surgeon).	CT ST SF CF	
7) I have a high tolerance for physical pain.	CT ST SF CF	
8) I can play a musical instrument or sing with skill.	CT ST SF CF	
9)	CT ST SF CF	
10)	CT ST SF CF	
11)	CT ST SF CF	
12)	CT ST SF CF	

Finish by ranking (under R#) each statement from most like you to least like you. Write (up to) your top four Completely True (CT) talents on your Identity Portrait in Chapter 15.

Now rate the following self-image statements. Then check the box for any statement that evokes strong negative feelings (such as sadness, anger, fear, or shame).

Physical Self-Image Statement	Rating	?
1) I take care of my body.	CT ST SF CF	☐
2) I like my appearance.	CT ST SF CF	☐
3) I'm comfortable in my own body.	CT ST SF CF	☐
4) I'm easily in touch with (aware of) my body sensations.	CT ST SF CF	☐
5) I have self-control; I can make my body to do what I want it to do.	CT ST SF CF	☐
6) I can depend on my body; I am healthy.	CT ST SF CF	☐
7) My happiness depends on my physical appearance.	CT ST SF CF	☐
8) I compare my appearance to others and find myself inferior.	CT ST SF CF	☐
9) I'm desperate to change (part or all of) my appearance.	CT ST SF CF	☐
10) I'm hopelessly physically defective.	CT ST SF CF	☐
11) I use my body to its fullest potential.	CT ST SF CF	☐
12) I accept God's design for my body.	CT ST SF CF	☐

Chapter 9

Your Gender Identity

"I'm not sure I like being female. I wonder if there was some mix-up and I was supposed to be male. Sometimes I feel like a man in a woman's body."

"You look like a woman to me. How can you feel like a man?"

"I don't know. I'm more like my dad than my mom. We have so much in common. I didn't get along with my mom very well, unlike my sister who's more of a girly girl. Ugh! I'll never be a girly girl."

"Maybe that explains it then — if you and your mom had a better relationship, maybe you could accept yourself as feminine, even though you have some typical male traits in common with your dad."

"That could be. But why does it have to be so complicated? I don't feel comfortable in Christian women's groups because I'm not like them. How can I be me but feel like I belong?"

"I'm sorry this is so hard for you. All of us suffer in one way or another when life doesn't line up with truth. The alternative, deviating from God's design, is much worse. Even though you're struggling, this doesn't change our friendship."

"Thanks, that means a lot to me."

God's Design

Your gender identity is healthy to the degree you accept the gender God has assigned to you. These three rules capture the essence of God's design for gender identity:
1. God created only two distinct genders (male and female).
2. God created sex and allows it only within marriage.
3. God created sex to occur only between one man and one woman.

Given these rules, what options do you have to accept God's design of gender identity?

Two Options for Accepting God's Design
1) Marriage and sex
2) Singleness and celibacy

Rejecting God's Design

Lusting, fantasizing, or coveting

Sex outside of marriage

Sex with the same gender

Altering your gender

Gender Distinction

After you realize you've been made in God's image and God loves you unconditionally, your gender has the most impact on your identity. Gender shapes every aspect of your life. Your gender isn't random — God chose your gender; it's inseparable from who you are.

God doesn't blur the boundaries between male and female. Their distinctiveness adds a beauty to life that shouldn't be erased. Can you imagine life without gender?

Gender is one part of creation meant to be black and white. Either you're male, or you're female. I believe God intends this part of identity to be obvious — a given fact that we don't have to question. Yet without truth to ground identity, a person can be so confused that they allow themselves to doubt their biological identity. What a burden this is!

At best, this confusion represents the inherent suffering of living in an imperfect, cursed world. Believing you shouldn't have to suffer can lead to all kinds of painful conclusions, not the least of which is that you don't have a Creator who intentionally designed you.

A gender is a specialized version of the divine nature. God gives gender so you can participate in life in specific ways. The time you have on earth is limited. What will you focus on with your time? Your gender helps simplify your decision.

Gender Equality

Your gender limits you in some ways to allow you to specialize in others. How do you feel about this? Are you able to equally value male and female qualities without possessing both qualities?

Jesus chose His 12 disciples to be male. He chose some of His closest relationships to be with women. He cared for them, and He let them care for Him. Jesus related to men and women differently, but He clearly valued both. He did nothing to indicate one is better than the other.

Unity without diversity is meaningless. Unity with diversity strengthens any endeavor. To deny or overemphasize male/female differences only weakens God's design. Both approaches fuel unhealthy competition rather than cooperation. Don't believe the lie that one gender is better than the other, and don't mess up God's plan for teamwork and unity.

Denying the differences destroys diversity and leads to glorifying a small subset of abilities. This polarizes people into "has-value" and "has-no-value" categories instead of "female" and "male." Paul addressed envy in the Body of Christ by pointing out God's self-balancing design:

> *But God has so composed the body, giving greater honor to the part*
> *that lacked it, that there may be no division in the body,*
> *but that the members may have the same care for one another.*
> —1 Corinthians 12:24b–25

Concerning gender, the principle is the same. God promotes gender equality, not gender envy. God designed male and female to work together, not independently or competitively. Each gender has its own strengths and weaknesses. Both are needed and valued. Neither is superior to the other.

Gender Attitude

Your identity as male or female carries with it a responsibility, at least during your earthly life. Your gender is an opportunity to reflect the order of creation. God has authority over all of us, and He placed men in authority over women. The authority holds to the degree it fits within a mutually desired, healthy relationship.

One application of gender is to communicate the attitude of your gender. God designed men to relate to women with an attitude of love, not indifference or harshness. Likewise, God designed women to relate to men with an attitude of respect, not independence or contempt. A woman who disrespects a man promotes disrespect of God. A man who doesn't love a woman represents that God is unloving. Love and respect aren't only needs; they are, first and foremost, the right way to relate that honors God (Ephesians 5:22–33)!

God intends for both genders to conform their attitudes to fulfill the purposes of His design. God is masculine compared to all of creation. Spiritually, we all have a heart that God can indwell. As we are prepared to submit to God and allow Him to live inside us, so should women be prepared in their attitude to highlight the best in men. As God is gentle — not harsh and not forcing Himself on us — so should men be prepared in their attitude to be gentle with women.

Marriage and Sex or Singleness and Celibacy

Because God designed sex to occur only within marriage, those who remain single have only one option: celibacy. Marriage isn't for everyone. Celibacy is a good thing.

Being single doesn't nullify gender. Celibacy excludes the act of sex but not the expression of one's gender.

Several people in the Bible chose singleness. Paul considered his singleness as a spiritual gift from God (1 Corinthians 7:7). As an apostle, he devoted his life to bringing the gospel to the Gentiles and writing much of the New Testament. John the Baptist devoted his life to preparing the way for Jesus. He was an important part of God's plan as a humble, selfless servant (Matthew 3). Anna became a widow after only seven years of marriage. She lived 84 years devoted to God through prayer and fasting (Luke 2:36–38).

Sex between One Man and One Woman

God didn't create additional gender options beyond Adam and Eve. God told Adam (one male) and Eve (one female) to be fruitful and multiply. He didn't provide for anything outside of this. Sexuality isn't like clothing that you can choose based on how you're feeling on any particular day.

So God created man in his own image, in the image of God he created him; male and female he created them. And God blessed them. And God said to them, "Be fruitful and multiply and fill the earth and subdue it, and have dominion over the fish of the sea and over the birds of the heavens and over every living thing that moves on the earth."
—Genesis 1:27–28

Requirements for a Confident Gender Identity

Living well means that your mind (thoughts and feelings), body, and gender identity are in harmony. To understand how your gender identity develops, consider God's three processes:
1. **God's design:** God's intentions for a human's gender
2. **God's biological process:** The way God made for an embryo to develop into the male or female sex
3. **God's developmental process:** The way God made for a human to internalize and identify with their biological sex

Of these three processes, only God's design is perfect. The other two are flawed to some degree. Most of the time, these flaws are not significant enough to result in a conflict (disharmony) between one's biological sex and one's emotionally identified sex. If the conflict exists and doesn't resolve, then, ultimately, a person chooses their flawed design over God's ideal design.

A confident gender identity starts with agreement with God's design for gender. God chose your distinct gender before you were conceived.

Beyond this, the strength of your gender identity depends on three factors:
- Physical, biological, and hormonal development
- Early childhood emotional development
- Acceptance and belonging

A stronger gender identity is one in which all three factors sufficiently support God's design. A weaker gender identity is deficient in one or more factors. Developing a strong gender identity later in life is possible if you are willing to seek help to strengthen all three areas.

Acceptance of God's Design

God intends for you, as a created being, to conform to His design. This means you don't have a choice with respect to your gender. God assigned it — end of story. Being created comes with implicit expectations:
- Serve God with all you are. Bring glory to God. Don't compromise the truth.
- Don't rebel against God's chosen gender for you.
- If you choose to engage in a sexual relationship, follow God's design.

Don't pursue life in a way that neglects your gender strengths. Give your primary effort to embracing your God-given gender. Don't expect men to do what God designed women to do. Likewise, don't expect women to do what God designed men to do.

The world's ever-changing definition of gender isn't the same as the biblical definition. If you're a married female, don't pass up the opportunity to become pregnant so that you can pursue something else like a career. If you're a married male, don't neglect your responsibility to provide for your wife. I'm not saying that women can't work or that men can't take care of children. I'm saying not to let a secondary interest become more important than fulfilling your primary calling as indicated by your gender.

Proper Biological Development

Males and females are different on the cellular level, not only because of developmental differences caused by hormones. Physiological research supports that every human cell is either male or female. From conception, every cell has two X chromosomes (XX for females) or one X and one Y (XY for males).

> Differences between the male and female brain have been a subject of study by philosophers, poets and scientists alike. It has long been held that sex differences in the brain are caused by differential exposure to gonadal secretions during fetal and neonatal development, with distinct sexual dimorphism particularly in sex-steroid concentrating regions. However, there is accumulating evidence that supports the notion of sexual dimorphism in the brain in the absence of gonadal secretions.

—Kalpit Shah, Charles E. McCormack, and Neil A. Bradbury[8]

God designed physical development so that at conception, the instructions exist to develop the person into one distinct sex. To the degree this biological process malfunctions, a person will be more likely to experience the conflict between outward appearance (biological identity) and internal experience (emotional identity).

Biology can impact a person's sense of their gender identity. A small percentage of people are born in an unclear gender state (through chromosome errors and/or lack of sufficient hormones). This is an unfortunate failure of the biological process. This doesn't mean God created more than two genders. God can use anything for His glory (John 9:3).

In cases where hormones are severely deficient, especially during childhood development, hormones should be supplemented to reinforce God's design. However, a lack of sufficient hormones doesn't nullify gender and certainly doesn't prevent one from serving God (Matthew 19:12).

God's truth remains absolute, despite the effects of the curse. This should bring hope that we live in an ordered world. God's ideals never shift or change — no matter how much we suffer because of sin or the curse. A mature person will accept God's power in their life, whether or not God provides relief from a physical problem.

Proper Emotional Development

A healthy gender identity requires both the infusion of needed positives and the absence of detrimental negatives. The more these are out of balance — if the negatives are severe and the positives are minimal —the more likely a person will be confused about their gender. If there's an imbalance, the solution isn't to go with the imbalance against God's design.

The primary needed positives are acceptance and belonging. The primary detrimental negative is anything that involves implicitly or explicitly being cast out from one's biological gender affiliation. This includes both parental and peer rejection. This also includes any form of neglect and abuse, although sexual abuse is particularly damaging.

Imagine lacking positive encouragement of your God-given biological gender identity and instead, receiving abusive behaviors, rejecting statements, or neglect. Growing up is hard enough already.

The First Three Years

Gender identification is a developmental process that normally takes place within the first three years of life. If the process is successful, a toddler emerges with a framework for a cohesive gender identity. Male children identify as male, and female children identify as female. This is primarily achieved through a relational bond.

Infants, whether male or female, are born ready to bond with their mothers. God designed mothers for this important first bonding experience. When the bond is good enough, the baby internalizes that their existence is good because they experience their needs being reasonably met. This lays the foundation for all future development.

Babies cannot remain completely dependent upon their mother forever. Prior to about eight months, babies generally cannot grasp the idea that they're separate from their caregivers.

---

[8] *American Journal of Physiology – Cell Physiology*. Published 6 November 2013. Vol. no. DOI: 10.1152/ajpcell.00281.2013; Lines 254–259

Developmentally, around the age of 16 months, a child must separate from their mother to form an identity of their own. This process culminates in what parents know as the "terrible twos."

The following table describes the developmental phases necessary to achieve an identity. The phases have some overlap. Each subsequent phase shows signs of beginning in the preceding phase, and earlier phases carry forward into later phases.

Developmental Phase	Age Range[9]	Phase Characterized By
Autism	0–2 months	No or little knowledge of self or other; incapable of relating; functions by reflex
Symbiosis *"Me as We"*	2–6 months	Beginning knowledge of self and other; capable of being aware of needs being met; beginnings of relating
Individuation *"Me as You and I"*	6–24 months	Developing knowledge of self and other; motivation to separate along with fear of complete separation
Identity *"Me as I, You as You"*	24+	Beginnings of security without an other's constant presence; recognition of one's sense of self

A baby girl will be able to identify as female as long as separation from her mom is allowed and tolerated. A baby boy has to go one step further. A boy must accomplish a transition from a bond with his mother to a bond with his father. To achieve a masculine identity, he must find peace in separating from the feminine without rejecting it. During this transition, a male child learns to accept and internalize the idea he is male, just like his father. As long as his mother doesn't interfere with her son's need to bond with his father, and as long as his father welcomes him as male, he can accept his identity as heterosexual male.[10]

If the bonding, separation, or identification processes are interrupted and not achieved, the child will have serious emotional difficulties. Let me emphasize that this doesn't guarantee gender confusion. However, if biological errors or abuse are involved, the chances greatly increase.

Gender confusion is excruciating and no less an identity crisis. If this occurs, a child will seek to fill their identity vacuum with whatever is attainable. For example, a boy who isn't accepted by his father but is accepted by his mother is in danger of identifying as female. For him, if identifying as male isn't easy or readily possible, the best alternative is to identify as female. Then, instead of associating with his male peers, he will find it easier to form relationships with female peers. Bonding and identifying with the opposite gender is better than nothing, but it introduces a distortion into identity that will eventually need correction.

Puberty

Affirmation of one's biological gender is especially important again during adolescence. God provides a way for each person to be affirmed in their biological gender identity. A rite of passage is a celebration of a youth's transition into adulthood. Older men welcome a young man into manhood. Similarly, older women welcome a young woman into womanhood. Affirmation is the final step in the emotional development and internalization of your biological gender identity.

---

[9] Hamilton, N. G. (1992). *Self and others: Object relations theory in practice.* New Jersey: Aronson.

[10] Focus on the Family recordings of Joseph and Linda Nicolosi, authors of *A Parent's Guide to Preventing Homosexuality*.

Acceptance and Belonging

Everyone has a deep longing to be affirmed for who they are. If you don't have this need met, you'll experience shame and doubt. Experiencing not fitting with your gender community can be devastating if you already have a weakened sense of gender identity. We shouldn't break God's design for distinct genders so we must accept everyone as biologically male or female, no matter how much they lack the proper biological or emotional development.

Be Flexible with Gender Stereotypes

Within the biblical definition, there is flexibility in how to live as male or female. You don't have to conform to a rigid one-size-fits-all stereotype. To see that God appreciates diversity, you only need to look at His creation. God is infinitely good, but creation's diversity has limits. Accept God's biblical truth (His laws of love, your gender, etc.), and be free to express your God-given personality. Make sure you don't fall into the trap of a negative interpretation of your gender and end up excluding yourself from your gender community.

Part of a conference I attended focused on the differences between men and women. The leaders asked us to separate by gender and then face each other. The men formed a single line, while the women bunched together (picture on the left). The men preferred to stand on their own, while the women preferred being part of a community. In keeping with these instincts, in a threatening environment, the men would likely form a circle around the women (picture on the right). The men

could interact with both the environment and the women, and the women would feel safe to interact with the men (and each other) while completing their work in the context of a community.

These words capture the essence of being female:
- Sensitive
- Helping
- Responding
- Strengthening
- Nesting
- Nurturing

If you are biologically female, find your own way to express these traits. You can be a feminine woman whether or not you fit a cultural stereotype. For example, *sensitive* has come to mean emotional, but it can also mean fine-tuned and therefore perceptive.

These words capture the essence of being male:
- Direct
- Powerful
- Initiating
- Pursuing
- Providing
- Protecting

If you are biologically male, find your own way to express these traits. You can be a masculine man whether or not you fit a cultural stereotype. For example, *powerful* means strength, and strength can be muscular, but it can also mean having a lasting influence on others.

Your *gender strength* is how well you can fulfill these basic gender roles. Specialization means limitation of the individual for the greater good of the team and those the team serves. This should be empowering, not restricting. Don't confuse gender traits with personality. For example, an outgoing woman might initiate things often; there's nothing wrong with this, unless she doing it solely to compare herself to and compete with men.

A male can have some stereotypical feminine traits and remain a man, and a female can have some stereotypical masculine traits and remain a female. This isn't a problem — it actually demonstrates what it means to be secure in one's sexual identity. Your behavior can't make you male or female. Gender is God-assigned and not meant to be changed.

Can women be direct and men be sensitive? Of course! But in living out your natural personality, do so while expressing your gender attitude. If you forget who you are at your core, you'll have difficulty following God's plan for your life. If a woman is direct, she shouldn't forget she's a woman. If a man is sensitive, he shouldn't forget he's a man. Maybe as a woman you are a gifted leader. That's great, so long as you respect God's chain of command and God's image.

Don't Be Shamed out of Your Gender

Everyone needs to feel they belong somewhere. One necessity of a confident gender identity is finding your clan — the group of people within your same gender where you feel you belong.

Often, if you don't fit into your gender's stereotype, you'll feel painfully rejected and excluded — by your peers, yourself, or both. When you don't belong, you're an outcast because you've been cast out.

Lack of belonging is a real problem. The need is so great that people will go against their created design to feel they belong. If a boy isn't identifying with his biological sex, he has nowhere else to go. Because he doesn't have the same biological makeup as a girl, he becomes an outcast.

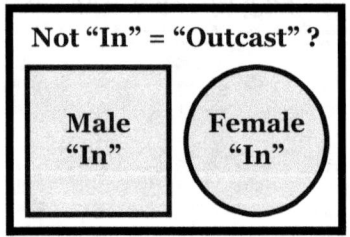

Gender confusion has become a worldwide problem, not a biblical problem. Society has abandoned the path to socialize everyone so that they can retain their biological gender. As a culture, we shouldn't leave anyone behind.

This is why an affirming homosexual community exists. These individuals have created a place to belong, which is an identity need everyone has. However, homosexuality is a human solution and isn't ordained by God. Is the only solution to affirm people as they go against God's design? What other choice is available if a person struggles to accept their biological gender?

The church has a responsibility to communicate acceptance of every person without compromising the truth. The church can be a place of belonging *and* a place of healthy conviction about sinful behaviors. You can love someone and acknowledge their worth without condoning and endorsing every action they choose.

Feeling like you don't fit in is a real identity problem. No one should be an outcast. Don't give up on your gender until you find a group that affirms you as "in." Gender identity is something that takes time to mature into. Everyone has a responsibility to meet this communal need. Those already "in" should accept those "out." Those feeling "out" should develop relationships with those already "in."

Rejection of God's Design

We are living during a period of great exploration. This means more opportunity to find significance. However, as the pressure increases to find a niche, so does the temptation to take experimentation too far. Out of desperation for identity, some people tamper with God's design by opening what they think is a new frontier.

Remember the invisible fence analogy from Chapter 7? I don't recommend experimenting with your gender. If you open the door to a lie, you could end up going down a path that takes you further away from God and into confusion.

God has a purpose in separating out female from male. God's design doesn't need modification. Trying to redefine who you are outside of God's design will only result in instability. You cannot find fulfillment outside of God's design. Don't let your unmet needs reject your God-given sexual identity. You must believe and trust that God created you with your gender for good reason.

God gives you the Holy Spirit to help convict you of your sin, not usually to identity others' sin. Because you cannot see another's heart like God can, you can primarily identify others' sin by their behaviors. Sexual sin can manifest in many ways:
- Indulging in sexual fantasies, including watching or reading explicit material
- Lusting after and objectifying people (but sexual attraction itself isn't sinful)
- Seducing someone to manipulate them
- Having sex with someone outside of marriage
- Altering your biologically assigned gender
- Forming a sexual relationship with someone of the same gender

Keep in mind that temptation and sin are two different things. Being tempted is being offered the opportunity to sin. You have to choose to sin. For Bible-believing Christians, temptation results in a conflict between the external, objective standard and the internal, subjective experience. Resolving this conflict means altering one of these to bring it into alignment with the other.

Extramarital Sex

Sex outside of marriage means any sexual behavior beyond what is healthy for a heterosexual, monogamous marriage. Extramarital sex dishonors God's design. In all cases, it's an expression of selfishness — a lack of self-control and a pursuit of instant gratification. Often someone ends up with damaged self-worth, bondage to further sin, or even ongoing spiritual attack.

Rejection of Assigned Gender

This includes same-sex attraction and gender alteration.

Same-Sex Attraction

God's design is heterosexual, but some people sexualize their relationship with the same gender. This is called same-sex attraction (SSA). God made sexuality to work by the attraction of two opposites. Those struggling with SSA are attracted to a gender quality they lack.

Essentially, SSA is a confused state of sexualizing one's need for emotional affirmation from the same gender. A deviation from normal biological or emotional development causes a person to feel out of sync with their assigned gender and therefore out of sync with God's design.

Gender Alteration

God designed only two distinct genders, but some people reject their assigned gender. Of those who reject their gender, some change only outer appearances (cross-dressing), but others go as far as they can by electing sex reassignment surgery.

World magazine recently published an article discussing how the push to go with impulses to alter gender frequently ends up in sadness and regret.[11] Surgically altering your gender is irreversible for the most part. As drastic as surgery is, there is no way to completely transform your gender. Every cell in your body is aligned to your God-given gender in some way.

Returning to God's Design

What happens when you go beyond God's boundaries? Can you recover? Cleaning up outward behavior is positive, provided the inward attitude of the heart is addressed also. No matter your struggle, God's expectations are the same: He works to put sin to death and to conform us to the image and character of Jesus Christ.

Those who struggle with sexual sin have an internal conflict between what feels right and what God says is right. You have four options to consider as ways to resolve your sin:

1. Ignore the conflict.
2. Attempt to find a compromise between feeling and truth to salvage most of both.
3. Decide that subjective feeling is more important than objective truth.
4. Decide that objective truth is more important than subjective feeling.

Option one doesn't resolve anything. Outright ignoring the truth or conforming by pretending to agree with the truth are both unproductive solutions. Instead, they delay or avoid the inevitable conflict. This is unsatisfactory because the only way to grow is to resolve the identity crisis. God

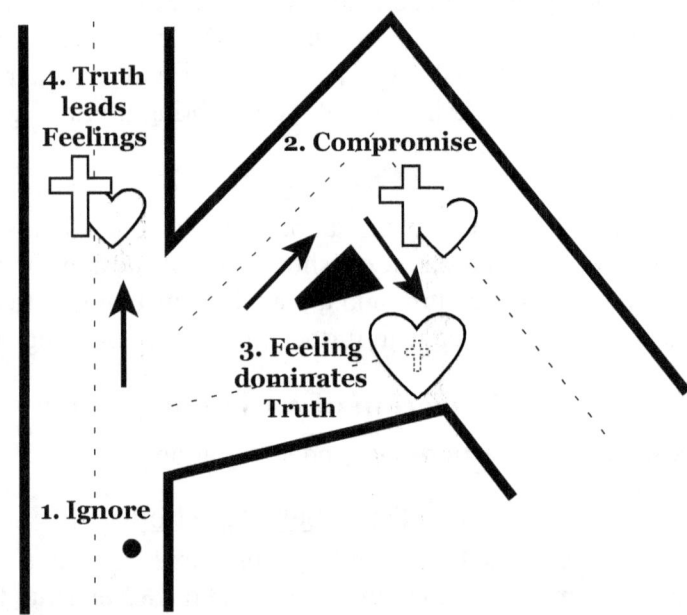

---

[11] "Sounding the alarm," *World*, April 15, 2017; p 30–41

made us to grow in our identity. Option two compromises the truth in some way, so it's effectively the same as option three (deciding subjective feelings are more important than objective truth).

The only intellectually sound way to resolve the objective/subjective conflict is to choose one standard to take precedence over the other. Truth comes from God and therefore, we can't make it up. God wants you to form beliefs — internal convictions based on the truth. But you can't declare your subjective beliefs to be more important than God's truth.

Those who favor their subjective feelings over God's standards might rationalize that the Bible isn't actually against certain sins (premarital sex, sex with the same gender, etc.). These individuals then proceed to interpret the Bible according to their beliefs. This assumes that all good-feeling experiences are God-intended, approved, and therefore ordained. This leads to the wrong conclusion that any behavior resulting in good feelings, no matter how unhealthy, is good to pursue.

Gender identity confusion is not sin, but it is an indication of a lack in one or more of the requirements for a Confident Identity. To be confused about gender is excruciating. But choosing your own version of truth over God's version is sin. All of us have to make choices at one time or another to deny what we desire. You can desire to eat five donuts for lunch, desire to have sex with someone you aren't married to, or desire to spend money that you don't have. For all of these, you first need to understand what is taking place in your heart. Just because it feels right doesn't make it right.

God's grace is sufficient for all, no matter the type of struggle. This means if you struggle with your gender identity, you shouldn't feel rushed to pick a direction. Forcing a decision only continues to promote an internal division, which isn't what God wants. You'll lack integrity, whether you feel God's disapproval of your sin and choose to embrace it anyway, or you feel compelled to follow what you know is true but must repress your honest but sinful desires.

God expects us to submit to the truth, but He gives us grace and time to work through our problems, as long as we're honest about our struggles and seek the appropriate remedy. Receive God's grace so that you can experience redemption, healing, and the fullness of your True Identity.

For Reflection

1. How are you using your gender to be a blessing to others?
2. If you struggle with your gender identity, give yourself time to gain what you missed developmentally.

Next Steps

- ☐ Complete the Gender Identity Self-Assessment on the following page.
    - The purpose of the Talent section is to identify exceptional abilities. While these areas can certainly be developed, you should base your answers more on raw talent.
    - The purpose of the Self-Image section is to identify areas where you can improve your self-worth with respect to the chapter focus.

    After completing the assessment, journal and talk to God about what you're learning about yourself. What areas are strengths? Weaknesses? What areas can you develop further? What areas need emotional healing? What areas are a priority and worth your time right now to improve? What's your plan for improving?
- ☐ Media for Further Learning
    - ☐ Music: *My Lighthouse* by Rend Collective

Gender Identity Self-Assessment

Instructions: Rate each statement as CT for Completely True, ST for Somewhat True, SF for Somewhat False, or CF for Completely False. If you are female, rate the word by the (F). If you are male, rate the word by the (M). Write in any gender-related talents you have that aren't included.

Gender Talent Statement	Rating	R#
1) I have exceptional ability to be Sensitive (F) / Direct (M).	CT ST SF CF	
2) I have exceptional ability to be Helping (F) / Powerful (M).	CT ST SF CF	
3) I have exceptional ability to be Responding (F) / Initiating (M).	CT ST SF CF	
4) I have exceptional ability to be Strengthening (F) / Pursuing (M).	CT ST SF CF	
5) I have exceptional ability to be Nesting (F) / Providing (M).	CT ST SF CF	
6) I have exceptional ability to be Nurturing (F) / Protecting (M).	CT ST SF CF	
7) Others look up to me as a strong representative of my gender.[12]	CT ST SF CF	
8)	CT ST SF CF	
9)	CT ST SF CF	
10)	CT ST SF CF	

Finish by ranking (under R#) each statement from most like you to least like you. Write (up to) your top three Completely True (CT) talents on your Identity Portrait in Chapter 15.

Now rate the following self-image statements. Then check the box for any statement that evokes strong negative feelings (such as sadness, anger, fear, or shame).

Gender Self-Image Statement	Rating	?
1) I'm glad I am the gender I am.	CT ST SF CF	☐
2) I'm attracted to the opposite sex.	CT ST SF CF	☐
3) The opposite sex is attracted to me.	CT ST SF CF	☐
4) I have a positive view of sexual relations in marriage.	CT ST SF CF	☐
5) I consider male and female to be of equal value.	CT ST SF CF	☐
6) My mind, body, and gender are all in harmony.	CT ST SF CF	☐
7) My gender puts me at a disadvantage.	CT ST SF CF	☐
8) I use my gender to its fullest potential.	CT ST SF CF	☐
9) I accept God's design for my gender.	CT ST SF CF	☐

---

[12] Some females are exceptional in how they represent women. They are like the "ultimate mother figure." Some males are exceptional in how they represent men. They are like the "ultimate father figure."

Chapter 10

Your Cognitive and Emotional Identity

"I'm not being mean."

"Yes, you are! You could have picked up Max from school today."

"I told you yesterday I wasn't going to have time to get him."

"That's what you say every week. Why do I always have to get him?"

"You don't always get him. I got him last week."

"Yeah, one time in the last three months."

"What am I supposed to do? Tell my boss I have to leave work early every day?"

"Harrghh! Nevermind. There's no point in talking about this anymore. You obviously don't care."

"Good! I'm glad this conversation is done."

"That's not what I meant and you know it."

Divided and Conquering

Arguments like this one take place when two people maintain different perspectives but can't figure out how to get on the same page. As arguments escalate, they can become more polarized. One person prefers to focus on their logical perspective (the "thinker") and another focuses on their emotional perspective (the "feeler").

Thinkers and feelers often have a hard time communicating. The thinker sees the feeler as inconsolable, irrational, or hopelessly overdramatic. The feeler sees the thinker as uncaring, harsh, or immovably cold.

What is the best way for thinkers and feelers to communicate? Neither person should eliminate their preference, nor should either person convert to the other person's preferences.

To answer this question, look at your own brain functioning for clues. Your brain has the capacity for thinking and feeling. If you aren't able to have your thoughts and feelings cooperate, you're less likely to understand and communicate well with someone else. Instead of seeking to have others function like you, work to reach your fullest cognitive and emotional functioning.

Your Brain Structure Mirrors Your Experiences

Whatever happens to you is stored somewhere in your brain. The brain wires similar experiences closely together. This allows you to easily recall memories that you consider to be significant. However, the very act of remembering starts to change and strengthen the memory. Older, less important memories become harder to retrieve. This is by design so that you aren't overwhelmed with irrelevant information. Additionally, this makes overcoming a False Identity a matter of rewiring the brain by focusing on the positives that will make the negatives obsolete.

An unhealthy brain has parts that are too disconnected from each other. If one part functions too much, it cripples the other parts. For example, your rational "doing" part could criticize and control your emotional "being" part with negative self-talk like Amy's ("I'm such a loser"). Or your emotional part could inflate and overwhelm your rational part, like when Amy's anxiety surfaced and her face twitched. An emotionally unhealthy brain is either overfocused or underfocused on emotions.

A healthy brain is well integrated. The thinking and feeling areas of the brain function optimally when they work cooperatively. This means each area performs what is best for the person, without interfering with other areas.

Brain Structure

Understanding a little about brain structure can help you see how the different parts work together. Here are some significant parts of the brain and what they do:

- The *brain stem*, which is situated directed above the spinal cord, controls the basic functions of life (breathing, heart rate, blood pressure, reflexes, sleep, balance).
- The *cerebral cortex*, which is situated around the brain stem, provides advanced cognitive and emotional functioning.
- The *frontal lobe* is the part of the cerebral cortex responsible for higher cognitive functions (problem solving, memory, language, motivation, judgment, and impulse control).
- The *prefrontal cortex* is a part of the frontal lobe and is involved with intellect, complex learning, mood, and personality.
- The *limbic system* is located near the center of the brain and is responsible for regulating emotion and memory. It's where senses and awareness are first processed.

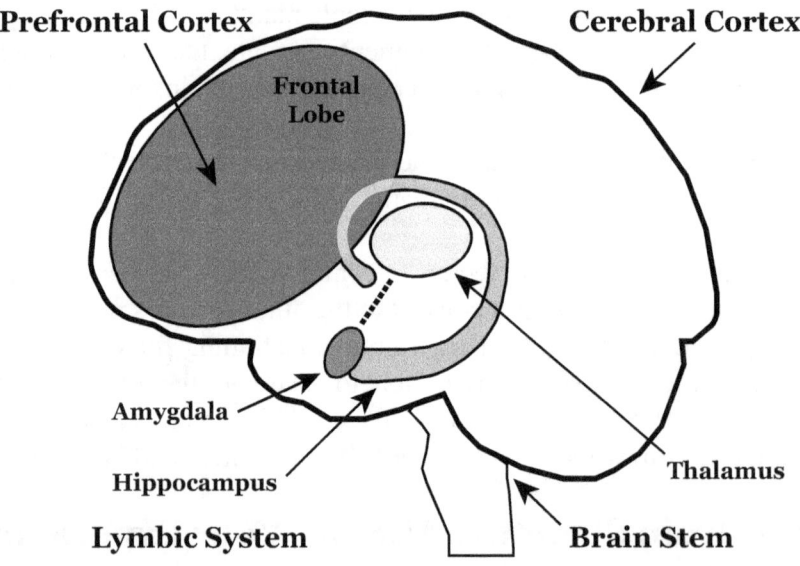

The amygdala and the hippocampus are part of the limbic system. They're significant because they process emotional information in different ways.

Amygdala: Faster but Inaccurate

The amygdala processes information related to emotions and decides what to do with it. During a potential threat, the *thalamus* (connected to the brain stem) sends general characteristics of the threat to the amygdala for quick processing (dashed line). If the threat appears to be real, the amygdala raises an alarm to prepare the body for action to restore safety. It stores implicit (unconscious) memories for future threat evaluation. This is how you can feel uneasy about a situation but not know why.

Hippocampus: Slower but Accurate

The hippocampus integrates emotional experience with cognition. It works with the cerebral cortex to help you understand experiences. The information from the hippocampus is much more detailed than what the amygdala can provide. This is why the hippocampus takes longer to respond. It stores the explicit (conscious) experiences into long-term memory according to what you've learned. If you've been through a traumatic event that isn't resolved yet, your hippocampus won't have information about the event.

Cognitive Identity

Cognition is the mental process of knowing, including aspects such as awareness, perception, reasoning, and judgment.[13] Your ability to think has many important uses.

Staying Objective by Keeping Truth

There's a time to be closed to persuasion and influence. Remaining objective allows you to filter through all the irrelevant or errant data and find the significant and raw truth. Thinkers can often remain calm in the midst of a stressful situation.

Eve was deceived by the serpent, and then Adam chose to join his wife rather than follow God's clear instructions. They both tossed aside God's clear directions in favor of an emotional argument. You're wired to be inspired by something. If you're not inspired by God, you'll look beyond God. Life would be amazingly different if you could always objectively discern when you were about to step into a trap and then avoid it.

Executive Functioning

God makes a clear distinction between humans made in His image and all the rest of Creation, including animals: He gives you the ability to achieve some degree of objective perspective on your behaviors and emotions. Being able to observe and evaluate your own thoughts and feelings is a powerful ability. The more you pay attention to what is going on within you, the more you strengthen the prefrontal cortex (the area responsible for executive functioning). *Executive functioning* includes things like paying attention, controlling your impulses, planning and organizing, and being flexible in thinking.

When you understand your own feelings, and learn to manage them, you can actually understand other people.
—Dan Siegal

---

[13] thefreedictionary.com/cognition

Cognitive Intelligence

People with exceptional abstract thinking might excel at advanced math, map reading, or problem-solving. They can see the big picture and generate ideas and solutions for complex problems. They often choose careers as inventors, scientists, or architectural designers.

People with exceptional concrete thinking enjoy detailed analysis and exercising precise strokes to make something intricate that functions well. They often see themselves as doers and enjoy solving physical problems like those of engineers, construction workers, or electricians.

Emotional Identity

Emotion is a mental state that arises spontaneously rather than through conscious effort; it's often accompanied by physiological changes.[14] How well can you tune in to your feelings and understand what is going on in the depth of your spirit? Can you also do this for others? Can you relate to others in such a way that they feel safe being vulnerable?

All of us need to be emotionally mature, but some people have exceptional abilities because of their unique emotional makeup. Being emotionally gifted means being sensitive along with having the ability to comfort others with a soothing voice, kind words, and a gentle touch.

Emotions make us open to relationship, change, and influence. They help us in discerning the right choice when making decisions.

Emotions Are Invaluable

God provides you with emotions to help you discern how your life is going. Emotions can be like a metal detector that provides feedback as to what makes life good. Also, emotions can be like a smoke detector that alerts you to danger. Without these detectors, you'd be left making decisions like a robot — with little interest, motivation, passion, or understanding.

God made us emotional and relational as part of His image. You're not emotional by accident. Emotions serve good purposes. The ability to be sensitive allows you to understand what is going on deep inside others. Emotions provide you a sense of safety, closeness, and connection — or the opposite when something is wrong.

However, feelings aren't completely reliable. Feeling good when something bad is happening and feeling bad when something good is happening are both possible:

- To feel good when your life is not going well, you must disconnect from your negative feelings and seek some form of pleasure. The seeking can quickly turn into an addiction if you don't address the underlying problem. Essentially, you're chasing positive feelings that you'll never quite catch. Eventually, you'll end up numb while trying to generate positive feelings from behaviors such as abusing drugs, viewing pornography, or overeating.
- To feel bad when life is going well, usually means you've associated a positive event with a similar event that was negative. For example, if you eat your favorite salad but get severely sick afterward, you might associate "salad" with "illness." Then, the next time you're presented with a salad, you'll have to work to override your instinct that it will be bad. The wiring is useful to prevent the same thing from happening again, but it also creates false negatives that require retraining the brain.

Unwavering Devotion

People who favor emotions tend to be more people-oriented. Emotionally gifted people are extremely loyal to a person or a cause that directly impacts people. Without emotion, there could

---

[14] thefreedictionary.com/emotion

be no passion. Without passion, no one would be willing to die for a cause. Passion motivates you to push through seemingly impossible odds.

Emotions used positively can lead to unconditional favor and love. They allow an irrational love, one that loves "just because" and despite betrayal and sin. Emotions used negatively can lead to disfavor, bias, unhealthy conflict, competition, contempt, or disgust.

Cognitive and Emotional Integration

Integrated means functioning at a higher level because you have more connections and perspectives.

An integrated brain is a healthy brain. If a strength is overdeveloped and overused relative to other abilities, it will start to function as a weakness. Instead of feelings taking center stage all the time, learn how to, as appropriate, defer your immature feelings by calmly trusting the rational-protector part of you. Instead of beating up yourself with your thoughts, learn how to, as appropriate, suspend critical judgement and allow yourself to simply exist without demand.

The well-integrated person knows when to defer to a nondominant function in order to achieve the best possible outcome. This is like a craftsman knowing exactly which tool will help him complete the task at hand.

The human brain is asymmetrical with respect to some of its abilities. This means that the left and right hemispheres specialize their functioning. However, the left brain is not exclusively responsible for logic, and the right brain is not exclusively responsible for emotion.[15] Actually, there appears to be more of a front (prefrontal cortex) to back (limbic system) split between reasoning and emotion. There's a time for certain parts of the brain to function together and a time for them to function separately.

Young adults tend to exhibit more logical/creative brain lateralization (the different brain hemispheres are specialized) than healthy, older adults. One possibility is that older adults have learned how to better integrate their logical and creative abilities.[16]

When Your Head Dominates Your Heart

A gifted mind can be powerful, but if the power is not properly regulated, it can result in a sick heart. Healthy self-analysis produces useful insights; overdeveloped analysis can result in destructive criticism. Hold to the reality of the truth, but be kind and compassionate with yourself. The head is prone to getting the details right but lacks in maintaining a healthy emotional relationship with others.

You might be emphasizing your head over your heart for a couple of different reasons. You could have grown up in an emotionally sterile environment where feelings were rarely processed. This leans toward neglect (not getting what you need). Also, you could have experienced harsh or shaming words that taught you that being vulnerable was not safe. This leans toward abuse (getting what you didn't need). The remedy for both scenarios is essentially the same. However, the journey will be different.

To develop your emotional skills, you need to devote time to identifying, feeling, expressing, and sharing your emotions. Ultimately, this requires spending more time getting close to others.

---

[15] dx.doi.org/10.1155/2015/908917 Hemispheric Asymmetry of Human Brain Anatomical Network
[16] npr.org/sections/13.7/2013/12/02/248089436/the-truth-about-the-left-brain-right-brain-relationship

If you experienced significant abuse, you might naturally resist feeling because it was associated with pain. Proceed with caution as you allow yourself to become in touch with difficult feelings.

If you experienced significant neglect, you might need to push yourself into contact with yourself and others. This can be overwhelming because you aren't used to feeling much of anything.

The following diagram illustrates emotional energy fluctuation over the course of one day. The optimal range is between the two dashed lines. Above the top dashed line is feeling too "on." Below the bottom dashed line is feeling too "off."

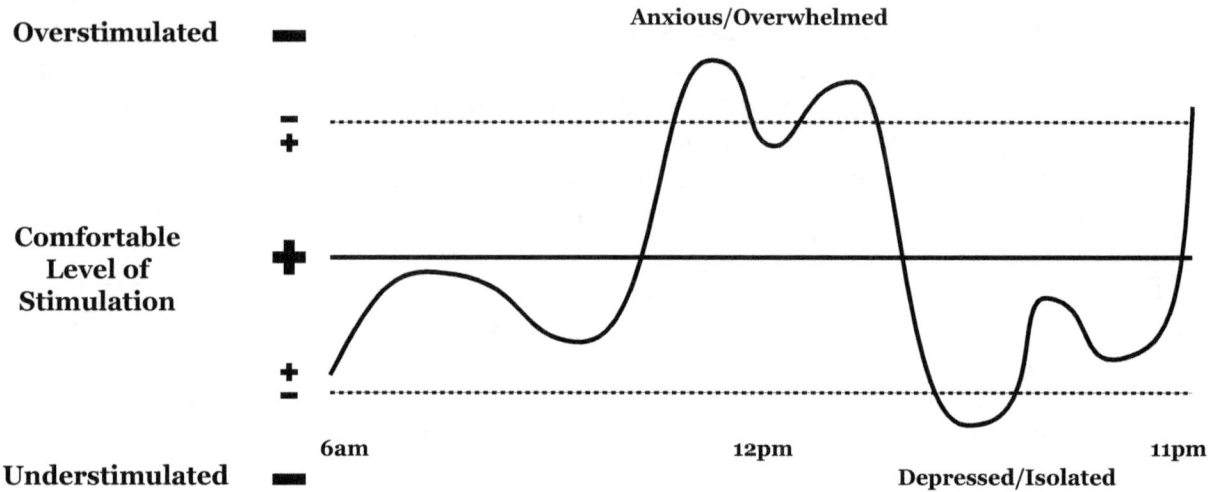

Paul

When Paul was Saul, he used his intellect to persecute Christians. After Paul became a Christian, he used his intellect to explain and defend the gospel. God also revealed to Paul deep truths and wonders concerning His identity. Paul acquired a passion for sharing the gospel like no other.

Paul contributed to the New Testament by writing in an abstract, procedural way to present the principles of the Christian faith. Even as a young Christian, he chose results over relationship by refusing to take Mark on a trip (Acts 15:38). As he became seasoned in his faith and experienced persecution, he focused more on relationships (2 Timothy 4:11).

When Your Heart Dominates Your Head

Although your emotions are indispensable, you can end up letting them wag the dog if you aren't careful. Once emotions have your active attention, switching them off can be difficult — like trying to stop a runaway train. Allowing emotions full control can be risky if you act impulsively. Your action relieves pressure, but you might regret your behavior later.

In this situation, the best thing to do is to intentionally choose a soothing activity and then focus on the emotion without acting on it. The activity could be physical exercise like going for a run, or it could be something calming like sitting in a comfortable chair in a quiet room. Allow your feelings to inform you of what is wrong, and then let your rational brain decide what to do. Whatever you choose to do to relieve the pressure, be sure to continue to pursue understanding; otherwise, you'll fail to correct the underlying issue.

David

David used his physical abilities to manage sheep, defending them from bears and lions. God also gifted David with passion, feelings, and the verbal ability to write most of the psalms. God called David a man after His own heart. For the most part, he was exceptionally loyal and faithful to God. However, he had some difficulty not letting his passions get the best of him, which resulted in adultery and murder (2 Samuel 11 and 12).

Balanced Head and Heart

Sometimes going with your gut is superior to going with your head. But sometimes it's much worse. The two need to cooperate by serving as checks and balances for each other. The heart can question the head's logic. The head can question the heart's instinct. The heart is prone to bias and can lead you to go against the truth. This might feel good initially, but it will only be worse later on.

If you learn how to let your head and heart defer to each other in optimal ways, you can learn to do it in a relationship. But if you can't find this balance within yourself, you probably won't be able to have a cohesive relationship.

Once you learn how, the balance between head and heart applies in many ways across your whole life. You can learn to calmly trust God, even when circumstances don't make sense. A husband can cease trying to control his wife's emotions. A wife can trust her husband.

A husband and wife can borrow each other's brains to reach a state of oneness. You grow and learn by being with others. The process of sharing life with someone else actually rewires the brain. As you experience love, you become better able to love others.

Abigail

Abigail (Nabal's wife and eventually David's wife) used her wisdom and quick thinking to avert a disaster. Whereas she was both discerning and beautiful, her husband Nabal was harsh and rude. David looked after Nabal's property. Nabal, being self-centered and prideful, repaid David's kindness with disrespect and insolence. David responded with anger and determined to kill Nabal. But Abigail, with her humility and emotional intelligence, intervened by giving David gifts of food and convincing him that he didn't need to have Nabal's blood on his conscience (1 Samuel 25:3–31).

Despite being in a tense predicament between two angry men, Abigail was able to think quickly and convince David not to immediately act on his anger. Someone with a less integrated brain might have yelled at her husband or shut down completely. Either would have resulted in a much different outcome.

For Reflection

1. How integrated are you? How dominant is one part of your brain at the expense of another part's growth and development? Do any of the following describe you on a regular basis?
   - ☐ Selfish
   - ☐ Domineering
   - ☐ Immature
   - ☐ Detached
   - ☐ Overly attached
   - ☐ Having to get your way

Next Steps

- Hand Dominance Exercise: Write out a somewhat personal question using your dominant hand. This could be something like "What do you want?" Then, using your nondominant hand, write the answer that naturally comes to mind. How hard is it to use your nondominant hand? What did you learn about your integration by attempting this exercise?
- Media for Further Learning (see Appendix B for more questions)
    - Movie: *Inside Out*. What role does emotion play in Riley's recovery from depression?
    - Music: *Keep Making Me* by Sidewalk Prophets
- Read more about Abigail at biblestudytools.com/bible-study/topical-studies/abigail-wise-and-determined-11633792.html
- Read more about the brain:
    - Memory: spring.org.uk/2012/10/how-memory-works-10-things-most-people-get-wrong.php
    - Brain hemispheres: npr.org/sections/13.7/2013/12/02/248089436/the-truth-about-the-left-brain-right-brain-relationship
    - The amygdala and fear: thebrain.mcgill.ca/flash/a/a_04/a_04_cr/a_04_cr_peu/a_04_cr_peu.html
    - Parts of the brain: askabiologist.asu.edu/parts-of-the-brain
    - Dan Siegel, clinical professor of psychiatry and Executive Director of the Mindsight Institute, explains the brain and relationships: youtube.com/watch?v=LiyaSr5aeho
- Complete the Cognitive and Emotional Identity Self-Assessment on the following page.
    - The purpose of the Talent section is to identify exceptional abilities. While these areas can certainly be developed, you should base your answers more on raw talent.
    - The purpose of the Self-Image section is to identify areas where you can improve your self-worth with respect to the chapter focus.

    After completing the assessment, journal and talk to God about what you're learning about yourself. What areas are strengths? Weaknesses? What areas can you develop further? What areas need emotional healing? What areas are a priority and worth your time right now to improve? What's your plan for improving?
- Use the Feelings Identification Worksheet to practice identifying how you feel. Periodically throughout the day, check in with your feelings.
    - First, identify if your emotion is positive or negative.
    - Second, identify which of the six major emotions you are feeling.
    - Third, find the intensity of the emotion.
    - Finally, log, journal, and/or share your findings with someone.

Cognitive and Emotional Identity Self-Assessment

Instructions: Rate each statement as CT for Completely True, ST for Somewhat True, SF for Somewhat False, or CF for Completely False. Regarding the letters after the statements, (I) is an Integrative statement, (C) is a Cognitive statement, and (E) is an Emotional statement.

Cognitive and Emotional Talent Statement	Rating	R#
1) I've trained myself to value and use my nondominant ability (I).	CT ST SF CF	
2) I can tap into my logical thinking to ground my emotions (I).	CT ST SF CF	
3) When I'm logical, I can tap into my emotions and feel passionate (I).	CT ST SF CF	
4) I have above average intelligence (C).	CT ST SF CF	
5) I can come up with creative solutions seemingly out of nowhere (C).	CT ST SF CF	
6) I can solve complex problems with my analytical ability (C).	CT ST SF CF	
7) I can manage strong emotions to make a fair, unbiased decision (C).	CT ST SF CF	
8) I can remain clear-headed when faced with stressful situations (C).	CT ST SF CF	
9) Others feel emotionally safe with me (E).	CT ST SF CF	
10) I know how to help someone who is deeply distressed (E).	CT ST SF CF	
11) I am especially sensitive to others' feelings (E).	CT ST SF CF	
12) I am especially aware of my feelings (E).	CT ST SF CF	
13) I can easily express what I am feeling (E).	CT ST SF CF	

Finish by ranking (under R#) each statement from most like you to least like you. Write (up to) your top four Completely True (CT) talents on your Identity Portrait in Chapter 15.

Now rate the following self-image statements. Then check the box for any statement that evokes strong negative feelings (such as sadness, anger, fear, or shame).

Cognitive and Emotional Self-Image Statement	Rating	?
1) I like my balance between thinking and feeling (I).	CT ST SF CF	☐
2) I am proud of my ability to think (C).	CT ST SF CF	☐
3) I use my cognitive abilities to their fullest potential (C).	CT ST SF CF	☐
4) I accept God's design of my cognitive ability (C).	CT ST SF CF	☐
5) I appreciate the times I'm in touch with my emotions (E).	CT ST SF CF	☐
6) I embrace my feelings and allow myself to fully experience them (E).	CT ST SF CF	☐
7) I use my emotional abilities to their fullest potential (E).	CT ST SF CF	☐
8) I accept God's design of my emotional ability (E).	CT ST SF CF	☐

Feelings Identification Worksheet

Loved	Secure	Connected	Hopeful	Significant	Compassionate
Celebrated	Safe	Included	Enthusiastic	Essential	Self-sacrificing
Cherished	Protected	Allied	Redeemed	Purposeful	Empowered
Precious	Solid	Bonded	Exhilarated	Powerful	Empathetic
Prized	Peaceful	United	Certain	Respected	Encouraged
Chosen	Free	Authentic	Encouraged	Important	Merciful
Approved	Relaxed	Attached	Motivated	Substantial	Passionate
Affirmed	Content	Loyal	Delighted	Successful	Generous
Treasured	Carefree	Reconciled	Worshipful	Strong	Giving
Wanted	Faithful	Whole	Inspired	Effective	Protective
Desired	Trusting	Together	Revived	Ambitious	Concerned
Admired	Calm	Alive	Eager	Confident	Sincere
Appreciated	At Ease	Present	Pleased	Capable	Kind
Special	Patient	Accessible	Energetic	Needed	Friendly
Valued	Focused	Receptive	Creative	Ready	Gentle
Accepted	Reassured	Aware	Cheerful	Serious	Self-controlled
Commended	Refreshed	Understood	Grateful	Decided	Helpful
Cared For	Restful	Grounded	Enlightened	Adventurous	Thoughtful
Liked	Comfortable	Interested	Curious	Courageous	Open
Remembered	Mellow	Sensitive	Persevering	Influential	Tolerant
Belittled	Restless	Distracted	Lethargic	Secondary	Bothered
Mistreated	Flustered	Dismissed	Down	Small	Closed
Criticized	Suspicious	Unrecognized	Hollow	Indecisive	Grumpy
Used	Guarded	Unsupported	Pessimistic	Unable	Stubborn
Ignored	Nervous	Foreign	Sad	Pointless	Irritable
Untouchable	Anxious	Distant	Broken-hearted	Unsuccessful	Controlling
Embarrassed	Worried	Lonely	Envious	Ordinary	Frustrated
Over-Exposed	Defensive	Abandoned	Disappointed	Incompetent	Bitter
Ugly	Pressured	Fragmented	Gloomy	Redundant	Judgmental
Inadequate	Alarmed	Shut-Down	Distraught	Disregarded	Harsh
Inferior	Intimidated	Withdrawn	Sorrowful	Invisible	Heartless
Defective	Overwhelmed	Out-of-Touch	Burned Out	Meaningless	Callous
Humiliated	Paranoid	Numb	Doubtful	Irrelevant	Furious
Neglected	Trapped	Lost	Depressed	Expendable	Explosive
Violated	Threatened	Rejected	Defeated	Unnecessary	Ruthless
Despised	Panicky	Outcast	Crushed	Powerless	Vicious
Devastated	Helpless	Forsaken	Hopeless	Impotent	Vengeful
Unwanted	Paralyzed	Disconnected	Desperate	Useless	Livid
Condemned	Terrified	Unreachable	Suicidal	Worthless	Murderous
Ashamed	Fearful	Isolated	Despairing	Insignificant	Angry

Chapter 11

Your General Spiritual Identity

Therefore, if anyone is in Christ, he is a new creation. The old has passed away; behold, the new has come.
—2 Corinthians 5:17

See what kind of love the Father has given to us, that we should be called children of God; and so we are.
—1 John 3:1

Blessed be the God and Father of our Lord Jesus Christ, who has blessed us in Christ with every spiritual blessing in the heavenly places . . .
—Ephesians 1:3

Now there are varieties of gifts, but the same Spirit; and there are varieties of service, but the same Lord; and there are varieties of activities, but it is the same God who empowers them all in everyone. To each is given the manifestation of the Spirit for the common good.
—1 Corinthians 12:4–7

You Are Spiritually Blessed

Christians, because of their spiritual connection with God through Jesus Christ, have spiritual blessings that define who they are. The Bible is the best resource to learn about your Christian identity because God inspired the Bible and it describes the blessings. All Christians gain the same spiritual benefits when God adopts them into His Family. You, along with other believers, can claim the truths found in the Bible, but by default, nonbelievers don't have access.

I've selected what I consider to be the top seven blessings of a Christian's identity. I ordered the blessings from the more foundational truths to the more action-oriented truths.[17] The blessings address seven questions every believer should know:

1. Where do I come from?
2. What is my status before God?
3. Does God care about me? If so, how much?
4. What is my relationship to other people?
5. How can I know who God is?
6. For what purpose did God create me?
7. How can I accomplish God's plan?

Spiritual growth is similar to physical growth. A new Christian must be born again spiritually. Being born again is a one-time occurrence of becoming a new creation in Christ. Then the developing Christian needs to be loved, made secure, and made to belong. As believers learn their

---

[17] Although I organized the blessings in a particular order, a strict sequential order is not intended.

significance, they can accept God equipping them for battle with power, love, and truth. Finally, a believer enters into the work prepared by God.

1) You Are Created by God

"Where do I come from?"

You have a point of origin: God. Before your parents conceived you, you existed only as an idea in God's mind. That boggles the human mind, but it's true. Your identity flows from the mind and intentions of your creator. God gives you a heart capable of being open to God.

> *And I will give you a new heart, and a new spirit I will put within you. And I will remove the heart of stone from your flesh and give you a heart of flesh.*
> —Ezekiel 36:26

God created you, which means:
- You are made in God's image — similar to Him (Genesis 1:27).
- You're fearfully and wonderfully made (Psalm 139).
- God is your Father; you're a child of God (1 John 3:1; Galatians 4:3–7).
- You're a new creation (2 Corinthians 5:17).

2) You Are Eternally Secure

"What is my status before God?"

Because you were adopted by God, you have the rights and privileges of a son or daughter of God, your Father and King. You have God's total acceptance because of Jesus's sacrifice. You can be secure in your salvation because God gives you the Holy Spirit as a guarantee.

> *In him you also, when you heard the word of truth, the gospel of your salvation, and believed in him, were sealed with the promised Holy Spirit, who is the guarantee of our inheritance until we acquire possession of it, to the praise of his glory.*
> —Ephesians 1:13–14

You can change and become like Christ. You already have a place with God in heaven. Ephesians 2:6 says that God "raised us up with him and seated us with him in the heavenly places in Christ Jesus."

God is your shepherd and shelter, which means:
- He protects you and provides for you (Psalm 23).
- You're safe and secure in His hands (Psalm 18).
- You don't need to fear or be anxious (Matthew 10:29–31).

3) You Are Loved Unconditionally

"Does God care about me? If so, how much?"

God's character is such that He will meet the needs of those He loves no matter the cost. Jesus experienced God's total acceptance during His baptism (Matthew 3:17). God communicated how pleased He was with Jesus.

God sings over His daughter Jerusalem in Zephaniah.

*The LORD your God is in your midst,
a mighty one who will save;
he will rejoice over you with gladness;
he will quiet you by his love;
he will exult over you with loud singing.*
—Zephaniah 3:17

God longs to express how pleased He is with you. Multiple examples from the Bible show how excited He is about His children (that's you!). God is the father who runs to greet His repentant son and celebrate his return.

And he arose and came to his father. But while he was still a long way off, his father saw him and felt compassion, and ran and embraced him and kissed him. And the son said to him, "Father, I have sinned against heaven and before you. I am no longer worthy to be called your son." But the father said to his servants, "Bring quickly the best robe, and put it on him, and put a ring on his hand, and shoes on his feet. And bring the fattened calf and kill it, and let us eat and celebrate. For this my son was dead, and is alive again; he was lost, and is found." And they began to celebrate.
—Luke 15:20–24

To find the true length of something requires an accurate ruler and an accurate measuring process. Measure yourself by God's extravagant love: Take a moment to consider how much God pursues you, no matter how ridiculous He might look (in the story of the prodigal son, the father's running to meet his son looked undignified). All other measurements will result in a False Identity.

God unconditionally accepts you, which means:
- You do not have to perform or change to be loved (1 Corinthians 13:4–7).
- You're valued, wanted, and inseparable from God (Romans 8:35–39).
- He will never reject or abandon you (Matthew 28:20).
- You can make mistakes without fear of abandonment (Hebrews 13:5).

4) You Are a Member of the Body of Christ

"What is my relationship to other people?"

You belong in God's family. You won't be able to reach your full potential if you're not connected to others. God made you to need your parents to help you develop. Once you reach a certain level of emotional development, you can function independently from your parents. However, this doesn't mean you're ready to move to a deserted island.

Your need for relationship is relatively constant over a lifetime, but your focus can shift between three different types of relationships:

1. *Receive* from parents.
2. *Relate* to peers.
3. *Be a resource* to children.

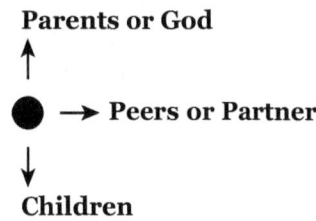

You're part of the Body of Christ, also called the Bride of Christ.

> *For the body does not consist of one member but of many. If the foot should say, "Because I am not a hand, I do not belong to the body," that would not make it any less a part of the body. And if the ear should say, "Because I am not an eye, I do not belong to the body," that would not make it any less a part of the body. If the whole body were an eye, where would be the sense of hearing? If the whole body were an ear, where would be the sense of smell? But as it is, God arranged the members in the body, each one of them, as he chose. If all were a single member, where would the body be? As it is, there are many parts, yet one body. The eye cannot say to the hand, "I have no need of you," nor again the head to the feet, "I have no need of you." On the contrary, the parts of the body that seem to be weaker are indispensable, and on those parts of the body that we think less honorable we bestow the greater honor, and our unpresentable parts are treated with greater modesty, which our more presentable parts do not require. But God has so composed the body, giving greater honor to the part that lacked it, that there may be no division in the body, but that the members may have the same care for one another. If one member suffers, all suffer together; if one member is honored, all rejoice together.*
> —1 Corinthians 12:14–26

God has gifted you spiritually so that you can be a blessing to other members. So this blessing also answers, "What is my identity in God's family?" The next chapter will help you specifically identify your gifting and function in the Body of Christ.

Other people need what you have, and you need what others have to reach your full potential. Your full potential requires interacting with and relating to others to achieve a purpose greater than what can be accomplished individually. The output of all the parts working together is greater than the output of all the parts working individually.

God includes you in his family, which means:
- You play a position for which He uniquely gifted you.
- You fit with the body of believers.
- You're needed and necessary for the Body of Christ to function properly.
- He made you to experience intimacy in relationships with Him and others.
- He and others can know and understand you, and you, them.

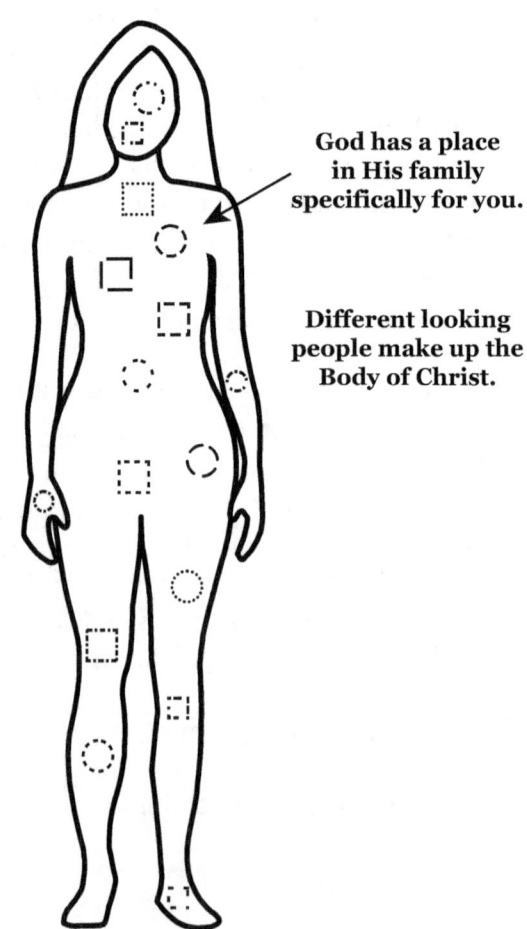

God has a place in His family specifically for you.

Different looking people make up the Body of Christ.

5) You Are a Dwelling Place for God

"How can I know who God is?"

You can know God because He is intimately close to you. He is able to communicate with you personally. Therefore, He can teach you directly who He is. Another benefit of this close relationship is that, as a place for God's spirit to dwell, you allow God's power to be evident.

For the Spirit God gave us does not make us timid,
but gives us power, love and self-discipline.
—2 Timothy 1:7

You are a dwelling place for God, which means:
- You have God the Holy Spirit living with you (2 Corinthians 1:21–22).
- The Holy Spirit is your powerful, intimate helper (2 Timothy 1:6–8).
- You have an intimate communication connection with God (Galatians 4:6).
- You are a dwelling place for power (Ephesians 3:16–21).

6) You Are Purposed for Significant Work

"For what purpose did God create me?"

God created you with purpose. You can use this divine purpose to direct your actions. God has an immediate, relevant purpose for you. You have something to contribute now.

God's purpose for you has long-term earthly and eternal ramifications. Therefore, He will continue to invest in you. You have a hope and a future. When you are stuck, you don't have to remain so; He will pick you up and set you on solid rock.

He drew me up from the pit of destruction, out of the miry bog,
and set my feet upon a rock, making my steps secure.
—Psalm 40:2

God wants you to thrive, so He nurtures and develops your gifts and talents until they're complete. Paul affirms God's commitment in Philippians 1:6: "And I am sure of this, that he who began a good work in you will bring it to completion at the day of Jesus Christ."

You are purposed for significant work, which means:
- You're predestined for good works prepared in advance (Ephesians 1:11, 2:10; Romans 8:29–30; Jeremiah 29:11).
- There is real work for you to do (John 14:12).
- You're unique and important. No one else can do the work God purposed for you because God custom-made you for the work (Acts 17:26).
- You're never beyond His reach or awareness (Psalm 139:7–16).

7) You Are Equipped for Battle

"How can I accomplish God's plan?"

God equips you with powerful spiritual blessings in addition to the Holy Spirit. As a Christian, you gain the following equipment to go along with your identity (Ephesians 6:10–18).

> *Finally, be strong in the Lord and in his mighty power. Put on the full armor of God, so that you can take your stand against the devil's schemes. For our struggle is not against flesh and blood, but against the rulers, against the authorities, against the powers of this dark world and against the spiritual forces of evil in the heavenly realms.*
> —Ephesians 6:10–12

Belt of Truth

God is absolute. You live in a world with absolute definitions of right and wrong. You can count on God and His truth to be reliable. God's truth doesn't shift and change depending on the circumstances; it's always true. Applying the truth lights your path; otherwise, you walk in darkness (Psalm 119:105, Isaiah 9:2).

Breastplate of Righteousness

Jesus provides your righteousness. You can shine with His glory. You have a new heart. You're no longer a slave to an unrighteous heart. You don't have to worry about accusations of unworthiness. God's got you covered.

Shoes of Gospel Readiness

The Gospel of Peace clears your way to God so you can be active in sharing your faith. 1 Peter 3:14 says, "Always be prepared to give an answer to everyone who asks you to give the reason for the hope that you have."

Shield of Faith

God calls you to live by faith. You're saved by faith, not by your efforts. You're meant to believe God by faith, not believe the words of the evil one. You don't have to entertain attacks of doubt. You can walk forgiven and unashamed.

Helmet of Salvation

Your salvation is secure. You don't have to entertain contrary thoughts that will attack the security of your mind. You belong to God.

Sword of the Spirit

You have a spiritual enemy, not a physical one. The spiritual word of God is the way to defeat a spiritual enemy. With the words of Scripture, you can push back evil spiritual forces.

Peter's Inspirational Identity

Jesus chose Peter to be His disciple. He believed in Peter despite his shaky start when he denied knowing Jesus (Luke 22:54–62).

> *Simon Peter replied, "You are the Christ, the Son of the living God." And Jesus answered him, "Blessed are you, Simon Bar-Jonah! For flesh and blood has not revealed this to you, but my Father who is in heaven. And I tell you, you are Peter, and on this rock I will build my church, and the gates of hell shall not prevail against it.*
> —Matthew 16:16–18

Jesus said to him, "Feed my sheep. . . Follow me."
—John 21:17b, 19b

Peter is a perfect example of someone living out his Christian identity. Filled with the Holy Spirit and convinced of Jesus's resurrection, Peter preached the gospel, healed many sick people, and led a growing group of believers (Acts 3–5). He stood up for the truth despite serious opposition. The Jewish leaders arrested him and put him in prison.

He didn't waver in his faith when persecuted. To stand firm as he did, he must have known the security of his salvation and God's love for him. God allowed him to escape prison so he could continue teaching about Jesus. Peter led a community of believers to share their possessions with one another for the common good. He clearly had God's power within him, and he accomplished God's purposes.

For Reflection

1. "The whole is greater than the sum of its parts." —Aristotle. What does this mean with respect to your identity?
2. You already have a place in heaven. How easy is it for you to tune in to this reality? The life you have now on earth is real, but the life you have in heaven with Jesus is a deeper reality.
3. If you feel lonely and aren't able to feel your connection with God, you probably need to spend some time with another believer who is feeling connected so you can catch a spark from them. There might be times when you need to learn how to connect with God through a relationship with another person.
4. God smiles at you.

Next Steps

☐ Core longings motivate babies and young children to cry out for relational interaction that is required for healthy emotional growth. See the figure in the Blueprint Space and consider how well your core longings are met. For each longing, mark the gauge to represent how full you feel. Then below it, write the reasons you chose that particular level. When you're done, make note of your lowest levels.

☐ Bring your unmet needs to Jesus and ask Him to show you how He can meet them.

☐ Media for Further Learning (see Appendix B for more questions)
  ☐ Movie: *I'm Not Ashamed.* How did Rachel make her Christian identity a priority?
  ☐ Movie: *Slumdog Millionaire.* What kind of community did Salim and Jamal have (or not have)?
  ☐ Music: *Never Been a Moment* by Micah Tyler

☐ Complete the Self-Assessment on the following page. The purpose of the Self-Image section is to identify areas where you can improve your self-worth with respect to the chapter focus. After completing the assessment, journal and talk to God about what you're learning about yourself. What areas can you develop further? What areas are strengths? Weaknesses? What areas need emotional healing? What areas are a priority and worth your time right now to improve? What's your plan for improving?

General Spiritual Identity Self-Assessment

Instructions: Rate each statement as CT for Completely True, ST for Somewhat True, SF for Somewhat False, or CF for Completely False. Then check the box for any statement that evokes strong negative feelings (such as sadness, anger, fear, or shame).

General Spiritual Self-Image Statement	Rating	?
1) I'm a child of God.	CT ST SF CF	☐
2) I'm a new creation.	CT ST SF CF	☐
3) I sense the Holy Spirit living within me.	CT ST SF CF	☐
4) I am secure in my salvation.	CT ST SF CF	☐
5) Jesus is my Lord and Savior.	CT ST SF CF	☐
6) God is my Father.	CT ST SF CF	☐
7) God is angry with me.	CT ST SF CF	☐
8) I'm spiritually gifted.	CT ST SF CF	☐
9) I cannot approach God.	CT ST SF CF	☐
10) I have a new heart.	CT ST SF CF	☐
11) I'm saved by grace, not because of what I do or don't do.	CT ST SF CF	☐
12) I can completely trust my general Christian identity.	CT ST SF CF	☐
13) I accept God's design of my general Christian identity.	CT ST SF CF	☐

Chapter 11 — Your General Spiritual Identity

BLUEPRINT SPACE

Core Longing Levels

Love
F
— Feeling Unconditionally Accepted

— Feeling Ashamed or Condemned
E

Security
F
— Feeling Safe and Protected

— Feeling Fearful or Overwhelmed
E

Connection
F
— Feeling Included and Understood

— Feeling Isolated or Lonely
E

Significance
F
— Feeling Purposeful and Essential

— Feeling Useless or Worthless
E

Hope
F
— Feeling Optimistic and Encouraged

— Feeling Doubtful or Despairing
E

Other
F
— Feeling _____

— Feeling _____
E

BLUEPRINT SPACE

Chapter 12

Your Specific Spiritual Identity

Your spiritual gifting is a significant aspect of your spiritual identity. The Holy Spirit gifts every believer with supernatural abilities. God created a world of needs and then the exact people with particular gifts to meet the needs. God's creativity shows up in the many possible combinations of:
- Needs (the problems)
- Gifting (the solutions)
- People (the solution delivery method)

God created a finite number of gifted people — only as many as He needs. This means you're significant. No one else can use your gifts in the way you were designed to use them. How are you doing at using your spiritual abilities to their fullest potential? You could possess supernatural power to meet needs in the following ways:
- Complete tasks with your hands
- Feel compassion and grant mercy to others
- Help others understand important truths
- Organize and bring order to chaos
- Communicate the gospel message to nonbelievers
- Pray and see powerful and sometimes even miraculous results
- Provide clear direction to others
- Advise others so they can make sound decisions
- Encourage others with hope
- Perform tasks behind the scenes

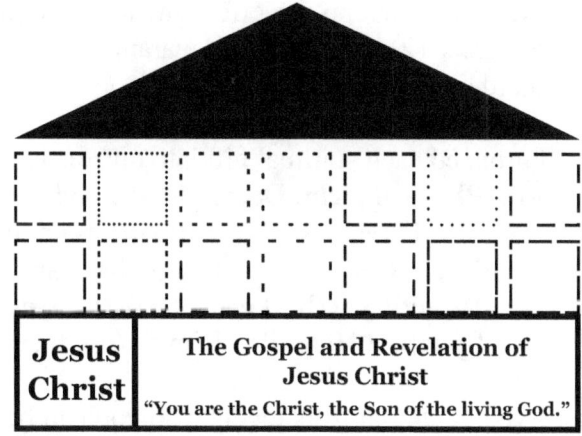

You're a living stone being built into a spiritual house with Jesus Christ as the chief cornerstone (1 Peter 2:5, Ephesians 2:20, 1 Corinthians 3:11). You're not alone. Your place in the house, in the Body of Christ, isn't random. Your position in the body is broader than your spiritual gift(s), but the two are tightly linked. You have a spiritual gift! You need others who are different from you to complete the spiritual home.

Every believer has at least one spiritual gift, or a form of grace (1 Corinthians 12:7). However, no believer has every gift (12:29–30). The Holy Spirit determines how the gifts are distributed in the body, so there aren't any specific rules to follow to find your gift. The gifts are positive spiritual power meant for the common good of building up the Body of Christ. They can't be used for evil purposes (Acts 8:19–21).

Spiritual gifts are spiritual power that God intends for you to use for spiritual (kingdom) purposes. Natural talent is the part of your identity which can be used for earthly and heavenly purposes. You can use spiritual gifts to build up the members of the church or proclaim who God is to nonbelievers. I believe the Holy Spirit considers each person's identity when He distributes the gifts. Your identity fits with the work God planned for you. Spiritual gifts fit with both your identity and your spiritual work to accomplish spiritual purposes.

You receive your gifts at the moment of spiritual rebirth, but this doesn't necessarily mean you will be completely aware of or skilled in using the gifts. As the entirety of the Christian life is spent learning about God and identity, you can always learn more about how to use your gifts.

Spiritual Gifts

I'm going to describe 18 spiritual gifts and three spiritual roles as found in the New Testament. However, the Holy Spirit is infinitely creative, so He might distribute gifts beyond those listed. Therefore, the gifts should be considered to be representative. Understanding what work God wants done is essential to understanding spiritual gifting.

The Holy Spirit will manifest in your life according to your unique identity. Just keep in mind that all spiritual power is for the benefit of others and not for selfish gain. The power comes from the Holy Spirit, who lives inside you. You plus the Holy Spirit are a new creation.

> *Having gifts that differ according to the grace given to us, let us use them: if prophecy, in proportion to our faith; if service, in our serving; the one who teaches, in his teaching; the one who exhorts, in his exhortation; the one who contributes, in generosity; the one who leads, with zeal; the one who does acts of mercy, with cheerfulness.*
> —Romans 12:6–8

The Holy Spirit might choose not to manifest certain types of gifts because they're no longer needed. The Holy Spirit determines all this, so I don't feel a need to censor the list of gifts. What I'm sure of, is that no one gift is guaranteed to be given to everyone (1 Corinthians 12). If gifts were guaranteed, they would be considered standard equipment, not gifts.

I grouped each spiritual gift into one of five categories:
1. **Physical Help:** Doers (use the body, hands, feet)
2. **Mind Help:** Advisors (use the mind, intellect)
3. **Heart Help:** Nurturers (use the heart, gut)
4. **Direction Help:** Leaders (use the eyes, vision, imagination)
5. **Spiritual Help:** Proclaimers (use the mouth, tongue, speech)

I've put similar gifts together so you can better see the correlation between your identity and the identity of the Body of Christ. This should help you understand how you can use your gifts in a church community.

As you read through the gifts, chances are you'll find that one of the categories fits your style more than the others. This doesn't mean you can't have gifts from multiple categories, but each group has a distinct purpose.

Read through the descriptions of all the spiritual gifts until you're sure you understand them. Each gift can have many different practical applications. Pay attention to *why* the gifts are used, and you'll start to understand the possibilities. The code in parentheses (X-X) links the gift with the Talent Self-Assessment at the end of the chapter. You can take the assessment while reading the descriptions or wait until the end of the chapter.

Physical Help: Doers

Purpose of Gifts: To provide help with the physical needs in this life
Physical Help Gifts: Service, helping, giving, healing

Service (Romans 12)

Definition: The ability to attend to details (often tasks) to keep the church community running smoothly. Serving in this way allows others to focus on their gifts without distraction. The word for *deacon,* which comes from the Greek, means "one who serves." (P-S)

Example: The disciples selected men to serve the needs in the church so they could devote themselves to preaching.

And the twelve summoned the full number of the disciples and said, "It is not right that we should give up preaching the word of God to serve tables. Therefore, brothers, pick out from among you seven men of good repute, full of the Spirit and of wisdom, whom we will appoint to this duty."
—Acts 6:2–3

Helping (1 Corinthians 12)

Definition: The ability to discern the needs of others and come alongside to support them, often without having to be asked. Like Service, this gift can be task-oriented, but it's often people-oriented. (P-H)

Example: Mark assisted Paul in his ministry. Paul sounded like he was lonely and wanted company as much as he wanted someone to help minister to others.

Luke alone is with me. Get Mark and bring him with you, for he is very useful to me for ministry.
—2 Timothy 4:11

Giving (Romans 12)

Definition: The ability to give generously, perhaps even sacrificially, to the needs of others. The giving should be from a willing and cheerful heart (2 Corinthians 9:7). The giving might be financial but could also be in time and effort. (P-G)

Example: A widow had very little, but she gave all she had to the temple.

And he called his disciples to him and said to them, "Truly, I say to you, this poor widow has put in more than all those who are contributing to the offering box. For they all contributed out of their abundance, but she out of her poverty has put in everything she had, all she had to live on."
—Mark 12:43–44

Healing (1 Corinthians 12)

Definition: The ability to pray on another's behalf and miraculously improve another's health. (P-HL)

Example: Peter healed a crippled man.

> *But Peter said, "I have no silver and gold, but what I do have I give to you. In the name of Jesus Christ of Nazareth, rise up and walk!" And he took him by the right hand and raised him up, and immediately his feet and ankles were made strong.*
> —Acts 3:6–7

Mind Help: Advisors

Purpose of Gifts: To make the truth clear to believers by promoting understanding
Mind Help Gifts: Wisdom, knowledge, discernment, teaching, interpreting tongues

Wisdom (1 Corinthians 12)

Definition: The ability to make truth applicable in the believer's life. (M-W)

Example: Two women disputed which one of them was the mother of a baby. Solomon found a way to determine who was lying. He ordered that the baby be cut in two. The real mother offered to give up her child if the child's life would be spared.

> *And all Israel heard of the judgment that the king had rendered, and they stood in awe of the king, because they perceived that the wisdom of God was in him to do justice.*
> —1 Kings 3:28

Knowledge (1 Corinthians 12)

Definition: The ability to understand God's intended meaning of deep and often difficult-to-understand truths that couldn't otherwise be known without God's help. (M-K)

Example: God gave the apostle Paul a special revelation of the gospel so he could write the scriptures and communicate the gospel to the Gentiles.

> *For I would have you know, brothers, that the gospel that was preached by me is not man's gospel. For I did not receive it from any man, nor was I taught it, but I received it through a revelation of Jesus Christ.*
> —Galatians 1:11–12

Discernment (1 Corinthians 12)

Definition: The ability to distinguish truth from falsehood. (M-D)
Example: Peter discerned that Ananias was deceptive.

> *But a man named Ananias, with his wife Sapphira, sold a piece of property, and with his wife's knowledge he kept back for himself some of the proceeds and brought only a part of it and laid it at the apostles' feet. But Peter said,*

> *"Ananias, why has Satan filled your heart to lie to the Holy Spirit and to keep back for yourself part of the proceeds of the land?"*
> —Acts 5:1–3

Teaching (Romans 12)

Definition: The ability to explain truth in a way that is easily understood by others. (M-T)

Example: Jesus taught the crowds using parables. He used parables so that His disciples and other believers would understand His spiritual message. He taught with authority, being both direct and compassionate. See the Sermon on the Mount for an example of Jesus's teaching (Matthew 5–7).

> *And when Jesus finished these sayings, the crowds were astonished at his teaching, for he was teaching them as one who had authority . . .*
> —Matthew 7:28–29a

Interpreting Tongues (1 Corinthians 12)

Definition: The ability to understand what is being said in another language — usually the self-edifying prayer language. To edify means "to instruct, especially so as to encourage intellectual, moral, or spiritual improvement."[18] (M-IT)

Example: On the day of Pentecost, listeners understood words in their own languages (Acts 2:1–12).

Heart Help: Nurturers

Purpose of Gifts: To strengthen a person's spirit so they can continue their life journey

Heart Help Gifts: Mercy, encouragement or exhortation, prophecy, speaking in tongues, shepherding or pastoring

Mercy (Romans 12)

Definition: The ability to communicate emotional understanding and comfort to an overwhelmed or distressed person; discharging grace and forgiveness to relieve the pressure of sin and guilt. (H-M)

Example: The Good Samaritan in Jesus's story took care of an injured man, even going so far as to pay for his medical bills.

> *Jesus replied, "A man was going down from Jerusalem to Jericho, and he fell among robbers, who stripped him and beat him and departed, leaving him half dead . . . But a Samaritan, as he journeyed, came to where he was, and when he saw him, he had compassion. He went to him and bound up his wounds, pouring on oil and wine. Then he set him on his own animal and brought him to an inn and took care of him."*
> —Luke 10:30, 33–34

---

[18] thefreedictionary.com/edify

Encouragement or Exhortation (Romans 12)

Definition: The ability to relieve a spirit of despair or hopelessness and replace it with a practical vision of one's potential. Also, the ability to motivate and challenge a person to persist amid life's struggles and pursue a course of action. (H-E)

Example: Barnabas's compassion (Acts 4:36–37; 11:22–23) or Peter's exhortation to the elders to fulfill their responsibilities (1 Peter 5:1–3). Barnabas was a spiritually gifted person who preferred to remain out of the spotlight.[19] He is best known as the "son of encouragement." He was gifted at strengthening others for God's work. He believed in Paul's conversion when others doubted (Acts 9:26–27), and he defended Mark (Acts 15:36–41).

Prophecy (Romans 12)

Definition: The ability to know the heart of God in a particular situation and communicate it to others: "But the one who prophesies speaks to people for their strengthening, encouraging and comfort" (1 Corinthians 14:3). Strengthening can include correcting and straightening. (H-P)

Example: Nathan rebuked David because of his unrepentant sin (2 Samuel 12:1–15), and the council of elders imparted Timothy with spiritual gifts (1 Timothy 4:14).

Why have you despised the word of the LORD, to do what is evil in his sight? You have struck down Uriah the Hittite with the sword and have taken his wife to be your wife and have killed him with the sword of the Ammonites. Now therefore the sword shall never depart from your house, because you have despised me and have taken the wife of Uriah the Hittite to be your wife.
—2 Samuel 12:9–10

Speaking in Tongues (1 Corinthians 12)

Definition: The ability to speak in another language (pray to God) such that one's spirit is strengthened (1 Corinthians 14:4, 13–17). (H-ST)

Example: New believers spoke in tongues after receiving the Holy Spirit (Acts 10:46).

Shepherding or Pastoring (Ephesians 4)

See later section on Spiritual Roles and Offices. (H-S)

Direction Help: Leaders

Purpose of Gifts: To make a way forward possible
Direction Help Gifts: Leadership, administration, faith, apostleship

Leadership (Romans 12)

Definition: The ability to consistently direct and motivate a church community in a particular direction ordained by God. (D-L)

Example: Joshua and Caleb acted in faith to take possession of the Promised Land (Numbers 13:30–33; 14:30), and Moses led the Israelites through the desert (Exodus, Numbers 27:17, Psalm 77:20).

---

[19] biblicalarchaeology.org/daily/people-cultures-in-the-bible/people-in-the-bible/barnabas-an-encouraging-early-church-leader

> *But Caleb quieted the people before Moses and said, "Let us go up at once and occupy it, for we are well able to overcome it."*
> —Numbers 13:30

Administration (1 Corinthians 12)

Definition: The ability to efficiently organize tasks and manage people. (D-A)

Example: Jethro's idea to help Moses govern the Israelites (Exodus 18:13–27) or the elders' appointing deacons (Act 6:1–7). Jethro told Moses that trying to resolve all of Israel's disputes on his own wasn't a good idea. He suggested that Moses organize Israel and appoint lesser judges to handle the easier cases.

> *So Moses listened to the voice of his father-in-law and did all that he had said. Moses chose able men out of all Israel and made them heads over the people, chiefs of thousands, of hundreds, of fifties, and of tens. And they judged the people at all times. Any hard case they brought to Moses, but any small matter they decided themselves.*
> —Exodus 18:24–26

Faith (1 Corinthians 12)

Definition: The ability to discern God's will and trust Him for a particular outcome, especially without concrete evidence or with contrary evidence. (D-F)

Example: Abraham believed God could raise his son Isaac from the dead (Hebrews 11:17–19). The centurion had faith Jesus would heal his servant (Matthew 8:5–13).

> *By faith Abraham, when he was tested, offered up Isaac, and he who had received the promises was in the act of offering up his only son, of whom it was said, "Through Isaac shall your offspring be named." He considered that God was able even to raise him from the dead, from which, figuratively speaking, he did receive him back.*
> —Hebrews 11:17–19

Apostleship (Ephesians 4)

See later section on Spiritual Roles and Offices. (D-AP)

Spiritual Help: Proclaimers

Purpose of Gifts: To help those outside the church put their faith in the Gospel of Jesus Christ.
Spiritual Help Gifts: Miracles, speaking in tongues, evangelism

Miracles (1 Corinthians 12)

Definition: The ability to clearly demonstrate God's power to nonbelievers by praying and seeing miraculous signs and wonders come to pass. (S-M)

Example: Philip performed signs and wonders (Acts 8:6, 7, 13).

Speaking in Tongues as a Sign (1 Corinthians 12)

Definition: The ability to clearly demonstrate God's power to nonbelievers by speaking in another language, perhaps even the language of a foreigner standing in your presence. (S-ST)

Example: New believers spoke in tongues after receiving the Holy Spirit (Acts 10:46).

Evangelism (Ephesians 4)

See later section on Spiritual Roles and Offices. (S-E)

Spiritual Roles and Offices

A spiritual role or office is filled by a believer who has certain gifts. However, you can have the gifts needed for a role without being elected to a church office. For example, women don't qualify to hold a church office, but they can use the same gifts in other roles within the church. A woman could have the gifting to shepherd a small group or Bible study but wouldn't be given the office of pastor.

God won't call you to fulfill a role without empowering and equipping you so that you can fulfill the role. When you take the Self-Assessment, consider whether you qualify for the role, not the office.

Ephesians 4:11 lists five roles or offices in the church: apostles, prophets, evangelists, shepherds/pastors, and teachers.

Apostle (Ephesians 4)

An apostle has the gift of *apostleship*, which is the ability to accomplish a unique, significant purpose ordained by God. While it's likely God won't choose any more apostles beyond the Twelve, the Holy Spirit might manifest in you or others in some extraordinary way to accomplish the work of the church.

Paul was an apostle of Jesus Christ by the will of God (Romans 1:1–5). He might have replaced Mathias, who replaced Judas as the twelfth apostle. Alternatively, he could represent someone who God gifted as an apostle beyond the Twelve Apostles.

Paul is an easy choice as an example of a gifted person because he had multiple spiritual gifts. He's also an intimidating example because while God allowed him great, surpassing revelation and giftedness, God also allowed great suffering and adversity.

As an apostle, Paul was a protector of the truth. The Holy Spirit clearly chose him for a specific mission and provided him with the power and ability to communicate the gospel to the Gentiles. I appreciate the depth of his writing. He explains the truth of the gospel and Christian faith in ways that make sense to me. (D-AP)

Prophet (Ephesians 4)

See earlier section on the spiritual gift of prophecy. (H-P)

Evangelist (Ephesians 4)

An evangelist has ability to clearly communicate the gospel message to meet nonbelievers at the place of their spiritual poverty, such that they put their faith in Christ. They must understand the scriptures well. For example, Philip explained the meaning of the scriptures and the gospel to an Ethiopian he had never met (Acts 8). Philip asked the Ethiopian, "Do you understand what you are reading?" All believers are called to share their faith, but an evangelist has a special role in the church and is likely specifically equipped for such a role. (S-E)

Shepherd or Pastor (Ephesians 4)

A shepherd is called to develop a healthy community that results in increased energy devoted to loving one another and accomplishing a greater purpose. A shepherd usually has the gift of teaching and likely other gifts such as encouragement or mercy. Jesus is the Good Shepherd, who saves and provides abundant life (John 10:1–10). (H-S)

Teacher (Ephesians 4)

See earlier section on the spiritual gift of teaching. (M-T)

For Reflection

1. What would the church community be like if it were missing one or more categories of spiritual gifting?
2. How well does your church use your members' spiritual gifts? Are all the gifts well-represented?
3. Because the power of spiritual gifts comes from the Holy Spirit, you don't have to be naturally talented in an area to be spiritually gifted. However, you should feel positively motivated and energized to use your gift(s). What gift group sparks the most interest and enthusiasm for you?
4. Are you aware of your gifts? Are you using your gifts? If you answer *no* to either of these questions, could you be spiritually sidelined from maturing? What is preventing you from using your gifts? God could work through a passive believer or an antagonistic nonbeliever, but you'll be most effective if you're aware of and are using your gifts.

Next Steps

- Practice using spiritual gifts. What happens? How does it feel? Can you tell which gifts God has given you? Can you tell something supernatural is happening? This is a joint effort between you and God.
- Complete the Specific Spiritual Identity Self-Assessment on the following page. The purpose of the Talent section is to identify spiritual gifts. After completing the assessment, journal and talk to God about what you're learning about yourself. What areas can you develop further? What areas are strengths? Weaknesses? What areas need emotional healing? What areas are a priority and worth your time right now to improve? What's your plan for improving?
- Learn more about spiritual gifts at the following websites. Keep in mind that there are different ways to think about how the gifts work in the 21st-century church. The websites I've selected are reputable and may offer paid assessments, which I think are worth the money (I don't receive a commission for these suggestions). You can also search online for "free spiritual gift test."
    - assessme.org (more information and paid assessment)
    - placeministries.org (more information and paid assessment)
    - spiritualgifts.wordpress.com/spiritual-gifts-test (more information and free assessment)
    - placeministries.org/jj---is-evangelism-a-spiritual-gift-.html (more information)
    - pastorrick.com/series/shaped-to-make-a-difference (more information)
    - spiritualgiftsresearch.blogspot.com (more information)
- Media for Further Learning
    - Music: *Overcomer* by Mandisa

Specific Spiritual Identity Self-Assessment

Instructions: Rate each statement as CT for Completely True, ST for Somewhat True, SF for Somewhat False, or CF for Completely False. Write in any spiritual gifts you have that aren't included.

Spiritual Gift Statement	**Rating**	**R#**
1) I'm motivated to complete tasks with my hands. (P-S)	CT ST SF CF	
2) I can discern others' needs and help and support them. (P-H)	CT ST SF CF	
3) I give generously and sacrificially. (P-G)	CT ST SF CF	
4) I pray and see others miraculously healed. (P-HL)	CT ST SF CF	
5) I can help another person apply important truths to their life. (M-W)	CT ST SF CF	
6) I understand the meaning of difficult-to-understand truths. (M-K)	CT ST SF CF	
7) I can readily distinguish what is true from what is false. (M-D)	CT ST SF CF	
8) I can help others understand important truths. (M-T)	CT ST SF CF	
9) I can interpret other languages to edify a congregation. (M-IT)	CT ST SF CF	
10) I communicate comfort to relieve the pressure of sin and guilt. (H-M)	CT ST SF CF	
11) I can help the hopeless see a practical vision of their potential. (H-E)	CT ST SF CF	
12) I can strengthen another's heart and correct their direction. (H-P)	CT ST SF CF	
13) I can speak in tongues to strengthen my spirit. (H-ST)	CT ST SF CF	
14) I can direct a group to accomplish God's work. (D-L)	CT ST SF CF	
15) I'm organized and enjoy bringing order to chaos. (D-A)	CT ST SF CF	
16) I can discern God's will and trust Him for a particular outcome. (D-F)	CT ST SF CF	
17) I pray and see powerful and even miraculous results. (S-M)	CT ST SF CF	
18) I can demonstrate God's power by speaking in tongues. (S-ST)	CT ST SF CF	
19) I have the gifting to fulfill a role of Apostle. (D-AP) I'm called to support the church in a special, significant way.	CT ST SF CF	
20) I have the gifting to fulfill a role of Evangelist. (S-E) I can clearly communicate the gospel message to nonbelievers.	CT ST SF CF	
21) I have the gifting to fulfill a role of Shepherd or Pastor. (H-S) I can develop a healthy, loving community.	CT ST SF CF	
22)	CT ST SF CF	
23)	CT ST SF CF	

Finish by ranking (under R#) each statement from most like you to least like you. Evaluate based on the level of passion or interest you have. Match the code at the end of each statement with the code in the chapter to identity the gift and the gift's group. Write your gift groups in order from most gifted to least gifted, on your Identity Portrait found at the end of Chapter 15. Then write (up to) the top five Completely True (CT) or Somewhat True (ST) gifts.

Chapter 13

Your Personality

Opposites attract!
When too selfish,
Opposites repel.

Opposites attack!
When two mature,
Opposites gel well.

Different personalities *can* get along and appreciate each other. However, God makes each person distinct for a reason. Where your personality is gifted, your opposite is weak. Where your personality is lacking, your opposite has talent. Every personality has strengths and corresponding weaknesses. *Different* doesn't equal *inferior*.

A weakness is the absence of a positive trait (such as being detailed), not the presence of a defect like carelessness. Carelessness is a failure to act responsibly — a failure to follow through on a promise. A limited ability to be detailed highlights a strength to see the big picture.

There are many ways to study personality. When you're learning about your personality, I suggest focusing on theories that utilize different but equal traits. These theories are said to have no bias. For example, God values extraversion just as much as introversion.

What if a personality theory evaluates you on whether you're "calm" or "anxious"? Because we can assume that being calm is better than being anxious, the theory is biased negatively. Would you want your personality to be labeled as "careless" or "detached" or "nervous"? There is no such thing as an "anxious personality." Being sensitive is a positive trait. Those who are especially sensitive might struggle with anxiety, but anxiety isn't part of someone's True Identity.

What Is Personality?

Your *personality* is the part of your identity that you express, usually with some consistency, while interacting with your environment. For example, you might be an extravert (who is focused more on environment), or you might be an introvert (who is focused more on thoughts). Knowing your personality is essential to having a Confident Identity.

Your personality is like a distinct flavor. When you flavor food, you add spice according to your taste. There isn't a right or wrong, only an "I like it" or "I don't like it." When God flavors your personality, there is only "I like it" or "I feel ashamed." God thinks it's good, but you may or may not feel that way.

God created and designed you intentionally. Therefore, you can't choose or spontaneously change your personality. Personality is more diverse and complicated to understand than other more well-defined characteristics, such as your physical, gender, or general spiritual identity. Your personality has a fixed definition, but the way you can express it has a flexible range.

A Young Personality Emerges

Your personality isn't created by your environment, but it needs an environment so it can emerge and become more clearly defined. God didn't make you and place you in a vacuum. Novel experiences help you grow by drawing out new aspects of your personality. You can feel like you know yourself, only to have another part of your personality surface later in life.

Some people make the distinction that *temperament* refers to the attributes you're born with and *personality* refers to the attributes that emerge over time. I see no difference because your personality is always within you and will emerge over time. Personality isn't open-ended and evolving (you can't become something God didn't intend). However, there are many different paths you can choose as you go through life.

Your choices make a difference in how you experience life but they don't change your identity. Your life will feel considerably different if you choose being single over being married or choose working over college. As your environment presents different opportunities, your choices determine what parts of your personality will emerge. The younger you are, the less you'll know your personality because you've had less opportunities for it to emerge. As you mature, your personality becomes more multidimensional.

Although God defined your personality when He created you, He hid it and you must discover it over time. Some personality attributes remain hidden until a specific event causes them to surface. Other attributes may never have a chance to surface in this life. Finally, some attributes emerge prematurely, during times of crisis (for example, abuse or neglect may cause a child to grow up too quickly).

If your environment doesn't change enough, you'll consistently express the same attributes, and then your sense of identity can become imbalanced. The circumstances that promote imbalances can be positive or negative. You need a healthy amount of change and stimulation in order to find your identity. For example, a teen girl might experiment with her environment by exaggerating her personality. She might try expressing anger frequently with her rational parent. Or she might mimic the rational parent. Either option overemphasizes some attributes and hides others.

A Mature Personality Is Flexible and Firm

You can mature by growing in character (for example: displaying more fruit of the Spirit). You can also grow by discovering your identity. You need both types of growth. Personality is independent of maturity. One particular personality is not more or less mature than another (even though it might seem that way at times). Regardless of personality, any person can be more or less mature than another.

Preferences imply flexibility. For example, to solve a problem, you may focus on thinking of a solution. But to relate to your spouse, you may focus on your feelings. The flexibility allows you to choose what to emphasize depending on your circumstances — like having multiple tools in your toolbox.

Your personality should be firm but flexible, not rigid or ambiguous. You can classify yourself as an introvert relative to the general population. However, you might be extraverted some of the time because different parts of who you are will surface depending on the situation you're in or the people you're with.

A husband and wife can both be introverted, but more than likely they would consider one of them to be the extravert of the relationship. A husband who thinks of himself as introverted might start to feel like he's now an extravert if his wife is more introverted.

Reevaluating yourself in a close relationship is normal, but losing your sense of identity isn't healthy. You'll be fine as long as you prioritize God's intentions for your identity above comparing yourself to others. Remember that your identity is a fixed target. Your identity shouldn't change around other people, but different aspects of your identity will emerge in different environments.

If you focus on the relationship role too much, you could forget who you are. A woman too focused on being a mom might feel she's lost her identity because she's focused her energy on her young children for so long. Or a man too focused on being an employee might feel he's lost his identity because he's focused his energy on the same job for years.

You can be a mom, wife, and extravert while also remaining true to your God-given Confident Identity. You shouldn't have to sacrifice one to keep the other. Sure, at different seasons of your life, different roles are more prominent. Raising children is a selfless act that demands a lot from you. But God never intends for you to lose your sense of identity in the process. Anything positive you do should ultimately help your Confident Identity grow.

How to View Personality

All personality theories simplify reality but some simplify it more than others. You can view personality as made up of types or traits.[20] Here's how they differ:

- **Types:** When someone speaks of personality types, they want to present the parts of personality as dichotomies. For example, a person is either an Introvert or an Extravert.
- **Traits:** When someone speaks of personality traits, they want to represent the parts of personality as a continuum. For example, a person falls somewhere along a continuum between Introversion and Extraversion.

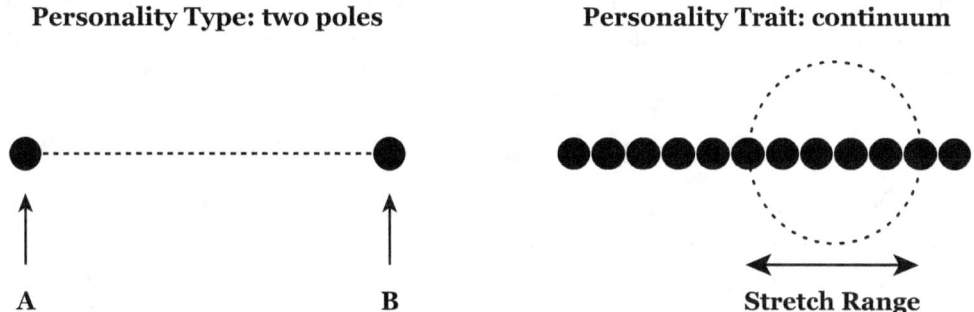

Personality as Types

You're a unique combination of many attributes and abilities. Dissecting and cataloging all of them isn't possible. A type theory simplifies personality so you can grasp and hold onto ideas with less effort. When first learning about yourself, you need more certainty, so focus on your personality type. You might appreciate believing the more definite "I'm an introvert" instead of the more ambiguous "I'm an introvert only when I'm at work."

Because there's always some unknown to personality, you have to be careful not to permanently label someone. A negative label cuts someone off from their potential but a positive label propels them forward into their potential.

I can't say, "I am definitely only an introvert." No one is 100 percent introverted or extraverted. If you spend the majority (greater than half) of your time functioning as an introvert, then you earn the label "Introvert." Labels make life easier, but labels don't reflect your True Identity. They aren't false, either. They're more like a pseudo identity.

---

[20] en.wikipedia.org/wiki/Personality_type

Claiming your best identity right now is infinitely more helpful than keeping your identity as vague and undefined — just keep in mind that new information could adjust your understanding. You have little to lose by trying to define yourself. At worst, you'll define yourself, experience life, and need to refine your self-understanding. That's what this book is about — growing in your Confident Identity.

Personality as Traits

When you're familiar with your personality, you can go deeper by considering personality traits. The goal of any theory is to help simplify what is complex; however, simplification is typically at the expense of accuracy. A dichotomy may simplify personality too much and can result in labeling — putting someone in a box that is true only part of the time at best.

Trait theory allows for a range of expression. You can be flexible with your natural preferences but eventually you'll reach your limit. For example, an introvert might act like an extravert when mingling with a crowd after giving a presentation. Or, abuse might force an extravert to become inwardly focused if it means survival.

Trait theory allows for expression of both poles at the same time. Thoughts can influence feelings, and feelings can influence thoughts.

I view personality as what you are "on average" or "most of the time." Attributes or traits exist on a continuum with a certain degree of variability — depicted on the preceding diagram as the range. If you were to evaluate yourself on the Thinker to Feeler continuum, you would specify a percentage for each such that the total is 100 percent. If you utilize thinking about three times as much as feeling, this would be expressed as 75 percent thinking and 25 percent feeling.

Discover Your Personality with a Four-Preference Theory

Carl Jung, a Swiss psychologist, conceived personality as a dichotomy in three dimensions (introversion/extraversion, sensing/intuition, and thinking/feeling), with a fourth (judging/perceiving) meant to evaluate the first three. The MBTI® theory improves upon Jung's original theory. Isabel Briggs Myers proposed that the fourth dichotomy be given a standalone status equal to the first three.[21]

These theories view personality as type. They consider the aspects of personality to be best measured using either/or poles, as in you either prefer A or you prefer B, where B is the opposite of A.

The following table lists the four dimensions of personality, along with the eight commonly used abbreviations for each pole. For each dimension, the Identifying Prompt helps you understand which pole you prefer.

The Four Dimensions of Personality	Identifying Prompt
Introversion (I) – Extraversion (E)	Where do you focus your attention?
Sensing (S) – Intuition (N)	How do you gain understanding?
Thinking (T) – Feeling (F)	How do you make decisions?
Judging (J) – Perceiving (P)	How do you experience and organize time?

---

[21] MBTI is a trademark or registered trademark of The Myers & Briggs Foundation in the United States and other countries. Visit https://www.myersbriggs.org for more information.

When you consider the various combinations of the four two-pole dimensions, the end result is 16 possible personality types:

ISFP	ISFJ	ISTP	ISTJ	INFP	INFJ	INTP	INTJ
ESFP	ESFJ	ESTP	ESTJ	ENFP	ENFJ	ENTP	ENTJ

Because no one is 100% of one pole and 0% of another, there are times when it is helpful to consider the four dichotomies as continuums. I use personality as a type theory when definition matters more than accuracy. I use personality as a trait theory when accuracy is more important than definition. For example, my personality type is INTJ but if I want to understand my personality using traits, I need to consider the strength of each pole. The strength of my "I" is about 90 percent ("E" is 10 percent). This means I fit the description of Introversion about 90 percent of the time. My "N" is about 70 percent. My "T" is about 80 percent. My "J" is about 70 percent.

Throughout this book I use "16PT" as a reference to the personality theories that utilize the sixteen types. I prefer the 16PT theories over other theories because they are sophisticated enough to make a significant distinction in personalities but still simple enough to understand.

Introversion–Extraversion

Where do you focus your attention?

This dimension describes a preference for an internal or external focus:
- **Introversion (I)**: Introverts focus on the internal workings of their minds. Their brains are wired to consider the possibilities and work toward a final answer before speaking. Their speech is often delayed (compared to extraverts). As such, they typically speak more concisely and dislike small talk. Any (others' or their own) talking can interrupt their thoughts.
- **Extraversion (E):** Extraverts focus on what is happening outside of their bodies. Their brains are wired to get ideas out of their mouths as quickly as possible. They refine their ideas as they speak. They enjoy talking, so they usually enjoy small talk. Talking usually results in greater understanding.

A common myth associates introversion with low self-esteem. Less talking is often associated with shyness, which is associated with low self-esteem; however, introversion doesn't mean shyness. Social anxiety can cause shyness, but that is something anyone can work to overcome. Both introverts and extraverts can suffer from anxiety, but an introvert might be considered reserved when compared to an extravert.

Sensing–Intuition

How do you gain understanding?

This dimension describes a preference for viewing reality:
- **Sensing (S):** A Sensing person accepts the facts provided by their senses (sight, sound, smell, touch, taste). They think things like, "Let the facts speak for themselves."
- **Intuition (N):** An Intuitive person will look at the same data but focus more on the relationships between the pieces of data and attempt to derive meaning. They think things like, "I wonder if a further explanation exists beyond the obvious."

The Sensing person might see the Intuitive person as trying to manipulate the data and not being practical enough. The Intuitive person might see the Sensing person as too narrow-minded and not wanting to invest in finding a deeper meaning.

Thinking–Feeling

How do you make decisions?

This dimension describes a preference for making decisions objectively or subjectively:

- **Thinking (T):** Thinkers focus on finding an optimal solution or a correct conclusion. They make decisions without considering extenuating circumstances. They're content to hold people accountable for their actions and therefore can be seen as judgmental or harsh.
- **Feeling (F):** Feelers focus on preserving relationships. They make decisions considering the impact on the relationship. They might ignore or bend the rules to show compassion and give someone another chance.

A Thinker shouldn't expect a Feeler to have easy, immediate access to logic, and a Feeler shouldn't expect a Thinker to have easy, immediate access to emotion. Both logic and emotion are needed. For example, when children make mistakes, sometimes they need firm correction, other times they need compassion, and often they need both. Personality is flexible, so you can cover a range, but only for so long. This makes it easier to appreciate that God made two parents.

Judging–Perceiving

How do you experience and organize time?

This dimension describes a preference for control over resources:

- **Judging (J):** Judging people instinctively exert control over their environment. They would rather proactively address an issue and put a plan in place. They might be heard saying, "Plan your work and work your plan."
- **Perception (P):** Perceiving people are content to let life run its own course within certain limits. They don't want to exert the effort to interfere until it's necessary. They might live by "Let's see what happens." They're patient with making decisions because they savor having options.

Perceivers love and are energized by options and possibilities. They don't like to feel restricted or forced into making a choice prematurely. This is why they don't make firm plans. It's not that they're lazy or don't want to make the effort.

Judgers experience decisions as items on a to-do list. The faster they get the decisions made, the faster they can rest and feel at peace. The more decisions they make, the more they accomplish.

Other Personality Theories

The DISC or Greek temperament theories are worth a look, too. These similar theories essentially consider only two dimensions, resulting in four distinct personalities.

Are you more task-focused or people-focused? Are you more reserved or outgoing? These categories should sound familiar, as they closely map to the 16PT personality dimensions of Thinking–Feeling and Introversion–Extraversion. Because these models are more simplified, you'll find that the four personalities don't exactly map to a 16PT type.

The following table is a starting place to understand the differences.

Focus	DISC	Greek	16PT (closest match)
Outward-Task	Dominant	Choleric	ExTx (ENTJ)
Outward-People	Influencing	Sanguine	ExFx (ENFP)
Inward-People	Steadiness	Phlegmatic	IxFx (ISFP)
Inward-Task	Competent	Melancholy	IxTx (ISTJ)

These theories are useful because they further simplify the details. The DISC model is often used in work environments. The Greek model is useful because it defines its four types in greater detail. More personality combinations exist if you're willing to consider blends (for example, a Dominant Influencer or a Melancholy Choleric).

For Reflection

1. Have you ever been made fun of for having a certain personality trait? Too shy? Too loud? Too emotional? Too analytical? Differences are often picked on, but they aren't wrong. If you're still hurting from these experiences, ask God to heal this wound to your identity. Reject the negative label and embrace the positive aspect of your identity.

Next Steps

☐ Complete the four-part Personality Self-Assessment on the following pages. As you rate each statement, keep in mind that you're selecting a preference. Then carry forward your scores to the Identity Portrait in Chapter 15.

☐ Complete the Self-Image Assessment on the page following the four-part personality assessment. The purpose of the Self-Image section is to identify areas where you can improve your self-worth with respect to the chapter focus. After completing the assessment, journal and talk to God about what you're learning about yourself. What areas can you develop further? What areas are strengths? Weaknesses? What areas need emotional healing? What areas are a priority and worth your time right now to improve? What's your plan for improving?

☐ How likely are you to find someone with the same four-letter type? The higher your percentage in any of the eight poles, the rarer you are. The following statistics might also help you understand your prospects for socializing and finding others who get you.
  - The ratio of Extraverts to Introverts is about 2:1.[22]
  - The ratio of Sensing to Intuitive is about 3:1.
  - The ratio of Male Thinkers to Female Thinkers is about 2:1.
  - The ratio of Female Feelers to Male Feelers is about 2:1.
  - There are slightly more Judging than Perceiving people.

☐ Media for Further Learning (see Appendix B for more questions)
  ☐ Web: *myersbriggs.org* (more information on the MBTI® personality theory).
  ☐ Web: *discprofile.com* (more information on the DISC personality theory).

---

[22] Some older statistics say 3:1 (see *Please Understand Me*) and some newer statistics say 1:1 (see mypersonality.info/personality-types/population-gender). I selected 2:1 with the understanding that the middle third of people are Ambiverts: frequently able to exhibit qualities of both.

- Site: *personality-testing.info/tests/O4TS* (more information on the Greek personality theory).
- Movie: *The Incredibles*. How do the various superhero personalities function together?
- Movie: *Bridge to Terabithia*. How does Jess remain true to himself and grow as a person?
- Music: *Greater* by MercyMe
- Book: *Please Understand Me: Character and Temperament Types* by David Keirsey and Marilyn Bates
- Book: *Your Personality and the Spiritual Life* by Reginald Johnson. Review the biblical characters and corresponding personality types found in this book:

16PT	Character	Example of Personality
ESxP	David	Quick to act as he killed Goliath; valued friendship with Jonathan
ISxJ	Mark	Wrote his gospel with a factual, realistic, and concrete style
ENxP	Joshua	Optimistic faith and vision in wanting to take the Promised Land
INxJ	John	Wrote his gospel with symbolism and depth
ExTJ	Solomon	Devised a clear plan to flush out a liar
IxTP	Matthew	Wrote his gospel focused on the inner principles in Jesus's teachings
ExFJ	Ruth	Loyal to her mother-in-law
IxFP	Luke	Wrote his gospel with a focus on Jesus's seeking solitude to pray

x=either trait is possible; for example, ESxP means ESTP and/or ESFP

Personality Self-Assessment — Part I

Instructions: Rate each statement as CT for Completely True, ST for Somewhat True, SF for Somewhat False, or CF for Completely False.

Introversion–Extraversion Statement	Rating	?
1) I'm energized by what goes on in my inner world.	CT ST SF CF	☐
2) I need to reflect to gain understanding.	CT ST SF CF	☐
3) I can be seen as subtle and difficult to know well initially.	CT ST SF CF	☐
4) I like to work quietly without interruption.	CT ST SF CF	☐
5) I often work to understand the world.	CT ST SF CF	☐
6) My interests often have depth.	CT ST SF CF	☐
7) I'd rather concentrate all day than interact all day.	CT ST SF CF	☐
8) I appreciate my space more than being around people all the time.	CT ST SF CF	☐
9) I can invest in only a small number of friends at one time.	CT ST SF CF	☐
10) I ration my social energies.	CT ST SF CF	☐
11) I'm energized by what goes on in the outer world.	CT ST SF CF	☐
12) I need to hear myself talk to gain understanding.	CT ST SF CF	☐
13) I can be seen as accessible and understandable.	CT ST SF CF	☐
14) It's difficult for me to just sit and listen.	CT ST SF CF	☐
15) I often work to change the world.	CT ST SF CF	☐
16) My interests often have breadth.	CT ST SF CF	☐
17) I appreciate interaction over focused alone time.	CT ST SF CF	☐
18) I'd rather socialize than protect my space.	CT ST SF CF	☐
19) If possible, I'd have an infinite number of friends.	CT ST SF CF	☐
20) I have social energy to spare.	CT ST SF CF	☐

Check the box next to the CT or ST statements that you consider significant enough to count in the results.

Number of statements checked in #1 to #10, multiplied by 10 = Introvert %:

Number of statements checked in #11 to #20, multiplied by 10 = Extravert %:

Personality Self-Assessment — Part II

Instructions: Rate each statement as CT for Completely True, ST for Somewhat True, SF for Somewhat False, or CF for Completely False.

Sensing–Intuition Statement	Rating	?
1) I'm practical; I focus on the realities of a situation.	CT ST SF CF	☐
2) I resonate with words like *actual, concrete, specific,* and *literal*.	CT ST SF CF	☐
3) I want to rely on what is tested and sure.	CT ST SF CF	☐
4) I prefer tradition over improving something.	CT ST SF CF	☐
5) I rely on and trust my five senses.	CT ST SF CF	☐
6) I'm past- and here-and-now oriented.	CT ST SF CF	☐
7) I focus on the details.	CT ST SF CF	☐
8) I'm patient with routine (perspiration).	CT ST SF CF	☐
9) I prefer to use skills I've already learned.	CT ST SF CF	☐
10) I prefer to learn by imitation and familiarization.	CT ST SF CF	☐
11) I'm innovative; I focus on meanings, relationships, and possibilities.	CT ST SF CF	☐
12) I resonate with words like *symbolic, abstract, general,* and *figurative*.	CT ST SF CF	☐
13) I add to what is already there to see something in a new way.	CT ST SF CF	☐
14) I prefer to improve something rather than leave it the same.	CT ST SF CF	☐
15) I look beyond the five senses.	CT ST SF CF	☐
16) I'm future-oriented.	CT ST SF CF	☐
17) I focus on the big picture.	CT ST SF CF	☐
18) I'm patient with complexity (inspiration).	CT ST SF CF	☐
19) I prefer adding new skills or expanding on the ones I have.	CT ST SF CF	☐
20) I prefer to learn by insight and experimentation.	CT ST SF CF	☐

Check the box next to the CT or ST statements that you consider significant enough to count in the results.

Number of statements checked in #1 to #10, multiplied by 10 = Sensing %:

Number of statements checked in #11 to #20, multiplied by 10 = Intuition %:

Personality Self-Assessment — Part III

Instructions: Rate each statement as CT for Completely True, ST for Somewhat True, SF for Somewhat False, or CF for Completely False.

Thinking–Feeling Statement	Rating	?
1) I make objective, principle-centered decisions.	CT ST SF CF	☐
2) I highly value rules, facts, policies, and procedures to make decisions.	CT ST SF CF	☐
3) I emphasize an objective standard of truth; I seek justice first.	CT ST SF CF	☐
4) I want to treat others fairly — they only get what they've earned.	CT ST SF CF	☐
5) I will expose wrongs without much consideration to feelings.	CT ST SF CF	☐
6) I'm often seen as detached and insensitive.	CT ST SF CF	☐
7) I value logic and focus on solutions.	CT ST SF CF	☐
8) I appreciate truthful communication.	CT ST SF CF	☐
9) I evaluate using performance criteria.	CT ST SF CF	☐
10) I enjoy analyzing and critiquing.	CT ST SF CF	☐
11) I make subjective, person-centered decisions.	CT ST SF CF	☐
12) I prefer the harmony of a win-win in making decisions.	CT ST SF CF	☐
13) I always consider extenuating circumstances; I'm merciful.	CT ST SF CF	☐
14) I want to treat others as they need to be treated.	CT ST SF CF	☐
15) I express care and concern.	CT ST SF CF	☐
16) I'm often seen as involved and sensitive.	CT ST SF CF	☐
17) I focus on human values and needs.	CT ST SF CF	☐
18) I communicate tactfully to help others save face.	CT ST SF CF	☐
19) I focus on personal encouragement and intimacy.	CT ST SF CF	☐
20) I sympathize and appreciate.	CT ST SF CF	☐

Check the box next to the CT or ST statements that you consider significant enough to count in the results.

Number of statements checked in #1 to #10, multiplied by 10 = Thinking %:

Number of statements checked in #11 to #20, multiplied by 10 = Feeling %:

Personality Self-Assessment — Part IV

Instructions: Rate each statement as CT for Completely True, ST for Somewhat True, SF for Somewhat False, or CF for Completely False.

Judging–Perceiving Statement	Rating	?
1) I have a strong work ethic (complete work, then play).	CT ST SF CF	☐
2) I like to live in a planned, orderly way.	CT ST SF CF	☐
3) I prefer to have closure and control.	CT ST SF CF	☐
4) I worry about being correct.	CT ST SF CF	☐
5) I want to have things settled.	CT ST SF CF	☐
6) I work well with structure.	CT ST SF CF	☐
7) I'm decisive and exacting.	CT ST SF CF	☐
8) I make decisions quickly with a sense of urgency.	CT ST SF CF	☐
9) I intentionally and proactively "run my life."	CT ST SF CF	☐
10) I prefer to make decisions and move on.	CT ST SF CF	☐
11) I have a strong play ethic (play some, work some, repeat).	CT ST SF CF	☐
12) I like to live in a flexible, spontaneous way.	CT ST SF CF	☐
13) I prefer to keep options open and to understand.	CT ST SF CF	☐
14) I relax even though I might miss some deadlines.	CT ST SF CF	☐
15) I want to experience and adapt.	CT ST SF CF	☐
16) I work well under pressure.	CT ST SF CF	☐
17) I'm curious and tolerant.	CT ST SF CF	☐
18) I postpone decisions with a sense of having plenty of time.	CT ST SF CF	☐
19) I let life happen.	CT ST SF CF	☐
20) I like "treasure hunting" — doing something for the fun of it.	CT ST SF CF	☐

Check the box next to the CT or ST statements that you consider significant enough to count in the results.

Number of statements checked in #1 to #10, multiplied by 10 = Judging %:

Number of statements checked in #11 to #20, multiplied by 10 = Perceiving %:

Personality Self-Image Assessment

Instructions: Rate each statement as CT for Completely True, ST for Somewhat True, SF for Somewhat False, or CF for Completely False. Then check the box for any statement that evokes strong negative feelings (such as sadness, anger, fear, or shame).

Personality Self-Image Statement	Rating	?
1) I like how introverted I am.	CT ST SF CF	☐
2) I like how extraverted I am.	CT ST SF CF	☐
3) I like how sensing I am.	CT ST SF CF	☐
4) I like how intuitive I am.	CT ST SF CF	☐
5) I like how thinking I am.	CT ST SF CF	☐
6) I like how feeling I am.	CT ST SF CF	☐
7) I like how judging I am.	CT ST SF CF	☐
8) I like how perceiving I am.	CT ST SF CF	☐
9) I'm using my personality to its fullest potential.	CT ST SF CF	☐

BLUEPRINT SPACE

Chapter 14

Your Strengths at Work

> You cannot be anything you want to be —
> but you can be a lot more of who you already are.
> —Tom Rath, *Strengthsfinder 2.0*

Your strengths (also called abilities) are further evidence of who you are. However, strengths provide less certainty of your identity than the more enduring aspects covered in previous chapters. You might need to try out a particular ability for a while to determine whether you have the potential to develop it into a uniquely defining characteristic. While this won't be a waste of time, you might find that some abilities are more like hobbies than clear strengths. Some people will want more variety in their repertoire, while others might choose more focused development.

This chapter will help you start to make the connection between your abilities and how you can contribute to society. Different kinds of work require different kinds of abilities. Different kinds of people have varying interests that influence their motivations. You can use the context of work to help you identify your strengths and abilities. Chapter 18 complements this chapter by focusing on your personal values, interests, and passions.

As you move through this material, remember that your identity is what is consistent over time and across circumstances. Your focus, or what currently interests you, can shift and change when circumstances change.

Strengthen Your Identity

The positive-psychology movement started as a response to the mostly negative focus on how to fix what is wrong with people. *Positive-psychology* tries to figure out what is right with people and strengthen it. Both areas of psychology are necessary, and the general ideas are biblical.

Positive psychology parts ways from biblical teaching when it becomes *humanistic,* which is essentially the idea that you can be anything you want to be and you don't even need God to do it. According to the Bible, each individual part must do its work. So you can't be anything you want to be; you can only be more of who God designed you to be.

> *And it was He who gave some to be apostles, some to be prophets, some to be evangelists, and some to be pastors and teachers, to equip the saints for works of ministry, to build up the body of Christ, until we all reach unity in the faith and in the knowledge of the Son of God, as we mature to the full measure of the stature of Christ. Then we will no longer be infants, tossed about by the waves and carried around by every wind of teaching and by the clever cunning of men in their deceitful scheming. Instead, speaking the truth in love, we will in all things grow up into Christ Himself, who is the head. From Him the whole body is fitted and held together by every supporting ligament. And as each individual part does its work, the body grows and builds itself up in love.*
> —Ephesians 4:11–16

Trying to improve an area of weakness is helpful, too; however, it has less marginal return, and you'll run into natural limits much faster. Not operating from your strengths has significant consequences:

> You're quite simply a different person. In the workplace, you are six times less likely to be engaged in your job... Gallup's research has shown how a strengths-based approach improves your confidence, direction, hope, and kindness toward others.
> —Tom Rath[23]

Strengths are not as broad as personality attributes like extraversion or introversion. Nor are strengths as spiritual as spiritual gifts. But strengths provide yet another window into your identity. They're more narrowly focused and specialized. This means as you find your strengths, they will more uniquely and clearly define you. The downside is that there are many more attributes to consider than the four pairs of the Meyers–Briggs.

One popular test, The Strengths Finder, considers and ranks 34 positive qualities. You can take this test online at strengthsfinder.com for a fee. There is a similar test for free at richardstep.com/richardstep-strengths-weaknesses-aptitude-test. The free test ranks 21 qualities. Both sets of strengths are listed at the end of this chapter.

If you identify your God-given unique design and invest in developing its potential, you'll be strong in your Confident Identity.

Raw Talent + Investment to Reach Your Potential = Strength = Confident Identity

Knowing your strengths will give you an immediate picture of how you compare with others. As with all the other clues you've discovered in Part II of this book, knowing your strengths isn't about seeing yourself as better than others. Instead, you need to know the unique contribution you bring to life.

Strengthen Your Life-Work Potential

Personality inventories (see the preceding chapter) provide good clues for career choices. However, they weren't designed to help people choose careers.

John Holland, an American psychologist, created a career development model based on six areas of interest (Holland's occupational themes): Realistic, Investigative, Artistic, Social, Enterprising, and Conventional (RIASEC).[24] Holland intentionally lists the areas in an order that keeps like areas next to each other. He believed a relationship exists between the six areas such that when they're placed on a hexagon, neighbors are similar and areas across from each other are opposites (or most dissimilar).

---

[23] Rath, Tom. *StrengthsFinder 2.0*. New York: Gallup Press, 2007.
[24] See en.wikipedia.org/wiki/John_L._Holland and en.wikipedia.org/wiki/Holland_Codes

In the following figure, the dashed lines connect opposites.

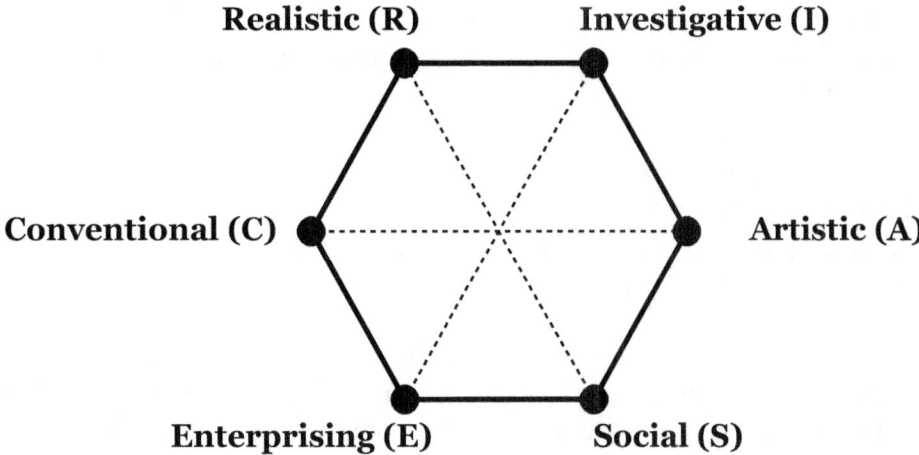

Opposite doesn't mean *incompatible*; however, you probably won't be able to use opposing abilities at the same time. The following table lists the three opposing pairs together so you can see how they contrast. A man with the Realistic (R) preference, by definition, usually doesn't like to interact with people. He can't focus on his task and be attentive to a customer at the same time.

Code	Primary Activity	Contrast of Opposites	Closest 16PT Attribute
R	Doing	Focus on completing a task	Thinking
S	Relating	Focus on meeting people's needs	Feeling
I	Understanding	Focus on how something works	Introversion
E	Persuading	Focus on something's usefulness to people	Extraversion
A	Creating	Focus on creating something original	Intuition or Perceiving
C	Organizing	Focus on organizing what already exists	Sensing or Judging

Combining areas yields different career options. As you can see in the following table, areas not next to each other can work well together and can be used simultaneously. The first exercise in Next Steps asks you to describe neighboring careers (R + I, I + A, A + S, S + E, E + C, C + R).

Code	Example When Combined	Code	Example When Combined
R + A	Design and craft custom furniture	R + I	
I + S	Help people understand themselves	I + A	
A + E	Create innovative ways to market and sell	A + S	
S + C	Help people organize their homes	S + E	
E + R	Sell outdoor equipment	E + C	
C + I	Program computers	C + R	

The better you know your abilities, the easier it will be for you to explore possible job matches without feeling forced into a particular job. Your top three areas will point to a variety of specific jobs. Following are the six areas described in more detail.

Realistic

Definition: This area involves concrete and hands-on experiences. Work is usually outside, away from an office, and doesn't focus on people. Realistic people have a high degree of mechanical aptitude. Being more practical, they would prefer to skip college and start working right out of high school.

Examples:
- An electrician rewires a residential home.
- An arborist trims or removes trees.
- An animal trainer prepares and shows dogs at a competition.
- An athlete competes in a tournament.

Investigative

Definition: This area involves the intellectual challenge of using the mind to understand real-world problems and then develop abstract ideas that become solutions. Investigative people have an insatiable desire to understand how and why something works the way it does. They design systems and would prefer to have someone else implement them.

Examples:
- A psychologist develops a new theory for helping people who've experienced trauma.
- A detective puts together clues to find out and prove who committed a brutal crime.
- A doctor studies how the human brain responds to medication.
- A software engineer designs a software's architecture.

Artistic

Definition: This area involves a high degree of self-expression to create something (often aesthetically pleasing) from nothing without having a rigid procedure to follow. Artistic people have a gifted imagination and a love and respect for others' creative work.

Examples:
- A writer creates a fiction book.
- A photographer takes portraits of high school students.
- A student learns and plays a musical instrument.
- A clothing designer creates a line of apparel with a new look.

Social

Definition: This area involves interacting with people to serve, teach, or help them relate better. Social people are eager to tune in to others' worlds and make a connection or friend. They work together with others in a cooperative and supportive way.

Examples:
- A teacher instructs a seventh-grade class.
- A counselor provides therapy to someone who is depressed.
- An aide helps disabled children to better manage their lives.
- A volunteer assists at a crisis pregnancy center to greet women and help them relax.

Enterprising

Definition: This area involves leading, making decisions, and persuading. Work usually has something to do with business and involves taking risks and assuming responsibility. Enterprising people are often competitive and ambitious. They work best with clearly defined goals and corresponding incentives.

Examples:
- A salesman presents the benefits of replacement windows.
- An entrepreneur opens a restaurant.
- A manager ensures her employees are following guidelines and meeting productivity.
- An inventor imagines an innovative design for video communication.

Conventional

Definition: This area involves keeping a steady routine, following clearly defined procedures, and organizing what is disordered. There's not much room for creativity or independent thinking. Conventional people handle details with efficiency and accuracy. They work well with structure but will probably rely on someone else to provide the structure.

Examples:
- An administrative assistant sends out invoices for work done.
- An accountant prepares tax returns.
- A purchaser orders enough supplies for a large company.
- A project coordinator puts together a presentation that summarizes business options.

For Reflection

1. Your identity = who you are. Your purpose, mission, or calling = how you contribute and make a difference. Remember that these are two different things.
2. By now, you should start seeing patterns and overlaps in the discoveries from Part II that emphasize God's design for you.

Next Steps

- ☐ Careers can be a mixture of the six areas. Find at least two areas that are needed to perform the following jobs: fire chief, nurse, astronaut, actor. Describe how you could use the following combinations in a job: R + I, I + A, A + S, S + E, E + C, C + R.
- ☐ Media for Further Learning (see Appendix B for more questions)
  - ☐ Movie: *How to Train Your Dragon*. How does Hiccup struggle with his identity?
  - ☐ Movie: *Simon Birch*. How does Simon manage not knowing his life purpose?
  - ☐ Music: *Tell Me* by Carrollton
- ☐ Complete the Career Interests Self-Assessment on the following page.

  Compare the preceding chapter's 16PT results to your Holland results. Are your results focused on one theme, or did you find several opposing characteristics? If you lack focus, that doesn't necessarily invalidate your results; just be sure it checks out. Try taking similar tests or take the same ones at a later time. If your results continue to lack consistency, perhaps you're multitalented. If so, can you identify a primary interest?
  - ☐ Various paid and free inventories are available online. Inventories requiring a fee include the Self-Directed-Search (SDS) and the Strong Interest Inventory (SII). Free inventories are available at personality-testing.info/tests/RIASEC and onetcenter.org/IP.html.
  - ☐ After you determine your top three abilities in order from most interest to least interest, you can use the three-letter code to look up matching careers at onetonline.org/explore/interests.

- ☐ Complete the Strengths Self-Assessment on the following page. How are your strengths different from your personality and career interests? Do they open up any new opportunities for you?
  - ☐ Review "How to Understand the Four Domains of Strength" at leadershipvisionconsulting.com/how-to-understand-the-four-domains-of-strength to help you map your strengths into areas similar to Holland's (Execute, Influence, Relationship Building, Strategic Thinking).
- ☐ After completing the assessments, journal and talk to God about what you're learning about yourself. What areas are strengths? Weaknesses? What areas can you develop further? What areas need emotional healing? What areas are a priority and worth your time right now to improve? What's your plan for improving?

Career Interests Self-Assessment

Instructions: Rate each statement as CT for Completely True, ST for Somewhat True, SF for Somewhat False, or CF for Completely False.

Talent means you possess the raw God-given ability. *Interest* means you would enjoy using the ability. *Skill* means you've already invested in developing the ability.

	Talent	Interest	Skill	Total	R#
1) Realistic (R)	CT8 ST4 SF2 CF	CT4 ST2 SF1 CF	CT3 ST2 SF1 CF		
2) Investigative (I)	CT8 ST4 SF2 CF	CT4 ST2 SF1 CF	CT3 ST2 SF1 CF		
3) Artistic (A)	CT8 ST4 SF2 CF	CT4 ST2 SF1 CF	CT3 ST2 SF1 CF		
4) Social (S)	CT8 ST4 SF2 CF	CT4 ST2 SF1 CF	CT3 ST2 SF1 CF		
5) Enterprising (E)	CT8 ST4 SF2 CF	CT4 ST2 SF1 CF	CT3 ST2 SF1 CF		
6) Conventional (C)	CT8 ST4 SF2 CF	CT4 ST2 SF1 CF	CT3 ST2 SF1 CF		

Total your results by adding all the numbers you circled in a row (CF = 0). Then order the six areas from most like you (#1) to least like you (#6). If there isn't a clear winner for first, second, or third place, use Talent, then Interest, and then Skill as tie-breakers. Write down your three-letter code. This is the representative letter from the top three areas put in order from highest to lowest (for example, IAS):

Strengths Self-Assessment

Instructions: To evaluate your strengths, you can pay for StrengthsFinder (strengthsfinder.com), take the free RichardStep Strengths and Weaknesses Aptitude Test (RSWAT, richardstep.com), or manually score the following words. If you take an online assessment, write in the percent (%) results. To manually score, choose a set of words, research the definitions, and then rank the words from most like you to least like you.

StrengthsFinder[25]	%	R#	StrengthsFinder	%	R#	RichardStep	%	R#
Achiever			Futuristic			Adaptability		
Activator			Harmony			Ambition		
Adaptability			Ideation			Balance		
Analytical			Includer			Communication		
Arranger			Individualization			Curiosity		
Belief			Input			Determination		
Command			Intellection			Faith		
Communication			Learner			Focus		
Competition			Maximizer			Innovation		
Connectedness			Positivity			Integrity		
Consistency			Relator			Leadership		
Context			Responsibility			Optimism		
Deliberative			Restorative			Problem-Solving		
Developer			Self-Assurance			Purpose		
Discipline			Significance			Resourcefulness		
Empathy			Strategic			Risk-Taking		
Focus			Woo			Self-Motivation		
						Strategic-Thinking		
						Salesmanship		
						Teamwork		
						Visionary		

Self-Image Assessment

Instructions: Rate each statement as CT for Completely True, ST for Somewhat True, SF for Somewhat False, or CF for Completely False. Then check the box for any statement that evokes strong negative feelings (such as sadness, anger, fear, or shame).

	Self-Image Statement	Rating	?
1)	I'm happy with my work ability (six area) rankings.	CT ST SF CF	☐
2)	I'm happy with my career options.	CT ST SF CF	☐
3)	I'm happy with my strength rankings.	CT ST SF CF	☐
4)	I'm using my strengths to their fullest potential.	CT ST SF CF	☐

---

[25] For detailed definitions see Rath, Tom. *StrengthsFinder 2.0*. New York: Gallup Press, 2007.

BLUEPRINT SPACE

Chapter 15

Assembling Your Identity Clues

In this chapter, you'll pull together everything you're learning and put it in one place so you can see the big picture of your identity. Then, you'll write an identity statement to capture the essence of your identity. In Part III of this book, you'll use your Identity Portrait to write a vision statement and a mission statement.

Directions

Follow these directions to fill in your Identity Portrait. Remember, you're capturing exceptional talents, so you might not fill in all the blanks. In fact, you might not have anything for one or more of the first three sections (Physical, Gender, and Cognitive/Emotional). As you fill in a section, list the individual items from most like you (strongest) to least like you (least strong).

Physical

List up to four physical talents you identified in Chapter 8 (if applicable).

Gender

Circle your gender. List up to three gender talents you identified in Chapter 9 (if applicable).

Cognitive/Emotional

List up to four cognitive or emotional talents you identified in Chapter 10 (if applicable).

General Spiritual

This section is pre-filled for you because it applies to all Christians. If you had additional insights into your spiritual identity (see Chapter 11), write them in this section.

Spiritual Gift Group

Copy your results from Chapter 12. List the *groups* in order from most like you to least like you.

Spiritual Gifts

Copy your results from Chapter 12. List the *gifts* in order from most like you to least like you.

Personality Preferences

Copy your results from Chapter 13. Write down your four-letter 16PT type. The first box is I or E; the second S or N; the third T or F; the fourth J or P. Consider any insights on thinking and feeling from Chapter 9.

Career Interest Areas

Copy your results from Chapter 14.

Top 5 Strengths

Copy your results from Chapter 14.

Identity Statement

Now that you've completed Parts I and II of this book, you're ready to write your preliminary identity statement. The *identity statement* is a summary of your best understanding of who you are. Remember, this will be a work in progress because you're a work in progress. You're still growing in understanding who you are. Also, some of the work in Part III might result in refinements you can make to your statement.

This space is also for you to write in specialized information you know about yourself that doesn't fit in one of the other boxes. You could use this for special ways God has spoken to you or significant life experiences. For example: "I attended a retreat and read about God giving us each a special name, and I sensed God giving me a new name."

You can also include significant personal struggles or limitations — even though you know this doesn't ultimately define you (because you'll be perfect in heaven someday), you can't get around this fact today. For example: "Being born without my left hand has helped me develop a sincere compassion for those who suffer." Remember, Paul recognized that when he was weak, he was strong. You can't help that some of your infirmities are part of who you are today. God is sufficiently powerful to work around any weakness.

> *But He said to me, "My grace is sufficient for you, for My power is perfected in weakness." Therefore I will boast all the more gladly in my weaknesses, so that the power of Christ may rest on me.*
> — 2 Corinthians 12:9

To write your identity statement, first take time to digest everything you've learned and all the information you've organized. Emphasize what multiple sources confirm about you. Remember the various tools from Chapter 7 (Digest Scriptural Truths, Look in the Mirror, Evaluate Relationships, Listen to the Holy Spirit, Remember Life Experiences, and Study Self-Assessment Instruments). Keep your statement specific to you, but avoid statements that tie you down to any actual tasks or actions, such as "I excel at washing dishes." Before you begin, pray and ask God to help you see His intentions for creating you. Use the following formula as a starting point or guide:

I am <fill in Christian truth>. I have <fill in abilities, talents, and gifts>. God created me with <personality attributes>. God created me to <fill in career interests, strengths>. I'm at my best when . . . What is really special about me is . . . I consistently . . .

After you complete this first draft, rewrite your statement in your own words, however it sounds best. Refine your writing until you have a concise statement that captures the essence of who you are. Your final statement should be one paragraph of three to six sentences.

If you're not feeling satisfied with the results, review the reflections in this chapter and possibly the previous chapters for the primary insights you gained. Then try again. Keep trying until your statement sounds inspiring and true. Don't settle for anything less. This is your personal identity statement. It has to inspire you, or something isn't right. For example, here is one of my attempts at my identity statement (see Appendix F for more examples):

I am a son of God: eternally secure and loved unconditionally. With my intelligence, I can understand truths quickly. I enjoy problem solving and making God's truth known to others through wise application. I work hard to provide complete and optimal solutions. I'm a life-long learner who takes risks and doesn't give up until God says stop or I've achieved my goal.

Identity Portrait

Name: **Date:**

Physical
1)
2)
3)
4)

Gender
M ♂   F ♀
1)
2)
3)

Cognitive/Emotional
1)
2)
3)
4)

General Spiritual
Created by God
Eternally secure
Loved unconditionally
Member of the Body of Christ
Dwelling place for God
Purposed for significant work
Equipped for battle

Spiritual Gift Group
1)
2)
3)
4)
5)

Spiritual Gifts
1)
2)
3)
4)
5)

Personality Preferences
Introvert (I)   %:
Extravert (E)   %:

Sensing (S)   %:
Intuitive (N)   %:

Thinking (T)   %:
Feeling (F)   %:

Judging (J)   %:
Perceiving (P) %:

Code: ☐ ☐ ☐ ☐

Career Interest Areas
1)
2)
3)
4)
5)
6)

Code: ☐ ☐ ☐

Top 5 Strengths
1)
2)
3)
4)
5)

Identity Statement

For Reflection

1. How has putting all this information about you on one page helped you see your identity? What patterns do you see? What conclusions are you forming? What consensus are you reaching? What confirmation are you realizing?
2. Take full advantage of your mind's ability to observe itself. What do you notice about you? What are you observing? How are you feeling about yourself? Write down (or tell someone) what you are noticing. Then look again. What else do you notice?
3. Read Revelation 2:17. Imagine Jesus is giving you a stone with a new name on it. You've made it through to the end. You persevered, and God is saying you're a good and faithful servant. What name would He write? Why would He write it? What does this mean between you and God?
4. Did you find a lot of reinforcement for a few attributes? Or does the fact that you have diverse talents stand out as what makes you unique? If so, you might be gifted at making connections. You can help translate for people who may not understand each other.
5. Be steady along the path. Resist doubt. Have confidence. God made you to accomplish specific work in a specific way, which no one else can do.

Next Steps

- ☐ Research your specific Myers–Briggs four-letter code. For example, if you're an ESFP, search for this type online and read at least two descriptions to make sure your codes are a best fit with who you are.
- ☐ Research specific careers for your Career Interests three-letter code from Chapter 14.
- ☐ Media for Further Learning (see Appendix B for more questions)
  - ☐ Movie: *Prince of Egypt*. How does Moses sort through his identity crisis of being a Jew raised as an Egyptian?
  - ☐ Music: *All That Matters* by Colton Dixon
  - ☐ Web: *assessme.org*. Pay to take the AssessMe set of personal assessments.
- ☐ If you aren't satisfied that you've captured the essence of your identity, try the following:
  - Repeat the inventories and tests. You won't get the same answer every time, but you will see some consistency across multiple evaluations. The consistency becomes a reliable description of your identity.
  - Ask others for candid feedback. Pick people you know well enough, but also ones who will be honest.
  - Revisit your life story — go deeper this time.

Part III – Using Your Identity

Chapter 16   **Vision: How Far I Can Go**

Chapter 17   **Consecration: Be Prepared to Go**

Chapter 18   **Mission: Go Make a Difference**

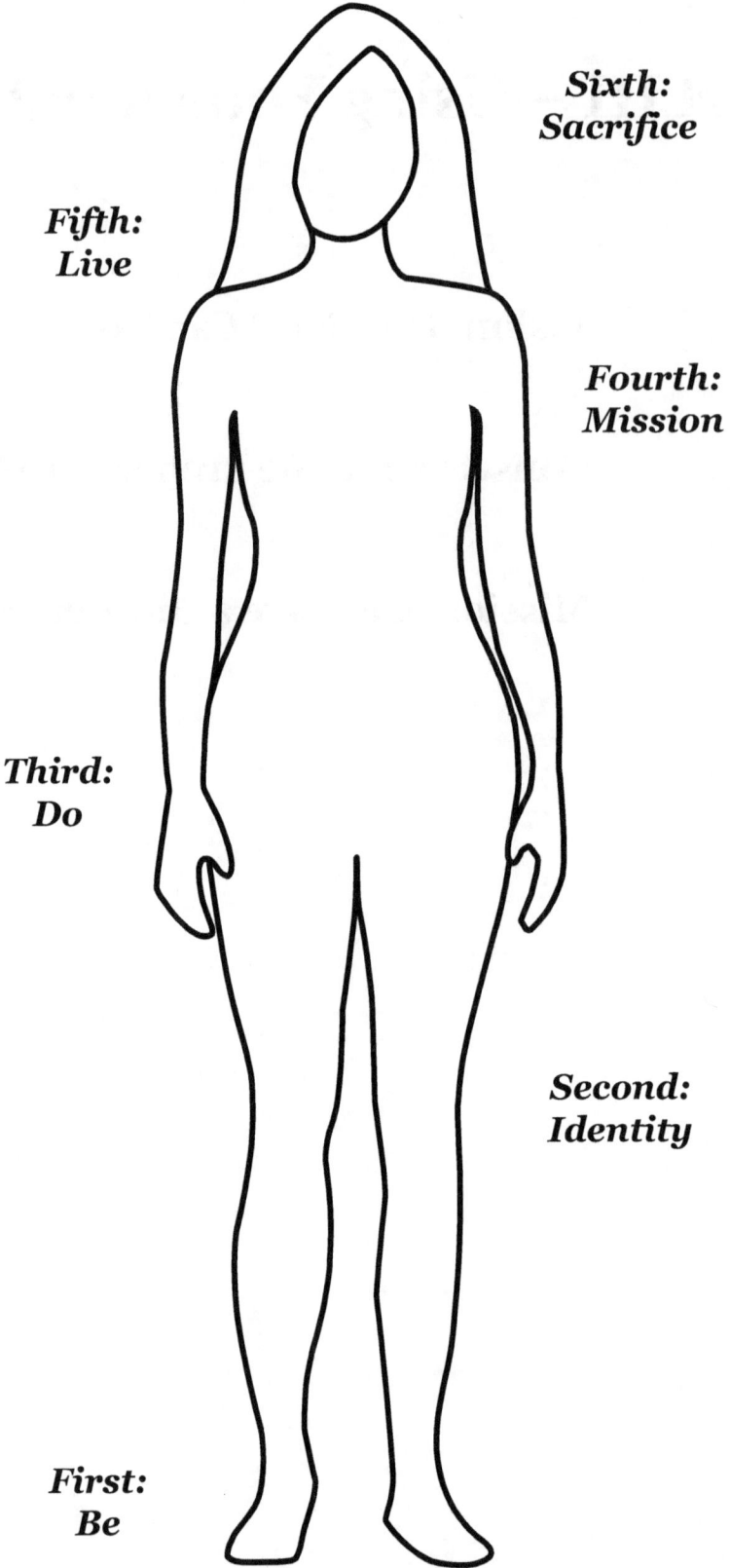

Using (God's Design of Your Identity)

Chapter 16

Vision: How Far I Can Go

In the movie *Batman Begins,* Bruce Wayne plays the role of an obnoxious playboy so no one will recognize his identity as Batman. When he bumps into his childhood girlfriend, Rachel Dawes, he tries to give her a clue that he is acting. But she doesn't understand. She tells him, "It's not who you are underneath — it's what you do that defines you." She is, in effect, saying she doesn't trust his words when his actions contradict his words.

Later in the movie, after Rachel witnesses Batman's heroic actions, she asks Batman his name. He responds with the often-quoted line, "It's not who I am underneath but what I do that defines me." This reveals to Rachel his identity as Bruce Wayne, but it also teaches her that appearances can be deceiving.

Maybe Batman is being ironic rather than sincere. If he is, then he's saying, "If you knew me underneath, you wouldn't judge me by appearances." That's an idea I can support because it demonstrates integrity. You can't have an identity without integrity. *Integrity* means consistency between the inside and the outside. A person with a Confident Identity moves toward stability and integrity by aligning their outside behaviors to their internal design (Ephesians 4:14, James 1:17).

Unfortunately, people without a life-context (God) for their identity believe the line means, "My identity is how I choose to behave at any given moment." This is the same as saying, "I am not bound to any particular identity. I am the god of my life. I can create my own identity." A chameleon changes its appearance to match its environment. An ever-changing appearance isn't stable, so an identity won't form and grow.

In the second Batman movie, *The Dark Knight,* the Joker — a chameleon of sorts — appears to have no identity (he can't be found in the system: no fingerprints, etc.). Because he's without an identity, no leverage exists to convince him to stop his evil plans. It's scary because that's exactly what fuels terrorism in real life.

The Joker is a disturbing picture of what someone would be like without an identity. He's got nothing to lose. Both the Joker and Satan are defined by their ability to aggravate and their desire to destroy. This is in direct contrast to Jesus, who has the most powerful identity — one that can't be destroyed. Jesus didn't lose even when He allowed evil to take its best shot. God resurrected Him and having defeated death, He has more than He started with.

What about Batman? Does he have an identity? At the end of the second movie, Batman concludes that he has to be "who Gotham needs me to be." He seems willing to use Batman's public image (Batman's identity in the eyes of the citizens of Gotham) to serve as a means to whatever end is expedient. Therefore, Batman is more of a symbol than an actual identity.

Bruce has a vision for Gotham and for Batman. One question remains, though: Who is Bruce Wayne? Does Bruce have a vision for himself?

Cast Your Vision

To maximize your Confident Identity, you must have a vision. Your vision is simply a future version of you that you can work to develop. When you know your destination (your vision), then you can take steps to realize your goals. If your vision isn't clear, you can test it by moving in a direction. Testing is a useful process to clarify your vision, but foggy conditions will slow you down. The more certain you are of your direction and the farther you can see, the more you can accomplish.

From Part I, you know what identity is and what it isn't. Your True Identity is who you are underneath, or how God defines you, not what you do. You can't "do" your way out of an empty or broken identity. Only God can move you toward His original design.

From Part II, you learned more specifically how you're unique. There are tasks God planned for you, which only you can do; no one else can accomplish them the way you can. You can participate with a unique contribution by reflecting God's image in a way no other can.

In Part III, you'll create a vision for your identity and your corresponding mission.

Doing flows out of *being* (not the other way around). Your True Identity determines your Mission. Your Mission is the reason God has you alive now — your purpose. Secure your identity (for example, "I'm a hammer"), and then you'll know your purpose ("I drive nails"). Know your purpose, and then you'll know what to do ("I'll build houses").

Your Vision is who you'll need to be in the future to fulfill your Mission. To the degree you understand your identity, you understand your uniqueness, significance, and purpose. Then you're ready to grab God's hand and take action.

To have a Confident Identity means you act on who you know yourself to be and therefore fulfill your purpose. True faith eventually requires action (James 2:14–26). Faithful action means remaining connected to God through prayer while you take steps forward.

Focus Your Vision

Vision is about planning ahead for where you want to be in the future. Once you have a target, you can focus on your goal. In order to attain more of your True Identity, you need to stretch yourself. Stretching and growing your Confident Identity allows you to pursue and achieve more of your purpose.

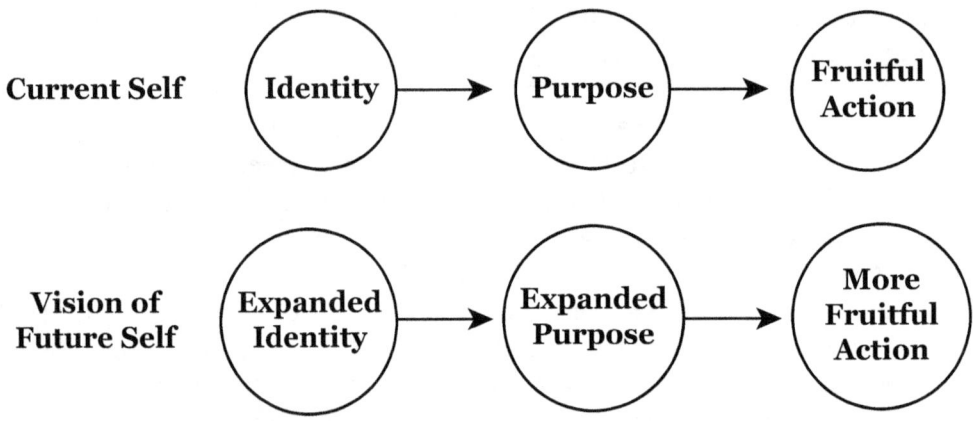

Increasing your capacity allows you to move closer to God and then rest more in God. While you're pursuing your vision, you're fulfilling God's plan for your identity. Your vision is the primary limiting factor in how fast you can grow. How clearly you see your True Identity makes all the difference in fulfilling God's plans. I know this is true because of the story of the Israelites spying on the Promised Land in Numbers 13:1–33.

God told Moses to send spies to the Promised Land — the land He was promising to give to the people of Israel. Most of the men Moses sent compared their capability (apart from God) to the capability of the people who occupied the land and concluded that seizing the land would be impossible. They saw that the land was fertile and would provide well for them, but they also reported with doubt and fear that "the people who dwell in the land are strong, and the cities are fortified and very large."

Two of the spies, Joshua and Caleb, chose a different focus. They aligned their vision and faith with God's ability to follow through on His promise. Caleb advised, "Let us go up at once and occupy it, for we are well able to overcome it." The others continued to focus on their weakness rather than their God as they spoke up again, saying, "We seemed to ourselves like grasshoppers."

God grants you a capacity and the corresponding faith according to the plans He has for you. Ask God to speak to you about the measure of faith He has assigned to you.

For by the grace given to me I say to everyone among you not to think of himself more highly than he ought to think, but to think with sober judgment, each according to the measure of faith that God has assigned.
—Romans 12:3

The following diagram illustrates that as you stretch your vision and take action, your Confident Identity will grow.

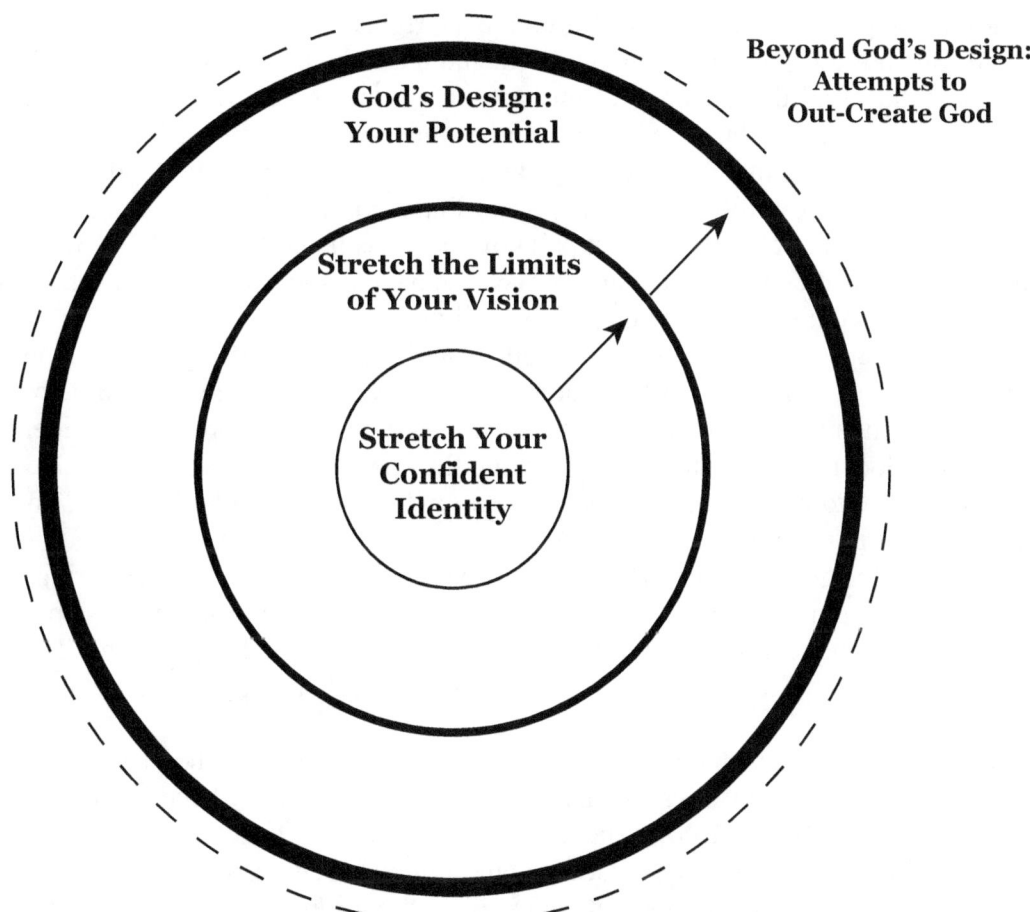

Don't attempt to go beyond God's design by taking on what you weren't made for. Instead, focus. Focus on what must be the very reason(s) God created you. Seek to know your identity as

God knows it. Your God-given identity is a fixed target that doesn't change over time. Your perception of your True Identity is a work in progress. Your understanding of who you are will change as you discover more of who God made you to be.

Seek God's vision for yourself and allow Him to lead you forward. Ask God for the faith to see yourself as He sees you. God's vision for you will always be well beyond your vision. As you fulfill your vision, recreate your vision to keep it future focused. Never stop stretching and growing!

If you're having trouble catching God's vision for you, keep in mind that God reveals your identity (among other things) through His Spirit. To see your identity, you must look through eyes of faith. These eyes are the same ones you use to believe Jesus is the Son of God.

But, as it is written,
"What no eye has seen, nor ear heard, nor the heart of man imagined, what
God has prepared for those who love him"—
these things God has revealed to us through the Spirit.
For the Spirit searches everything, even the depths of God.
—1 Corinthians 2:9–10

Don't hesitate to push yourself to be all you can be. Originality is attractive, respected, and just plain needed. Be your own person. Break out of the mold of who others say you should be.

Clear your mind of all distractions. If you have commitments and responsibilities to others, keep them, but don't allow others' wishes to compromise your identity. Make sure you don't become distracted by needs that don't actually exist — don't fight battles with others inside your head. Instead, determine to fulfill your identity according to your faith.

What blocks you from being you? What parts of you do you keep out of sight? What parts of you seem to be not good enough, not wanted? We all have parts we keep hidden behind a mask. What you have covered up might be your greatest ability.

Your place of deepest wounding is likely your place of greatest gifting. Where you're most easily hurt, is where you have the most potential. The most vulnerable parts of your identity need redemption and validation — not hiding in shame. As you feel secure in your identity and relationship with God, bring the vulnerable parts into the open so others can see that God's power is made perfect in your weakness. When others witness the combination of power and vulnerability, they will be drawn to God.

Where you're vulnerable, you'll suffer, but you need not suffer in vain. Your suffering is unique to your identity. Different people respond differently to the same life difficulties. Your suffering is a big clue to your unique design. When you're hurting, you've found a gold mine. To borrow a line from the short movie *The Butterfly Circus*: The greater your struggle, the more glorious your triumph.

You can't be hurt in places that you don't have. You hurt because of the places you do have. For example, Amy from Part I was especially sensitive to feeling rejected and abandoned. As she learned more about herself, she realized she had the relational gift of encouragement.

Therefore, welcome your uniqueness. Coax it out of hiding. Settle into who you are. Be free to be your real self. Don't be afraid to find out who you are. Be aware of who you are, but stop short of anxious observation and spectating. Be bold. Confront your fears of failure and success.

To accomplish all of this requires a healthy vision, calculated risks, and positive support from others. Realizing the vision of a Confident Identity doesn't happen overnight and doesn't happen without some bumps and bruises along the way. If you feel overwhelmed, you only need to move forward one step at a time. Practice being the real you in safe, predictable places before confronting your greatest fears.

Correct Your Vision

If you're nearsighted, you can see close up but have trouble seeing far away. If you're farsighted, you see far away but have trouble seeing close up. As eyes age and become less flexible, they often need correction for both nearsightedness and farsightedness.

Nearsighted and *farsighted* have meaning in the context of your identity:
- Nearsighted vision can be thought of as low self-worth, or a lack of ability to envision your future self closer to your True Identity.
- Farsighted vision can be thought of as an inability to view your current self; instead, you focus on a prideful, unrealistic vision of your future identity — one that you can't possibly attain but might boast about anyway.

Both perspectives are disconnected from reality.

Valuing others *and* yourself results in clear vision. A lack of either one results in fuzzy vision. When your values are out of balance, you'll be tempted to compare yourself to others in an unhealthy way.

The disciples struggled with comparison all the time, but Jesus consistently checked their prideful thoughts. By declaring that the least are great, He essentially said, "Don't worry about being great. Be concerned about receiving God."

An argument arose among them as to which of them was the greatest. But Jesus, knowing the reasoning of their hearts, took a child and put him by his side and said to them, "Whoever receives this child in my name receives me, and whoever receives me receives him who sent me. For he who is least among you all is the one who is great."
—Luke 9:46–48

Jesus restored Peter for denying that he knew Him (Luke 22:54–62). Even when Jesus told Peter how his death would glorify God, Peter had to ask about John. Jesus's response diverted Peter away from unhealthy comparison and back to his calling. Your calling is specific to you. Follow Jesus in the way God ordains for you.

When Peter saw [John], he said to Jesus, "Lord, what about this man?" Jesus said to him, "If it is my will that he remain until I come, what is that to you? You follow me!"
—John 21:21–22

The diagram on the following page contrasts four possible attitudes resulting from comparing your value against another's value:
1. Blind: No Vision
2. Nearsighted: Devalue-Self Vision
3. Farsighted: Devalue-Others Vision
4. Healthy: Clear Vision

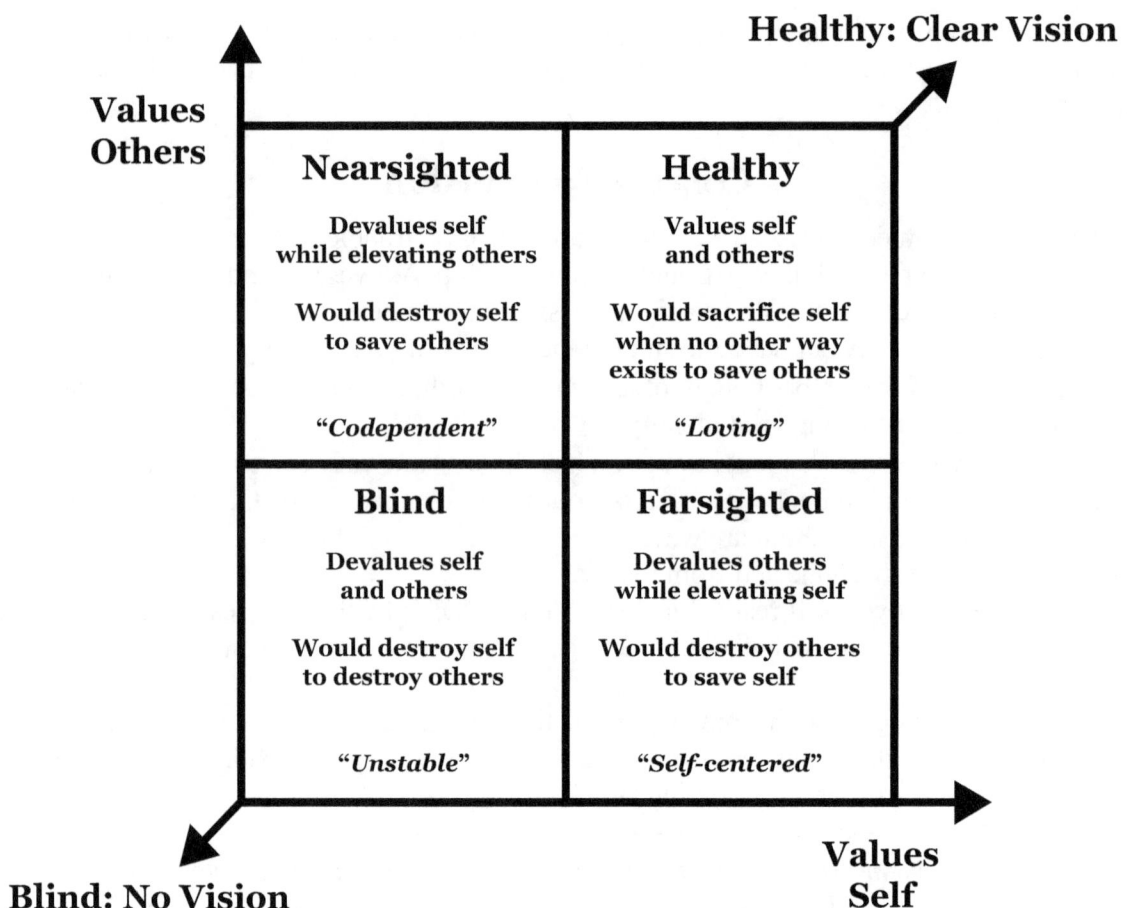

Blind: No Vision

Unhealthy comparison occurs any time you appraise your value or another's value as unequal or less than what God intended. When comparison is used the wrong way, it's a perfect example of fruitless labor. Unhealthy comparison is concluding you're better or worse in a way that would seem to indicate one person is redundant. This can lead to suicidal or homicidal thinking. A terrorist like the Joker acts destructively because he is out of touch with his True Identity. He is blind and unstable.

Nearsighted: Devalue-Self Vision

Nearsighted vision means you compare yourself to others and consistently find yourself not measuring up. How much do you doubt your identity? If you have doubts, you're in good company. But now is the time to resolve any inner conflict between who God says you are and how you feel about yourself. Don't run and hide from who God made you to be. Self-rejection and self-hatred are debilitating. Instead, experience the truth by accepting God's affirmation.

You're in training to be like Jesus, but you aren't Jesus, so you can't be prepared for every life difficulty that comes your way. You aren't responsible for everything that happens to you, but you are responsible for what you do next.

In a moment of crisis, you might have to choose between your identity and your life. Some life circumstances are so overwhelming that you have to give up a part of yourself in order to survive.

Before you think this doesn't apply to you, consider all the experiences you've been through in your lifetime. Some events are small and subtle but no less destructive; the total impact simply takes more time to accumulate.

When you face an event beyond your ability to manage, you have at least five possible responses:

1. **Fight:** Be in touch with your anger and attempt to fight your way out of danger.
2. **Cry:** Be in touch with your despair and make an earnest plea for help.
3. **Flee:** Be in touch with your fear and attempt to escape the danger.
4. **Submit:** Be in touch with your shame in your attempt to avoid danger; fully cooperate as a means to bargain for your life.
5. **Freeze:** Be in touch with both your fear and your shame and attempt to become invisible to danger; in hiding, remain vigilant if you need to flee.

Responses to Overwhelming Situations

Fight like a lion (anger)

Cry like a child (despair)

Flee like a deer (fear)

Submit like a possum (shame)

Freeze like a rabbit (fear/shame)

Each of these options serves to help you survive. During a crisis, you can't afford the luxury of having everything go the way you want. Compromise is often necessary for survival — especially for the most vulnerable: the young and less spiritually aware. When you're faced with an experience that threatens to break your spirit, you must find a way to cope with the overwhelming circumstances beyond your control. The breaking of your spirit compromises your sense of identity.

The shame response is most aligned with nearsighted vision. Shame is the process of shutting down your sense of self, including both strengths and weaknesses, in order to preserve yourself. You must ignore your feelings or be numb to survive. Shame leads to the belief *I don't matter* or

There's no reason for me to exist or *I'm worthless junk.* Ashamed people attempt to eliminate themselves.

In the midst of an overwhelming event, you must compromise your identity in order to gain the needed sense of safety. However, after the crisis is over, you need to regain your identity if you want to be healthy again. Something must be done to revive yourself, or you'll never reach your potential.

Breaking free from this weakened psychological/emotional state isn't easy. When you're wounded by relationship, you need relationship to heal. Seek the help you need; don't remain in a state of compromise or learned helplessness.

Farsighted: Devalue-Others Vision

Farsighted vision means you compare yourself to others and consistently see yourself as unrealistically superior. Your vision becomes exaggerated because of an unmet emotional need to sense your uniqueness. When you devalue others, meeting your need comes at others' expense. Seeing yourself as superior to others is destructive. Prideful people attempt to eliminate the competition.

> *Do nothing out of selfish ambition or empty pride, but in humility consider others more important than yourselves. Each of you should look not only to your own interests, but also to the interests of others.*
> —Philippians 2:3–4

The point of this passage is to never do anything at the expense of others. Actions done out of selfish ambition and empty pride would hurt others. So Paul makes the point to consider others interests while considering your own. *Considering* others as "more important" doesn't mean you *are* worth less or they *are* more important; instead, Paul is telling you to adjust your attitude so that you can see that others are worth serving. Jesus communicated the same truth when He said, "Love your neighbor as yourself" (Mark 12:31).

Healthy: Clear Vision

A confident person who values their identity and retains humility by valuing others can choose personal sacrifice. They can stand for who they are and what they believe, and they can willingly sacrifice themselves if doing so brings something good to others.

Healthy comparison is seeing how you're different without concluding you're better or worse overall. This allows you to focus on what you can be, which others cannot be, but without bragging or boasting. You celebrate others' positive differences as much as or more than your own.

You can achieve a clear vision and healthy comparison by recognizing the authority inherent in your identity. The creation story illustrates this well.

God created the first marriage and instructed Adam and Eve to have dominion over His creation. To have dominion means to rule by power and authority. As God's steward, you need to fully understand the awesome responsibility He gives you. With authority over the physical and spiritual realms, you can bring order to the earth.[26] This is God's first commission.

---

[26] When Jesus had to choose, He prioritized the spiritual realm over the physical realm (Matthew 4:1–11).

Chapter 16 — Vision: How Far I Can Go

> *God blessed them and said to them, "Be fruitful and increase in number; fill the earth and subdue it. Rule over the fish in the sea and the birds in the sky and over every living creature that moves on the ground."*
> —Genesis 1:28 (NIV)

God's identity is also His authority. He doesn't answer to anyone. He didn't remove someone from power or steal someone's authority. He is self-sustainable. He calls Himself the great I AM because He has always existed without help from anyone.

> *God said to Moses, "I AM WHO I AM."*
> *And he said, "Say this to the people of Israel:*
> *'I AM has sent me to you.'"*
> —Exodus 3:14
>
> *Jesus said to them, "Truly, truly, I say to you, before Abraham was, I am."*
> —John 8:58

God made you in His image. While you aren't self-sustainable like God, you do retain some authority. God means for you to carry your identity like a sheriff's badge. You have authority to be you. Imagine a badge with a picture of you, your name, and the words, "In God I Trust" on it. Trust God with the authority He has given you. Your identity is your authority. This idea means you have both the authority to become all God has designed you to be and the authority to act.

Your sense of authority from your identity peaks at a certain age. At the peak, you have both confidence and awareness of your identity. This time varies widely; however, a good estimate is around midlife. By midlife, you've experienced enough to know who you really are and how you want to prioritize the rest of your life — or at least, figuring this out resolves a midlife crisis. You can fulfill a mission to help others, and you can also invest in your vision of growth and development.

Queen Esther is an excellent example of someone who used all she was to further God's plan. As she learned about opportunity, she took appropriate steps forward (Esther 1–5):

- **Esther knew who she was.** She understood she had beauty and faith. She acted with humility by considering Mordecai's counsel.

- **Esther found a purpose within reach of her abilities.** When the king sought beautiful women, she was available. When her people were threatened, she made herself available and spoke with poise and self-control.
- **Esther took action by faith.** When she realized she was her people's only hope, she boldly approached the king's throne, taking a calculated risk. Her motive wasn't for her own interests. She was honorably focused on saving her people. God clearly and specifically chose her to save His people.

Securing your identity secures your personal authority to fulfill your mission and your destiny. God reveals Jesus's identity only to those God chooses. Be wise with your identity, revealing it only when the time is right. Wait for God to reveal it to you and to others.

> *[Jesus] said to them, "But who do you say that I am?" Simon Peter replied, "You are the Christ, the Son of the living God." And Jesus answered him, "Blessed are you, Simon Bar-Jonah! For flesh and blood has not revealed this to you, but my Father who is in heaven."*
> —Matthew 16:15–17

For Reflection

1. Ask your friends, "But who do you say that I am?"
2. "It's not who you are underneath. It's what you do that defines you." —Rachel from *Batman Begins*. Is this a falsehood, or is she saying that if your outside appears healthy but your insides are sick, you're still sick? Consider Jesus's statement in Matthew 15:18: "But what comes out of the mouth proceeds from the heart, and this defiles a person."
3. "It's not who I am underneath but what I do that defines me." —Batman. What's wrong with this philosophy when you compare it to your Confident Identity?

Next Steps

☐ Remember your top five positive experiences. Capture both facts and feelings. Do these experiences enhance or detract from your Identity Portrait from Chapter 15?

1	
2	
3	
4	
5	

☐ Media for Further Learning (see Appendix B for more questions)
  ☐ Movie: *The Dark Knight*. What would it be like without an identity?
  ☐ Movie: *Butterfly Circus*. How are you inspired to pursue your vision?
  ☐ Music: *Tell the Mountain (About Your God)* by Back Home

- ☐ Mask Exercise: Draw a face shape (or use the Blueprint Space shape). On the front, write words and decorate the face to depict your public self (who you want everyone to believe you are). On the back, depict your private self (who you really are, your vulnerable self). Reflect on what you learn about yourself by doing this exercise. Consider sharing your creation and thoughts with someone you can trust.
- ☐ Are you feeling good about who you are? If not, you might have some obstacles blocking your ability to see your identity. Journal about these. What negative beliefs are blocking you? If they're large or deeply rooted, make a commitment to see a mentor, counselor, or trusted friend so you can move beyond your low self-esteem.
- ☐ Create a Vision Statement that describes who you will be when you're closer to God's design. Consider areas where you're most in touch with your hurt. Allow this closeness to motivate you to expand the limits of your identity toward your True Identity. Review your Identity Portrait from Chapter 15. Ask God for His input and insights into who you are. Then ask for a picture of the plans He has for you. What is God saying about who you are and who you'll be?

Revisit the Self-Image assessments from Part II. Review the statements you checked. Are these potential strengths you can develop or God-given limitations? Consider including potential strengths in your statement but don't try to improve a God-given limitation.

Write your Vision Statement in your Blueprint Space. You can use the following prompt to get you started:

I will be my best self when I'm . . .

For example, Amy might write a statement like this (see Appendix F for more examples):

I will excel at encouraging all kinds of people in all kinds of situations. Others will feel strengthened to pursue exactly who God made them to be. Whether I'm feeling strong or weak, I can both be there for others and allow others to be there for me.

BLUEPRINT SPACE

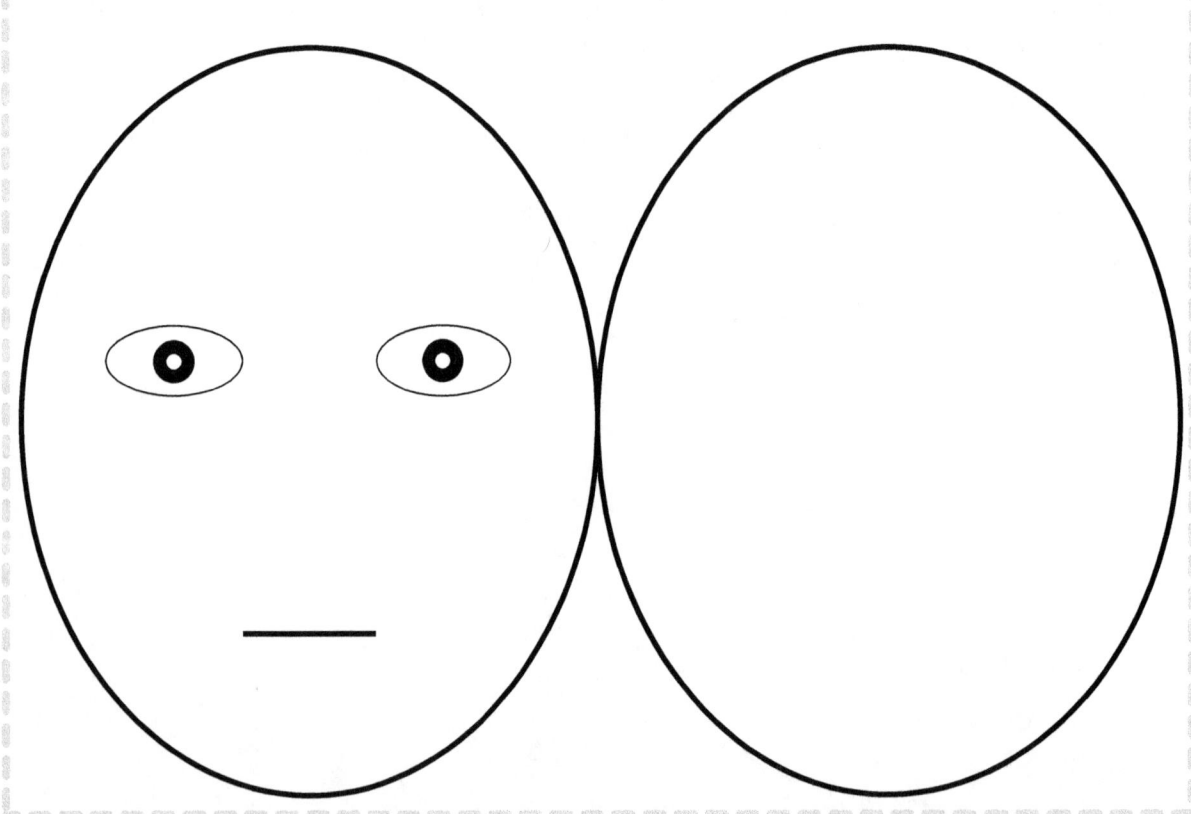

Chapter 17

Consecration: Be Prepared to Go

Then the kingdom of heaven will be like ten virgins who took their lamps and went to meet the bridegroom. Five of them were foolish, and five were wise. For when the foolish took their lamps, they took no oil with them, but the wise took flasks of oil with their lamps. As the bridegroom was delayed, they all became drowsy and slept. But at midnight there was a cry, "Here is the bridegroom! Come out to meet him." Then all those virgins rose and trimmed their lamps. And the foolish said to the wise, "Give us some of your oil, for our lamps are going out." But the wise answered, saying, "Since there will not be enough for us and for you, go rather to the dealers and buy for yourselves." And while they were going to buy, the bridegroom came, and those who were ready went in with him to the marriage feast, and the door was shut. Afterward the other virgins came also, saying, "Lord, lord, open to us." But he answered, "Truly, I say to you, I do not know you." Watch therefore, for you know neither the day nor the hour.
—Matthew 25:1–13

Consecration means to sanctify yourself by setting yourself apart as dedicated to God.[27] This chapter is an opportunity to break free from whatever prevents your devotion to God. In the Parable of the Ten Virgins, five prepared wisely and five prepared foolishly. To prepare wisely means to prepare enough for what God has planned.

For you to move toward your vision (as discussed in Chapter 16), God must prepare you. To be prepared to go fulfill your mission, you need to examine your motives so you can be reasonably sure they're clear of distractions and distortions.

Distortions come from life experiences, often in early childhood. What you grow up with is what you consider to be normal, even if it's unhealthy. Your childhood experiences can drive you to choose behaviors that seem holy but are actually unhealthy. You have a choice. You can proceed down a path that leads away from your identity (foolish living) or down one that leads toward fulfilling the purposes of your identity (wise living).

Foolish Living

Idolatry is depending on something (career, parents, spouse, friends, drugs, sex, etc.) beyond its capacity to fulfill you. An idolater prioritizes these things, giving them higher importance than God. When you idolize something, you value it more than it's worth, and in the process, you end up devaluing God as less than He's worth.

There is a way that seems right to a man, but its end is the way to death.
—Proverbs 16:25

[27] freethesaurus.com/consecration

Some substitutes for God are true surrogates that help you grow closer to God. God provides parents, mentors, friends, and/or counselors as a way for you to experience God, even though the experience will always be incomplete.

God ultimately fulfills every desire (Psalm 145:19). He often does this through others, but this rarely works through just one person because one person can't meet all your needs. If you attach to the wrong things — or to the right things in the wrong way — you'll become disappointed and increasingly dysfunctional. Are you aware of any idols in your life?

Giving up who God made you to be prevents you from maturing into an emotionally healthy adult. Two practical ways exist to block the maturation process and keep you from living in a state of preparedness: addiction and codependency. Even though the paths are different, both addicts and codependents lose their identities to idolatry.

Addiction

Compromising your identity for short-term gain doesn't prepare you for life's challenges. Instead, it supports an environment that can produce an addiction. Addicts sacrifice their identity and choose illegitimate substitutes such as drugs, alcohol, work, food, or pornography. Consider this story of a mother, Julie, and her 12-year-old daughter, Sally:

> "Sally, you take care of your father, brother, and sister while I'm gone," says Julie. "After you finish making dinner don't forget the laundry."
>
> From the other room, Sally's father yells to Sally, "Bring me another beer."
>
> Julie drives away from the house, excited to have time with her friends. *Having children right out of high school sure took all the fun out of life. At least now I'm making up for lost time. We're going to have so much fun tonight at the party. James scored us some Oxy . . .*

Julie is hurting herself and her family instead of finding a healthy way to meet her legitimate emotional needs.

Codependency

Codependents sacrifice their identity by taking over an addict's responsibilities. The codependent focuses on serving others, pleasing others, and giving to others. Under normal circumstances, these are good things. However, a codependent is just as addicted as an addict — except their drug of choice is acceptance through an unhealthy relationship.

As you grow in your identity, you can sacrifice for others, but you can't sacrifice what you don't have. Attempting to obey the Bible by thinking, *I must sacrifice my life for others,* along with lacking the understanding of how much you're worth, results in self-destructive sacrifice. Consider Sally's perspective:

> "Sally, bring me another beer," says her father.
>
> Sally interrupts dinner preparations to bring her father a beer the way he likes it. Then she hurriedly finishes making dinner for her father and her siblings. While they satisfy their hunger, she transfers the clothes they need for tomorrow from the washer to the dryer.

> As she works, she thinks, *I have a lot to do to keep this family together when my mom is out with her friends. Mom sure needs my help. I like helping, but I wonder if I'll ever have a birthday like we gave Mom last week. Making the yard look pretty the way she likes is hard work. At least she was happy. I better start my homework. So, this is what it's like to be twelve.*

Sally sacrifices herself, but she has limited understanding of her family's dysfunction. She bears the consequences of her mother's immaturity. The following figure illustrates the transformation from healthy responsibility before an addiction to dysfunctional responsibility during an addiction.

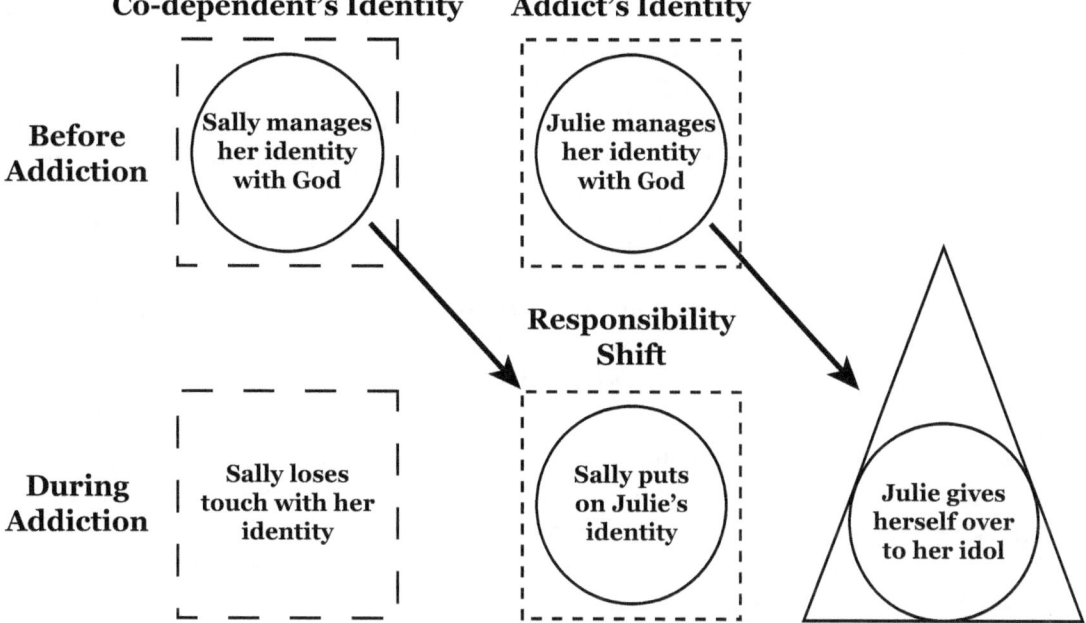

Children can't handle adult responsibility, but because most children are innocent and vulnerable, they instinctively offer to give up their lives. We're not supposed to heap adult responsibilities on a child. For example, we don't ask a child to go to war because it would rob them of their natural development. Chances are they would consider fighting as their identity.

An adult has many cares of the world — securities and ambitions — that they might not be willing to surrender in order to build God's kingdom. Jesus said, "Truly I tell you, unless you change and become like little children, you'll never enter the kingdom of heaven" (Matthew 18:3). God wants you to be an adult, knowing the power of your identity, *and* be like an innocent child, willing to sacrifice what you have.

Wise Living

Having a Confident Identity doesn't mean instant fulfillment. On the contrary, having a Confident Identity means accepting progress through life, as God provides it. When you have a Confident Identity, you can find meaning and contentment in day-to-day life while maintaining a vision for the future.

> *Wealth gained hastily will dwindle,*
> *but whoever gathers little by little will increase it.*
> —Proverbs 13:11

Identity before Sacrifice

First secure your identity; then you'll have something to sacrifice for a cause greater than yourself. God doesn't want you to give yourself away because you're worth so little. No, it's because you're worth so much. Knowing your worth is a prerequisite to true sacrifice.

Hearing from God, our Creator, that He values and loves you as you are is a craving you have and need. You don't have to stretch in order to gain others' acceptance. This won't strengthen your identity. You shouldn't compromise your identity in an effort to serve others.

Self-abuse or giving prematurely decreases your worth, and then you have less to give to others. Self-sacrifice demonstrates your worth and the worth of the person you help by your sacrifice. God sacrificed His son, who has great value, for us, who have nothing of value to offer in return.

> *For while we were still weak, at the right time Christ died for the ungodly. For one will scarcely die for a righteous person—though perhaps for a good person one would dare even to die—but God shows his love for us in that while we were still sinners, Christ died for us.*
> —Romans 5:6–8

Jesus had awareness of His significant value and then offered His life for others. He chose the right time, as led by God the Father, to give away His life. Self-sacrifice in Jesus's style is having the awareness of your significant value, and then offering your life for others.

Offering your life refers to more than dying; it includes living *for* something, too. Jesus's sacrifice was also in his ministry leading up to the cross.

> *For whoever will save his life shall lose it:*
> *and whoever will lose his life for my sake shall find it.*
> —Matthew 16:25

Focus your life on a greater purpose. If you can see beyond your earthly life and invest in your future heavenly life by participating in God's kingdom on earth, you live with your Confident Identity. But if you seek only earthly pleasures and comforts, you fail to know your True Identity. To have an identity is to have something you can lose or sacrifice. God created us to love.

> *Greater love has no one than this: to lay down one's life for one's friends.*
> —John 15:13

> *This is how we know what love is: Jesus Christ laid down his life for us. And we ought to lay down our lives for our brothers and sisters.*
> —1 John 3:16 (NIV)

God's relationship with us makes us valuable. Identity is valuable only because we were created with purpose and meaning.

Active Waiting by Faith

Every moment of life consists of either preparation or fulfillment. You can find much of your life purpose in the time you spend preparing for the (usually briefer) moments of fulfillment.

Preparation means active waiting. During this period of waiting, you should be intentionally seeking God but not attempting to force something to happen. God trains you and develops the roots you need to grow fruits (to fulfill your mission).

Fulfillment happens when God prepares you to the right degree and then brings you to the right opportunity at the right time. This kind of fulfillment is destiny and God's timing.

> *For while we were still weak, at the right time Christ died for the ungodly.*
> —Romans 5:6

God has plans for you now and plans for you in heaven. Everything you're going through prepares you for what will come next in your life. Sometimes the preparation is direct and intense, and sometimes it's subtle but no less disruptive (in a positive way).

As God's people, we are called to be actively waiting. We do our part and then wait for God's timing. Sometimes the wait is short, but sometimes the wait is longer than a lifetime.

> *but they who wait for the Lord shall renew their strength;*
> *they shall mount up with wings like eagles;*
> *they shall run and not be weary; they shall walk and not faint.*
> —Isaiah 40:31

If you want to be prepared for ministry, you need to go through training, trials, and testing to build up your Confident Identity (1 Peter 4:12). Jesus lived this way. He knew His identity and God's purpose for His life, so He didn't concern Himself with others' plots and schemes. He often said, "My time has not yet come" (John 7; 10:22–39). Jesus waited 30 years before entering ministry. Before His ministry, He entered a time of training and testing in the desert.

> *Then Jesus was led up by the Spirit into the wilderness to be tempted by the devil. And after fasting forty days and forty nights, he was hungry. And the tempter came and said to him, "If you are the Son of God, command these stones to become loaves of bread." But he answered, "It is written,*
> *"'Man shall not live by bread alone,*
> *but by every word that comes from the mouth of God.'"*
> —Matthew 4:1–4

Dying to self requires strong faith. Freedom and security are inseparable. You can make leaps of faith as long as you're securely attached to God. True freedom is being securely tied to God as a "slave to righteousness" (Romans 6:17–18).

> *Very truly I tell you, unless a kernel of wheat falls to the ground and dies, it remains only a single seed. But if it dies, it produces many seeds.*
> —John 12:24

Many others went before us actively waiting in faith for something greater beyond this life.

> *These all died in faith, not having received the things promised, but having seen them and greeted them from afar, and having acknowledged that they were strangers and exiles on the earth. For people who speak thus make it clear that they are seeking a homeland. If they had been thinking of that land from which they had gone out, they would have had opportunity to return. But as it is, they desire a better country, that is, a heavenly one. Therefore God is not ashamed to be called their God, for he has prepared for them a city.*
> —Hebrews 11:13–16

Anchored to God

John, the young missionary from Chapter 7, knew something had to change as he stood looking at the ground far below. When his fear of jumping became less than his fear of rejection, he spread his arms like an eagle and jumped off the bridge. Air hit his face for what would have seemed like forever, if it weren't for the objects below rapidly growing larger. Fortunately, he felt the tugging of the bungee cord on his legs. He gradually slowed and then reversed his descent. What a thrill!

Anchored to God means both 1) securely attached and 2) connected so you're able to receive what is good. If your attachment to others hasn't been good, this makes it extremely difficult to attach and receive from God. Being attached is the only way to be prepared and therefore, the only way to realize your vision and life purpose.

To have a Confident Identity, you need a positive enough view of yourself, others, and ultimately, God. The more negative your views, the slower you progress. But there is always hope if you're desperate enough to trust someone who genuinely wants to show you love.

In order to develop enough capacity to attach to God, you need a surrogate — someone made in God's image who temporarily stands in for God. Parents and other mother and father figures are meant to be transitional objects. As children mature, they need to transfer their longings from earthly parents to God. But you'll continue to need to be able to attach to others to give to and receive from them.

This life is a short breath that passes quickly. Make the most of every opportunity (1 Peter 3:15–16). To make life count, you need to see the big picture of where you come from. By anchoring to God, you can see your life from His perspective. When you're anchored to other stuff, you're limited to an earthly perspective. Part of being consecrated is shifting the context of your life from an earthly origin to a heavenly one. Being anchored is like being bungee-corded to God in heaven and diving into the messiness of this life.

The longer I live, the more I derive my security from the coming life in heaven rather than this life on earth. This life is imperfect and incomplete. God asks us to give our all in this life in order to make a difference to others. This is truly meaningful, especially in a world that is slowing passing away.

> *Therefore, since we are surrounded by so great a cloud of witnesses, let us also lay aside every weight, and sin which clings so closely, and let us run with endurance the race that is set before us, looking to Jesus, the founder and perfecter of our faith, who for the joy that was set before him endured the cross, despising the shame, and is seated at the right hand of the throne of God.*
> —Hebrews 12:1–2

For Reflection

1. To make any real progress in life, to be prepared for greater things, you need a pathway to receive from others.
2. Trust yourself before you trust others, but trust others enough to be able to receive more love. Use discernment to determine who to trust. Believe what God says about you over what you or others believe about you. Be vulnerable so you can internalize God's love, but be wise and minimize your risk.
3. People-pleasing keeps you from your identity when you define yourself by what others need instead of by what God designed you to provide. You lose touch with who you are and neglect to learn who you are. A Confident Identity is the best antidote to this unhealthy behavior.
4. Anything can become an idol if you use it beyond its intended purpose. Whatever you're looking to — to attach to and be your anchor — if it isn't God, it's an idol (or at least it has the potential to become one).

Next Steps

- Who or what are you anchored to? Are you depending on any one person or thing more than you should? Are any of the following idols a struggle for you?
    - Possessions or money
    - Food, drugs, or alcohol
    - Performance, achievement, or fame
    - Relationships, love, pornography, or sex
    - Other:
- Read John Gill's commentary on Matthew 16:25 (see biblehub.com/commentaries/gill/matthew/16.htm)
- Media for Further Learning (see Appendix B for more questions)
    - Movie: *Curious George*. Describe George's attachment to the Man in the Yellow Hat.
    - Movie: *The Ultimate Gift*. Describe Jason's transformation.
    - Music: *Live It Well* by Switchfoot
- Remember your top five negative experiences. Capture both facts and feelings. Do these enhance or detract from your identity portrait from Chapter 15? Is there a hidden strength within your experience?

1	
2	
3	
4	
5	

☐ Evaluate your image of God. Describe your God based on your actions (not head knowledge). Actions can't define who you are, but they can reveal what you believe about yourself and God. How does what you do reveal who you understand God to be?

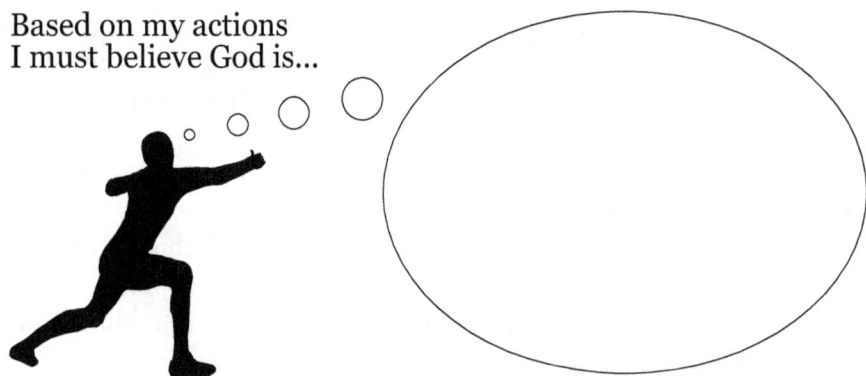

How do your parents continue to influence your God-image? Choose the top ten words that describe your earliest positive and negative childhood impressions of your father and mother. Be completely honest. Mark an X in the column if the word fits with your image of that particular person (including your self-image). If the word doesn't represent your self-image, write in a word that does. Reflect on your answers in your Blueprint Space. What new experiences do you need to move toward positive images?

Descriptive Word(s)	Father-Image	Mother-Image	God-Image	Self-Image
Example: *Distant*	X		X	*Loner*

BLUEPRINT SPACE

Chapter 18

Mission: Go Make a Difference

When you have God's affirmation and your Confident Identity, all that remains is pursuing enduring work. Now is the time to put into practice all that you are by addressing real-world problems. What kind of work should you pursue? Your identity indicates what you're capable of, but the options for enduring work must be narrowed down. Current world events, life circumstances, economic circumstances, and life experience all narrow down the infinite possibilities to what is available in your lifetime. Your values, interests, and passions can further filter the possibilities to a specific focus.

The perfect mission for you is the intersection of:
1. **Your identity:** Who God made you to be
2. **Current world problems:** The world's urgent needs
3. **Your values, interests, and passions:** What is important and exciting to you

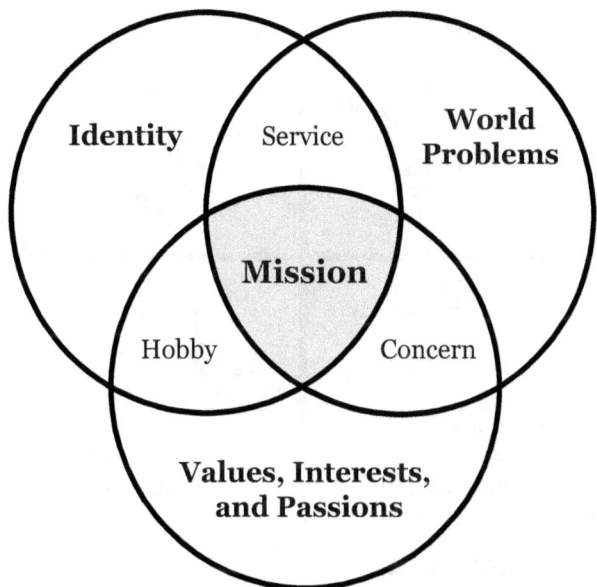

What if you're passionate about something the world doesn't appear to need? You could decide to keep the passion as a hobby and pick a different one that the world needs for your mission. Some passions may take years to plan and bring to fruition. Dream big anyway.

Your *identity statement* (see Chapter 15) is a stable description of who you are. Your *vision statement* (see Chapter 16) is a description of who you will become so you can achieve your mission. Your *mission statement* is a description of your God-given calling or vocation — how you'll use your Confident Identity to make a difference in the world. You'll write a personal mission statement in the Action Plan at the end of this chapter.

Your mission will change somewhat frequently because it depends upon your identity, vision, values, interests, and passions as well as current world problems. This might not sound very stable, but that only keeps life more interesting. Your mission will evolve over your lifetime; it should become considerably more focused, stable and predictable the longer you live.

The Four Seasons of a Missional Life

Your passion is your motivation. Without genuine passion, you'll end up burned out, broken down, or bored. God gives you the ability to be passionate about a cause so you'll be unstoppable. When your passion for life or your career runs out, this is a sign that something needs to change.

To pursue a life mission, you need passion, ability (experience), and opportunity. Ability can be learned. Opportunity can be found or created. But passion can only come from within. Because all of these can change, your mission will cycle through four stages throughout your life:

1. **Sidelined (Winter):** Low passion, with no ability and no opportunity
2. **Rookie (Spring):** Passion and opportunity, with low ability
3. **Pro (Summer):** Optimal passion, ability, and opportunity
4. **Stalled (Autumn):** Depleted passion, with declining ability or restricted opportunity

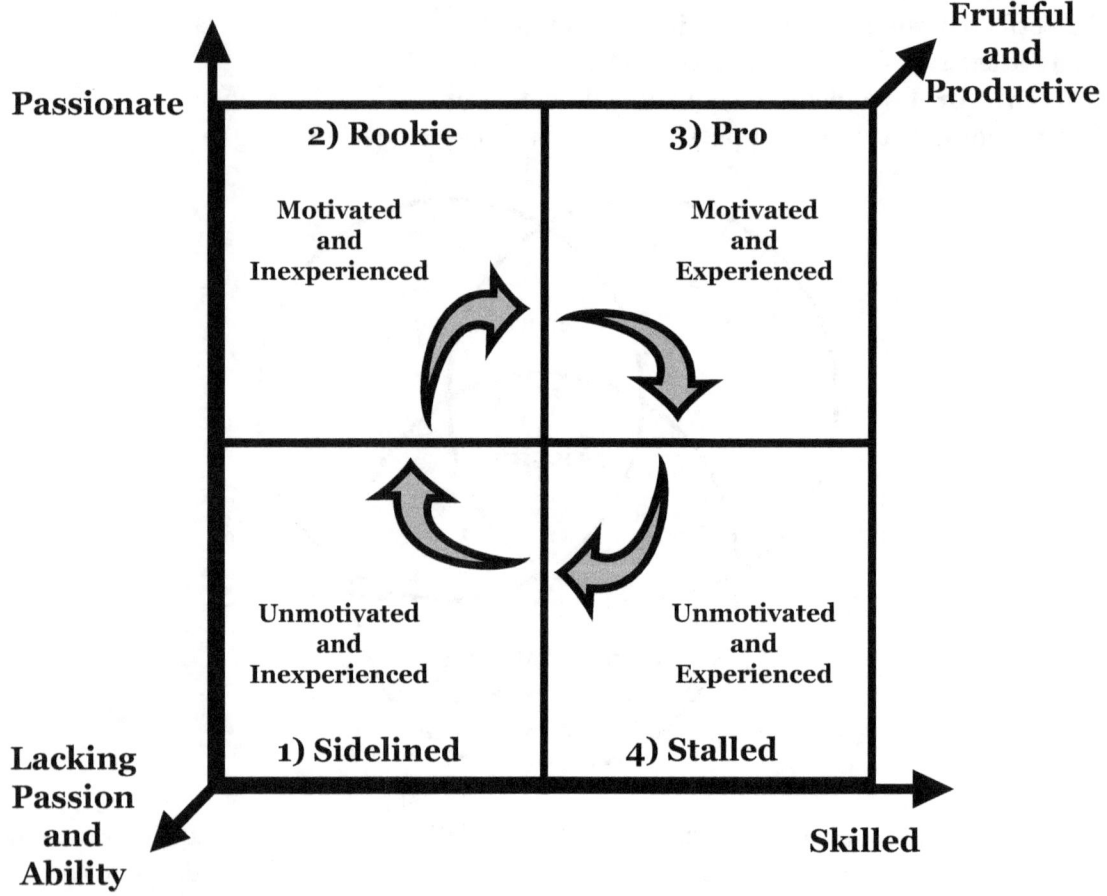

Sidelined (Winter Waiting)

Everyone will find themselves lacking direction and experience at least once in their life. You might have a sense of your identity but lack the passion to pursue a particular calling. You're sitting on the bench waiting for God to put you into the game.

> *Have you not known? Have you not heard?*
> *The Lord is the everlasting God, the Creator of the ends of the earth.*
> *He does not faint or grow weary; his understanding is unsearchable.*
> *He gives power to the faint,*
> *and to him who has no might he increases strength.*
> *Even youths shall faint and be weary, and young men shall fall exhausted;*
> *but they who wait for the Lord shall renew their strength;*
> *they shall mount up with wings like eagles;*
> *they shall run and not be weary; they shall walk and not faint.*
> —Isaiah 40:28–31

While you're waiting on the Lord, you can still be active in moving forward. God can steer a moving sailboat. Unless you are hearing from God to stay put, your best option is to put yourself into a position where you'll be able to experience a variety of options without having to make a commitment.

Rookie (Spring Action)

Rookies bring enthusiasm to a task because they can see the potential of their identity. Enthusiasm is from the Greek word *entheos,* which means "in God" or "possessed by God" or "God within." Rookies have a heightened level of faith and are ready to act.

> *His divine power has granted to us all things that pertain to life and godliness,*
> *through the knowledge of him who called us to his own glory and excellence,*
> *by which he has granted to us his precious and very great promises, so that*
> *through them you may become partakers of the divine nature, having escaped*
> *from the corruption that is in the world because of sinful desire.*
> —2 Peter 1:3–4

Being a Rookie means having an abundance of energy without the experience to efficiently direct it. You can see God clearly and without inhibition, you act boldly. While you can enjoy this stage, you should make gaining wisdom a goal so you can accomplish more with the same effort.

Pro (Summer Fruit)

Pros have achieved a level of competence that allows them to be fruitfully productive. Being in this stage means you are functioning optimally. However, you aren't a machine, so you need to make adjustments along the way to stay in the pro zone. Find ways to stay challenged so you'll continue to grow.

> *For this very reason, make every effort to supplement your faith with virtue,*
> *and virtue with knowledge, and knowledge with self-control, and self-control*
> *with steadfastness, and steadfastness with godliness, and godliness with*
> *brotherly affection, and brotherly affection with love. For if these qualities are*
> *yours and are increasing, they keep you from being ineffective or unfruitful in*
> *the knowledge of our Lord Jesus Christ. For whoever lacks these qualities is so*
> *nearsighted that he is blind, having forgotten that he was cleansed from his*

> *former sins. Therefore, brothers, be all the more diligent to confirm your calling and election, for if you practice these qualities you will never fall.*
> —2 Peter 1:5–10

Whenever you stop growing, you won't be far from stalling. This doesn't have to be a negative. It might only mean God is done preparing you for the next step.

Stalled (Autumn Surrender)

You might find yourself stalled when you once again lack passion or when your opportunity is gone. This is the time to recreate yourself or take your ministry to the next level. God always has something new for you to do. A loss of opportunity might be a sign that God wants you working on something else.

> *"Do not call to mind the former things, Or ponder things of the past.*
> *"Behold, I will do something new, Now it will spring forth;*
> *Will you not be aware of it?*
> *I will even make a roadway in the wilderness, Rivers in the desert.*
> —Isaiah 43:18–19

When you start to feel stalled, make an accounting of what you've accomplished and learned as a Rookie and a Pro. Prepare to surrender these things to God so you'll have room for what God is bringing into your life. Then move into a time of waiting on God.

Finding Motivation to Change the World

The world changes everyone in some way, and everyone changes the world in some way. Make your efforts personal so you can be invested in changing the world! Values, interests, and passions are all personal choices that determine your priorities.

- **Values** are what you consider to be the most important ways to live
- **Interests** are the proven subjects and activities you focus on during recreation
- **Passions** are the subset of world problems that you want to personally invest in solving

Exercise: Identify Your Values

Values, which can change with stages of life, maturity, and circumstances, can help you discover your passion. Values are all positive. Because you might appreciate all of them, you have to prioritize them by importance so you can bring focus to your life mission. Prioritizing your values doesn't mean you hate one in comparison to another. You choose your focus because you can't do everything. Having a focus brings meaning and purpose to your life.

> *The kingdom of heaven is like treasure hidden in a field, which a man found and covered up. Then in his joy he goes and sells all that he has and buys that field. Again, the kingdom of heaven is like a merchant in search of fine pearls, who, on finding one pearl of great value, went and sold all that he had and bought it.*
> —Matthew 13:44–45

Chapter 18 — Mission: Go Make a Difference

Values are often deeply held, so it may be painful if you choose work that conflicts with your values. Be clear about your values so that whenever possible, you can choose work that doesn't create this conflict for you.

Your values are determined when you make decisions — when you have to choose one thing over another. You will know your values by the choices you make.

Review the values in the following list. If any of your values are missing, add them to the list. Taking time to define what each value means to you will produce more satisfying results. Your values are personal — determined and prioritized by you. Choose what you believe is important, desirable, or good. What brings meaning and purpose to your life? Then rank the values in order from strongest to weakest.

To make this exercise easier, first eliminate about half the words you know aren't that important to you; you'll be left with your top 50 or fewer values. Then put each value on a small piece of paper and write in a definition if it helps (see Appendix D for a template you can photocopy). For example:

Faith	Rank:
Sustaining belief in God despite difficult circumstances	

Spread them out and sort and rank your values until you are satisfied. When you're done, write your top seven values on your Action Plan, putting the strongest first.

Aesthetics	Dependability	Honesty	Perseverance
Accountability	Determination	Honor	Positivity
Accuracy	Diligence	Humility	Practicality
Achievement	Discipline	Humor	Preparedness
Advancement	Discretion	Influence/power	Recognition
Adventure	Diversity	Independence	Responsibility
Ambition	Efficiency	Integrity	Security
Artistic expression	Elegance	Joy	Self-control
Authenticity	Empathy	Justice	Selflessness
Balance	Excellence	Learning	Sensitivity
Challenge	Fairness	Legacy	Service
Commitment	Faith	Leisure	Simplicity
Community	Family	Location	Speed
Compassion	Financial security	Love	Stability
Competency	Fitness	Loyalty	Strategy
Competition	Friendship	Mastery	Structure
Contentment	Flexibility	Nature	Success
Continuous-improvement	Freedom	Obedience	Thankfulness
	Fun	Openness	Thoroughness
Contribution	Generosity	Order	Thoughtfulness
Control	Giving back	Organization	Tolerance
Conversation	Growth	Originality	Tradition
Cooperation	Happiness	Patriotism	Understanding
Creativity	Hard work	Peace	Uniqueness
Curiosity	Health	Perfection	Unity
			Variety

Exercise: Identify Your Interests

Interests include things like recreation, rest, and hobbies. What do you enjoy doing, learning, or talking about? What energizes you and holds your attention so much you lose track of time?

Write down at least three interests for each decade of your life. For your current decade, write all your interests. Then rank your interests and write your top seven interests on your Action Plan, putting the strongest first.

Decade	Interests
1 0–9 years	
2 10–19 years	
3 20–29 years	
4 30–39 years	
5 40–49 years	
6 50–59 years	
7 60+ years	

Exercise: Identify Your Passions

Passion is the savor in the salt and the wavelength of the light. It's the way you'll shine and bring glory to God. While considering your identity, reflect on the following questions to find your passion(s). Write your top seven passions on your Action Plan, putting the strongest first.

How do you want to enjoy the life God has given you?
What's going on in the world that needs to be addressed?
What would you volunteer to do (even if you know you wouldn't be paid)?
What heart-wrenching experiences have you witnessed or gone through personally?
What's the best way you're going to be able to show Christ to the world?
How do you want to make a difference in the world?
What cause are you willing to die for?

Exercise: Write Your Mission Statement

If you haven't already done so, copy your identity statement from Chapter 15 and your vision statement from Chapter 16. Then, considering your identity, vision, values, interests, and passions, write a mission statement. Keep it as short as possible, without sacrificing anything meaningful. Don't repeat your identity statement or your vision statement. Instead, consider the ways you can make a difference and leave the world better than you found it.

This will likely be an iterative process — meaning you might find that after you write a mission statement, you'll need to improve your vision statement to aim high enough to be able to fulfill your mission. Then you might want to adjust your mission statement or even your identity statement — never to embellish any of them but to make them accurate, clear, and concise.

Your mission statement is a statement of your purpose for existing, but it's focused outside of yourself. If you need help starting, use this prompt:

At this time and for my foreseeable future, I can best fulfill God's purpose for my life and have the most positive impact on the world by focusing my efforts on <describe action>. As a result, <describe the desired outcome>.

For example (see Appendix F for more examples):

God's purpose for my life is to communicate the gospel message to the next generation in their language. This includes developing a curriculum on how to successfully communicate the gospel to teens and young adults and teach it to other believers. As a result, many people will come to know God and their True Identity.

BLUEPRINT SPACE

| Name: | **Action Plan** | Date: |

Identity Statement (Chapter 15)
Who I am but not specifically what I do

Vision Statement (Chapter 16)
Who I can be in the future, seeing myself through God's loving eyes

Top 7 Values	Top 7 Interests	Top 7 Passions
1)	1)	1)
2)	2)	2)
3)	3)	3)
4)	4)	4)
5)	5)	5)
6)	6)	6)
7)	7)	7)

Mission Statement
How I'll use my Confident Identity to make a difference in the world

For Reflection

1. "A winner is someone who recognizes his God-given talents, works his tail off to develop them into skills, and uses these skills to accomplish his goals." —Larry Bird
2. Are you prepared to dedicate your life to what you're passionate about?
3. What will it take to attain your vision and your mission?
4. Does your mission include being married or being single?
5. As all Christians grow in their Confident Identity, the time will pass quickly as God's plans will come to fruition. Then, we'll all be together in heaven, fully knowing each other and fully knowing God.

Next Steps

- Review your Action Plan. What themes stand out to you? What is consistent across multiple areas? Pray and ask God for understanding. If you've gained any new insights, revise your plan accordingly. Remember to regularly revisit your identity, vision, and mission statements to make sure you're still moving in the right direction — do this especially when you sense your passion is fading. Your values, interests, and passions are the most volatile clues to your identity. You should reassess them about every three to six months. They can point to your identity, but they aren't part of your identity.
- Put together a plan for reaching your mission's goals. What help (people, resources, etc.) do you need?
- If you're trying to find a career direction, read The Next Step for Your Career on the next page.
- Media for Further Learning (see Appendix B for more questions)
  - Movie: *The Passion of the Christ*. Note how Jesus stays focused on His mission.
  - Movie: *Gladiator*. Note how Maximus stays focused on his mission.
  - Music: *Nothing Is Wasted* by Jason Gray
  - Read "Make Your Passion Follow You" at successmentor.com/make-your-passion-follow-you
  - Read Frank Borg's sermon "Godly Enthusiasm" at fcogl.org/english/christian_living/enthusiasm.pdf

The Next Step for Your Career

Are you reading this book to decide on a college major or a new career? Now that you've developed a mission statement, you should revisit Chapters 13 and 14 in the context of your mission. Search online using phrases like "MBTI career choices" and "Holland career choices."

Many people are unsatisfied with their jobs. When this happens, what is the first thing most people do? They look for another job. Frequently, this approach results in the person being dissatisfied again in months or maybe one or two years down the road. Why? Because a "job" is primarily a means to cover the bills that need to be paid in order to survive. While this idea is important, it emphasizes a short-term outlook on a life made for God's purposes.

Instead, I suggest a long-term approach that involves more up-front work. With this approach, you'll do well if you can identify your "life mission" apart from any specific career or job.

While the purpose of this book isn't necessarily to help you find your next job, examining how job relates to mission will help you understand how to define your mission:

- **Mission (or "Calling" or "Vocation"):** The purpose(s) for which God created you.
- **Career:** An area of occupational focus which you're well-suited to work in; however, career stops short of looking at any specific job. A person may have multiple careers in a lifetime.
- **Job:** A job at a specific company at a specific location. A person may have multiple jobs while pursuing a career.

Knowing your life mission will allow you to most effectively find satisfying careers and ultimately best-fit jobs. There will be more than one career that can fulfill your life mission, and there will be more than one job that will match your career choice.

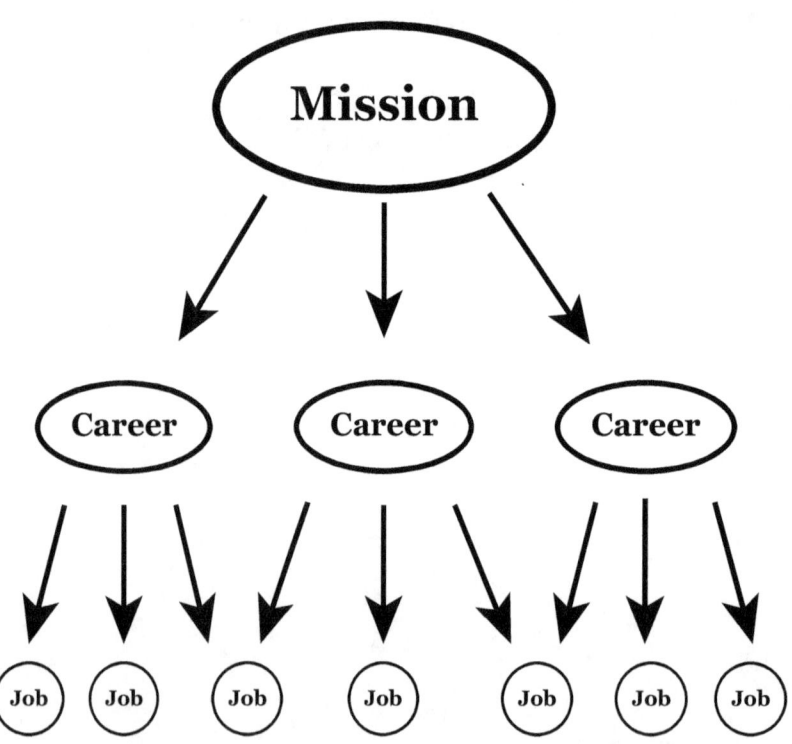

Supplemental Material

                          Closing Thoughts

Appendix A   **You 2.0 Prayer**

Appendix B   **Movie and Music List**

Appendix C   **Spiritual Identity Scriptures**

Appendix D   **Values Cutouts**

Appendix E   **Discover More Interests**

Appendix F   **Example Statements**

                          Selected Bibliography

                          Index of Scriptures

Closing Thoughts

For this reason I remind you to fan into flame the gift of God, which is in you through the laying on of my hands. For the Spirit God gave us does not make us timid, but gives us power, love and self-discipline. So do not be ashamed of the testimony about our Lord or of me his prisoner. Rather, join with me in suffering for the gospel, by the power of God. He has saved us and called us to a holy life—not because of anything we have done but because of his own purpose and grace. This grace was given us in Christ Jesus before the beginning of time, but it has now been revealed through the appearing of our Savior, Christ Jesus, who has destroyed death and has brought life and immortality to light through the gospel. And of this gospel I was appointed a herald and an apostle and a teacher. That is why I am suffering as I am. Yet this is no cause for shame, because I know whom I have believed, and am convinced that he is able to guard what I have entrusted to him until that day.

What you heard from me, keep as the pattern of sound teaching, with faith and love in Christ Jesus. Guard the good deposit that was entrusted to you—guard it with the help of the Holy Spirit who lives in us.
—2 Timothy 1:6–14

Does achieving your vision sometimes feel far away? Press on. Don't hesitate. Don't hold back. The truth that God entrusts you with is special and of the utmost importance.

God blesses you with the gift of physical and spiritual life which is essentially your identity. God has set you free. Use your identity to make a difference. He deposits with you revelation of the truth through His Holy Spirit so you can in turn entrust God with your whole self.[28] Your life is in God's hands. At the same time, the gospel message is in your hands.

Grow where God plants you. Your environment is always changing. A changing environment is food for the hungry brain. You can fulfill God's calling no matter where you're physically located. You can find outcasts who need Christ next door, or you can find them around the world.

What Jesus has done for us goes beyond saving us from a negative, to providing entrance into glorious life and immortality. This is too amazing to completely comprehend. When you choose to be friends with God, you'll experience suffering because the world will reject you (John 15:18–19). Hold tightly to the truth because it anchors you in the midst of the storm.

Don't stop seeking to understand God's identity. Don't stop seeking to understand and use your identity. God created you to do great things. Be confident in the identity God gave you.

And I am sure of this, that he who began a good work in you will bring it to completion at the day of Jesus Christ.
—Philippians 1:6

---

[28] biblehub.com/commentaries/2_timothy/1-12.htm

Next Steps

What next? How can you continue to position yourself to grow and become everything God made you to be? Seek out other people who want to grow in their identity and learn from each other.

Identity Checkup

Return at least once a year to this book for a checkup. We all tend to drift off center when we take our eyes off the goal. During your checkup, review the past year and then plan for the next year. These questions will help with that process. In the past year, with respect to your identity:

- What are the top positive and negative experiences you endured? What unexpected blessings did you have? What difficulties or challenges? Append your experiences to your Life Experiences Exercise from Chapter 7. Have your experiences illuminated your True Identity any further?
- What are the most significant things you wanted to accomplish but didn't?
- What are the most significant things you learned about yourself?
- Review your identity, vision, and mission statements. How have you grown? How has your perspective changed? How have your values, interests, or passions changed in the past year? Is God moving you in a new direction? Update your statements based on everything that has changed.

Further Study Resources and Help

ConfidentIdentity.com

Visit for: More about identity, including bonus material for this book. I'm planning to have an online assessment that pulls together all the ideas from this book into one place.

ChristianConcepts.com

Visit for: News and information about upcoming publications and products. Additional material about individual and marital growth. Opportunities to ask questions and post comments.

NewReflectionsCounseling.com

Visit for: Coaching, counseling, and other more intensive help is available. Do you need career counseling or life coaching? Would intensive counseling be of value to you?

MarriageFromRootsToFruits.com

Visit for: Information about my first book on preparing for and having a better marriage.

MattPavlik.pro

Visit for: Learning what else I'm up to as an author, counselor, and software developer.

Feedback

I hope you found *Confident Identity* to be a helpful tool on your growth journey. If you've enjoyed this book, will you consider sharing the message with others?

- Recommend this book to those in your small group, book club, workplace, or classes.
- Write a book review on Amazon or Goodreads.
- Mention via a Pinterest pin, Facebook post, blog post, or picture on Instagram.
- Tweet "I recommend reading #confidentidentity by @newreflectionz."

I'll gladly receive your comments and feedback about this book. If you have a specific question you're wondering about or need some further direction, don't hesitate to contact me — I'll do the best I can to help. Contact me at mpavlik@nrcounseling.com or visit one of the websites above for more information.

Appendix A — You 2.0 Prayer

"Lord Jesus, I know that I have fallen short of your perfect standard and I don't deserve eternal life. But I believe you paid the full penalty for my sin when you died and rose from the grave. I surrender control of my life to You. Jesus, come into my life, take control of my life, forgive my sins, and save me. I place my trust in You for my salvation, and I accept Your free gift of eternal life. Now, having accepted Your gift, I'm a new creation that will live with You for all eternity. I further welcome Your Holy Spirit into my heart to mold my identity into Your image."

If you prayed this prayer for the first time, all the blessings of a Confident Identity are yours.

Appendix B — Movie and Music List

This appendix lists the movies and songs found in each chapter.

Movies

For each movie, I've included a few words to describe its theme and any cautions. The ratings span from G to R. The R movies are rated for intense violence or trauma necessary to tell the story. However, some movies have offensive material. If you have concerns, research the movies before you watch them.

Use these questions to help you organize your experience into a plan for growth:
1. What are the main themes and principles of the movie?
2. With which character do you identify most? Least?
3. How does the movie support the current chapter you're reading?
4. How does this movie speak to the reason you're reading this book?
5. How has your understanding of identity changed?
6. In what ways did the movie inspire you?
7. How will you live differently based on what you learned?

Chapter	Movie	Year	Themes	Rating
1	The Lion King	1994	Finding your identity	G
2	Evan Almighty	2007	Leading, following; faith, trust	PG
	Toy Story	1995	Discovering and accepting who you really are	G
3	The Shawshank Redemption	1994	Hope and perseverance	R; graphic pictures of prison rape
	The Matrix	1999	Choose what is true over what is false	R; sci-fi violence and brief language
4	The Truman Show	1998	Confidence vs self-doubt	PG
	The King's Speech	2010	Confidence vs self-doubt	R; some language
5	Groundhog Day	1993	Self-awareness; growth is fun	PG
	The Lord of the Rings trilogy	2001	Perseverance; teamwork, trust	PG-13
6	Back to the Future trilogy	1985	Confidence vs self-doubt; self-control	PG
	A Beautiful Mind	2001	Sorting fact from fiction	PG-13
7	Ragamuffin	2014	Inadequacy; addiction	PG-13
	Up	2009	Enjoying the moment you have; no regrets	PG
8	Beauty and the Beast (Disney)	1991	Intimacy; beauty isn't skin deep	G
9	none	-	-	-
10	Inside Out	2015	Emotion's role in healing	PG
11	I'm Not Ashamed	2016	Making Jesus a priority	PG-13
	Slumdog Millionaire	2008	Growing up without parents; perseverance	R; graphic pictures of abuse and neglect
12	none	-	-	-
13	The Incredibles	2004	Distinct abilities; teamwork	PG
	Bridge to Terabithia	2007	True friendship	PG

14	*How to Train Your Dragon*	2010	Be yourself; use your strengths	PG
	Simon Birch	1998	Purpose; significance	PG
15	*Prince of Egypt*	1998	Choosing between Earthly and True Identity	PG
16	*The Dark Knight* (Batman trilogy)	2005	What is identity?	PG-13
	The Butterfly Circus	2009	Overcoming limitations	NR (PG)
17	*Curious George*	2006	Innocence; attachment	G
	The Ultimate Gift	2006	Finding meaning and purpose	PG
18	*The Passion of the Christ*	2004	Jesus' life and sacrifice	R; graphic depiction of crucifixion
	Gladiator	2000	Fighting for what is important; self-sacrifice; legacy	R; war violence

Additional movies to consider: Sybil, Identity, Dances with Wolves, Nacho Libre.

Music

Most of these songs can apply to any chapter, but I listed them one per chapter so you can gain encouragement from music throughout the book.

Chapter	**Song**	**Year**	**Theme**	**Artist**
1	*I'll Lead You Home*	1995	Don't worry; God will lead you	Michael W. Smith
2	*You Are I Am*	2012	God is sovereign, almighty	MercyMe
3	*I Have This Hope*	2016	Don't despair or fear; have hope	Tenth Avenue North
4	*Hard Love*	2016	Let your old self die	Needtobreathe
5	*Remind Me Who I am*	2011	Be reminded of your true identity	Jason Gray
	Who I am	2015		Blanca
6	*No Longer Slaves*	2015	You're a child of God	J Helser; M Helser
7	*One Step Away*	2016	Don't be ashamed	Casting Crowns
8	*Beautiful*	2013	You're beautiful even at your worst	Plumb
9	*My Lighthouse*	2014	God is absolute truth, peace	Rend Collective
10	*Keep Making Me*	2012	Empty to be filled by God	Sidewalk Prophets
11	*Never Been a Moment*	2016	I'm always loved by God	Micah Tyler
12	*Overcomer*	2013	You're an overcomer	Mandissa
13	*Greater*	2014	Redeemed (not wrong)	Mercy Me
14	*Tell Me*	2015	Tell me who I am (loved)	Carrollton
15	*All That Matters*	2017	You matter to God	Colton Dixon
16	*Tell the Mountain*	2013	God is bigger than your problems	Back Home/Collingsworth
17	*Live It Well*	2016	Life is short; live it well	Switchfoot
18	*Nothing Is Wasted*	2011	God uses all of you	Jason Gray

Appendix C — Spiritual Identity Scriptures

I am redeemed from the curse of the law.	Galatians 3:13–14
I am free from the written code, the law, and its regulations.	Colossians 2:14
I am free because of the truth.	John 8:32
I am a new creation.	2 Corinthians 5:17
I am redeemed and forgiven.	Ephesians 1:7
I am dead to sin but alive to God.	Romans 6:2, 11
I am free from all condemnation.	Romans 8:1
I am holy and blameless in God's sight.	Ephesians 1:4
I am a royal priest. I belong to God.	1 Peter 2:4–10
I am the dwelling place of God.	Ephesians 2:19–22
I am God's workmanship, created in Christ Jesus to do good works.	Ephesians 2:10
I am saved by God's grace, not by anything I do.	Ephesians 2:9
I always triumph in Christ.	2 Corinthians 2:14
I am the righteousness of God through Christ	2 Corinthians 5:21
I am enriched in every way; I do not lack any spiritual gift in Christ.	1 Corinthians 1:5–7
I have the mind of Christ.	1 Corinthians. 2:16
I have been rescued from the dominion of darkness, brought into Christ's kingdom.	Colossians 1:13
My God will meet all my needs according to the glorious riches in Christ Jesus.	Philippians 4:19
I can do everything through God who gives me strength.	Philippians 4:13
I am being made into God's image . . . the completion of which is guaranteed.	Philippians 1:6
I am a child of God; God is my Father; I am an heir of God, co-heir with Christ.	Romans 8:16–17
I am sealed with the Holy Spirit, a deposit guaranteeing my inheritance.	Ephesians 1:13–14
I am born again of imperishable seed. I will live forever.	1 Peter 1:23
I am complete in Christ.	Colossians 2:10
I am chosen and loved by God.	1 Thess. 1:4
I have abundant life.	John 10:10
I know Christ, His voice, and He knows me.	John 10:14–16
I am a conqueror.	Romans 8:37
I have all I need to abound in every good work.	2 Corinthians 9:8
Designs to harm me shall fail.	Isaiah 54:17
My worries are over.	1 Peter 5:7
Fear is not my practice.	2 Timothy 1:7
I have plans, a hope, and a future.	Jeremiah 29:11

Appendix D — Values Cutouts

Appendix E — Discover More Interests

Things you really love doing

1)
2)
3)
4)
5)
6)
7)
8)
9)

Hobbies you love or would love to try

1)
2)
3)
4)
5)
6)
7)
8)
9)

Things that make you feel good

1)
2)
3)
4)
5)
6)
7)
8)
9)

Activities that energize you

1)
2)
3)
4)
5)
6)
7)
8)
9)

Things you like to do while on vacation

1)
2)
3)
4)
5)
6)
7)
8)
9)

Activities that de-stress you

1)
2)
3)
4)
5)
6)
7)
8)
9)

Things you enjoy learning or want to learn

1)
2)
3)
4)
5)
6)
7)
8)
9)

Skills you have, things you know you're good at

1)
2)
3)
4)
5)
6)
7)
8)
9)

Subjects you most enjoy reading about

1)
2)
3)
4)
5)
6)
7)
8)
9)

Appendix F — Example Statements

I provided the following examples to help you write your statements. But don't closely model your statements after these. Remember, identity is who you are (not what you do specifically). Vision is who you will be according to God's design. Finally, mission is specifically what you'll do to make the world a better place.

Example #1

Identity Statement

I'm known and befriended by the king of everything; therefore, He helps me according to my needs. I am both smart and merciful, and I can easily use my fun-loving intuition to:
- Think of awesome ideas
- Encourage people with my optimistic spirit and sense of humor
- See the big picture as I go through life

I enjoy a challenge and the satisfaction of giving my all, so I try my hardest in most everything I do. A community with good friends is important to me.

Vision Statement

I will be my best self as I show others hope and joy. I'll meet more people and become more open to relationships. Wherever God has me living, playing, or working, I will brighten another's day and allow them to brighten mine.

Mission Statement

I help people who are hurting by giving them a chance. I encourage unlikely people who are feeling lonely by loving them and showing them that they matter. I use my creativity to invent new ideas that help others enjoy living.

Example #2

Identity Statement

I'm saved and loved by God. He has given me talents such as being sensitive to the needs of others and being loyal and caring. I'm intelligent and willing to help others with anything they might need. I'm able to encourage my friends when they have an emotional problem or serve them if they need some work done.

Vision Statement

I will grow in my ability to be sensitive to others' needs. With God's help, I'll become more aware of what they need before they ask. I'll be closer to God, stronger in my identity, and ready to be there for those around me who need it.

Mission Statement

God's purpose for my life is to help people with their emotional or physical problems. By doing so, I will show them God's love. I will use my love for animals to help others overcome their emotional wounds.

Example #3

Identity Statement

I am a daughter of God. God created me in love and purposed me for significant work. God blessed me with artistic ability, strength, coordination, and flexibility. I enjoy teaching others in ways they can easily grasp the ideas that are important to their lives.

Vision Statement

I will work hard to stay in shape. My goal is to continually increase my skills so that I'm able to teach others what I've learned. I will grow in my identity and character by studying the Bible with other women.

Mission Statement

God's purpose for my life is to bring joy to others through physical arts. I share the image of God through beautifully choreographed dance. As an expert choreographer, I teach others the skills they need to excel in the physical arts. While pouring my life into others, I will share God as the great Choreographer. As a result, many people will praise God and put their faith in Jesus.

Example #4

Identity Statement

I am a son of God: God created me with love and purposed me for significant work. With my analytical ability, I can understand how anything works. God has gifted me with the ability to discern right from wrong in another's heart.

Vision Statement

I will grow in understanding God's truth so I can communicate it to others who are thinkers like me. Others will feel they are not alone when I'm around. I will use my gift of discernment to protect others from those influenced by evil.

Mission Statement

God's purpose for my life is to lead the hearts of others, first and foremost my wife and children. I devote my effort to discipling others so they can genuinely understand who God is. As a result, many people will become strong in their True Identity.

Selected Bibliography

Alberti, R., & Emmons, M. (2008). *Your Perfect Right*. Impact Publishers.
Allender, D. B. (1990). *The Wounded Heart*. NavPress.
Allender, D. B., & Longman III, T. (1994). *The Cry Of The Soul*. NavPress.
Benner, D. (2003). *Surrender To Love*. InterVarsity Press.
Bolles, R. N. (2015). *What Color Is Your Parachute 2016*.
Carter, L., & Minirth, F. (1993). *The Anger Workbook*. Thomas Nelson Publishers.
Clarke, J. I., & Dawson, C. (1998). *Growing Up Again*. Hazelden.
Clinton, T., & Straub, J. (2010). *God Attachment*. Howard Books.
Cloud, H. (1995). *Changes That Heal*. HarperPaperbacks.
Cloud, H. (2011). *The Law Of Happiness*. Howard Books.
Cloud, H., & Townsend, J. (2001). *How People Grow*. Zondervan.
Covey, S. R. (1990). *The 7 Habits Of Highly Effective People*. Simon & Schuster.
Craab, L. (1991). *Men & Women*. Zondervan Publishing House.
Crabb, L. (1988). *Inside Out*. Navpress.
Dallas, J. (2003). *Desires In Conflict*.
Dolan, Y. (2000). *One Small Step*. Authors Choice Press.
Eggerichs, E. (2004). *Love and Respect*. Thomas Nelson.
Eldredge, J. (2011). *Beautiful Outlaw*. Hachette Book Group.
Erikson, E. H. (1968). *Identity Youth and Crisis*.
Erikson, E. H. (1993). *Childhood and Society*. W W Norton & Company.
Groom, N. (1991). *From Bondage to Bonding*. NavPress.
Grudem, W. (2002). *Biblical Foundations for Manhood and Womanhood*. (W. Grudem, Ed.) Crossway.
Hamilton, N. G. (1990). *Self and Others*.
Heller, D. P. (2014). Somatic Attachment Trainings (dianepooleheller.com).
Hemfelt, R., & Warren, P. (1990). *Kids Who Carry Our Pain*. Thomas Nelson.
Horner, A. J. (1979). *Object Relations and the Developing Ego in Therapy*.
Jakes, T. D. (2015). *Identity*.
Johnson, R. (1995). *Your Personality and the Spiritual Life*.
Jung, C. G. (1990). *Psychological Types*.
Keirsey, D., & Bates, M. (1984). *Please Understand Me*.
Kise, J. A., Stark, D., & Hirsh, S. K. (2005). *Discover Who You Are*.
Kolk, B. v. (2014). *The Body Keeps the Score*.
Lahaye, T. (1991). *Transforming Your Temperament*.
McGee, R. (1998). *The Search For Significance*. Thomas Nelson.
Medinger, A. (2000). *Growth Into Manhood*.
Morgan, R. L. (2002). *Remembering Your Story*.
Myers, I. B. (1995). *Gifts Differing*.
Nicolosi, J., & Nicolosi, L. A. (2002). *A Parent's Guide to Preventing Homosexuality*.
Pascal, B. (1958). *Pascal's Pensees*.
Posthuma, D. A. (2008). *Made for a Mission*.
Pulaski, M. A. (1971). *Understanding Piaget*. Harper & Row.
Rath, T. (2007). *Strengths Finder 2.0*.
Seamands, D. (1990). *Living With Your Dreams*. Victor.

Shapiro, F. (2012). *Getting Past Your Past.* Rodale.
Siegel, D. J. (2012). *The Developing Mind.* The Guilford Press.
Smedes, L. (1993). *Shame & Grace.* HarperOne.
Smith, H. W. (1994). *The 10 Natural Laws of Successful Time and Life Management.* Warner Books.
Springle, P. (1994). *Trusting.* Servant Publications.
Stoop, D. (2004). *Making Peace With Your Father.*
Thrall, B., McNicol, B., & Lynch, J. (2004). *TrueFaced.*
Wardle, T. (2005). *Wounded.* Leafwood.
Wardle, T. (2009). Formational Prayer Seminar. Healing Care Ministries (healingcare.org).
Warren, R. (2002). *Purpose Driven Life.*
Wilson, S. (1992). *Shame Free Parenting.* InterVarsity Press.
Wilson, S. (2002). *Released From Shame.* InterVarsity Press.

Index of Scriptures

Genesis
- 1:27 — 13, 116
- 1:27–28 — 95
- 1:28 — 171
- 3:1–7 — 20
- 3:8 — 50
- 4:8 — 55
- 3:14–24 — 50, 51
- 15:1–6 — 64

Exodus
- 3:14 — 171
- 14:16 — 30
- 18:13–27 — 131
- 18:24–26 — 131
- 31:1–6 — 90

Leviticus

Numbers
- 13:1–33 — 164
- 13:30 — 131
- 13:30–33 — 130
- 27:17 — 130

Deuteronomy

Joshua

Judges

Ruth

1 Samuel
- 25:3–31 — 111

2 Samuel
- 11 — 111
- 12:1–15 — 130
- 12:9–10 — 130
- 23:8–39 — 89

1 Kings
- 3:28 — 128

2 Kings

1 Chronicles

2 Chronicles

Ezra

Nehemiah

Esther
- 1:12 — 89

Job
- 13:15 — 63

Psalm
- 18 — 116
- 23 — 116
- 23:6 — 30
- 40:2 — 119
- 42 — 70
- 55 — 64, 70
- 56:3–4 — 28
- 77:20 — 130
- 118 — 25
- 119:105 — 120
- 127:1a — 1
- 139 — 19, 59, 116
- 139:13–16 — 20
- 139:15 — 12
- 139:7–16 — 119
- 139:23–24 — 12
- 145:19 — 176

Proverbs
- 11:22 — 88
- 13:11 — 178
- 15:22 — 3
- 16:7 — 46
- 16:25 — 175
- 22:24–25 — 38
- 24:3–4 — 1

Ecclesiastes

Song of Solomon

Isaiah
- 9:2 — 120
- 40:28–31 — 185
- 40:31 — 179
- 43:18–19 — 186
- 54:17 — 201

Jeremiah
- 2:13 — 53
- 17:9 — 80
- 29:10–14 — 61
- 29:11 — 61, 119, 201
- 30:11–17 — 62

Lamentations

Ezekiel
- 36:26 — 116

Daniel

Hosea

Joel

Amos

Obadiah

Jonah

Micah

Nahum

Habakkuk

Zephaniah
- 3:17 — 117

Haggai

Zechariah

Malachi

Matthew
- 3 — 95
- 3:16–17 — 67
- 3:17 — 116
- 4:1–4 — 179
- 5 — 12, 129
- 5:13–16 — 12, 13
- 6:33 — 67
- 7:1–5 — 67
- 7:28–29a — 129
- 8:5–13 — 131
- 10:14 — 65
- 10:29–31 — 116
- 12:43–44 — 66
- 13:24–30 — 16
- 13:44–45 — 186
- 16:15–17 — 172
- 16:16–18 — 121
- 16:25 — 28, 178, 181
- 17:20 — 69
- 18:3 — 177
- 19:12 — 97
- 25:1–13 — 175
- 25:14–30 — 76
- 25:23 — 76
- 25:26–27 — 77
- 28:20 — 117

Mark
- 12:31 — 170
- 12:43–44 — 127

Luke
- 2:36–38 — 95
- 6:47–49 — 29, 31
- 9:46–48 — 167
- 10:30 — 129
- 12:15–21 — 32
- 15:11–32 — 14
- 15:20–24 — 117
- 16:19–31 — 35
- 22:54–62 — 120, 167

John
- 3:1–16 — 23
- 4:34 — 67
- 7 — 179
- 8:32 — 201
- 8:39–47 — 16
- 8:58 — 171
- 9:3 — 97
- 10:1–10 — 133
- 10:10 — 30, 201
- 10:14–16 — 201
- 12:24 — 179
- 14:12 — 22, 25, 119
- 14:12–14 — 22, 25
- 15:13 — 178
- 15:18–19 — 195
- 15:1–11 — 24
- 15:18–25 — 65
- 16:13 — 44, 80
- 21 — 15, 167
- 21:17b, 19b — 121
- 21:21–22 — 167

Acts
- 2:1–12 — 129
- 3:6–7 — 128
- 4:36–37 — 130
- 5:1–3 — 129
- 6:2–3 — 127
- 8 — 132
- 8:19–21 — 125
- 8:6, 7 — 131
- 9:17–18 — 24
- 9:26–27 — 130
- 10:46 — 130, 132
- 15:36–41 — 130
- 15:38 — 110
- 17:26 — 19, 119

Romans
- 1:1–5 — 132
- 4:16–25 — 64
- 5:6 — 179
- 5:6–8 — 178
- 5:12, 15 — 23
- 6:17–18 — 179
- 6:2, 11 — 201
- 6:23 — 55
- 8:1 — 10, 201
- 8:1–11 — 10
- 8:16–17 — 201
- 8:23–25 — 29
- 8:28 — 28, 61
- 8:29–30 — 119
- 8:35–39 — 13, 117
- 8:37 — 201
- 9:19–21 — 22
- 12 — 53, 126, 127, 129, 130
- 12:2–3 — 54
- 12:3 — 78, 165
- 12:6–8 — 126

1 Corinthians
- 1:5–7 — 201
- 2:9 — 22, 166
- 2:9–10 — 166
- 3:10–15 — 68
- 6:18–20 — 90
- 7:7 — 95
- 12 — 13, 126, 127, 128, 129, 130, 131, 132
- 12:14–26 — 118
- 12:24b–25 — 94
- 12:4–7 — 115

12:7	125	1:16–17	24
13:11–12	24	2:10	201
13:12	10, 79	2:14	201
13:4–7	117	1 Thessalonians	
14:3	130	2 Thessalonians	
14:4	130	1 Timothy	
15:33	38	4:14	130
2 Corinthians		2 Timothy	
1:21–22	119	1:6–8	119
1:22	13	1:6–14	195
2:14	201	1:7	119, 201
5:17	115, 116, 201	3:16a	80
5:21	201	4:11	110, 127
6:14	16	Titus	
9:7	127	Philemon	
9:8	201	Hebrews	
10:4–5	28	4:13	46
12:1–10	24	11:6	34, 77
12:7	9	11:13–16	180
12:9	22, 158	11:17–19	131
Galatians		12:1–2	180
1:11–12	128	13:5	117
3:13–14	201	James	
4:3–7	13, 116	1:17	163
4:6	119	2:14–26	164
Ephesians		1 Peter	
1:3	115	1:23	201
1:4	201	2:4–10	201
1:7	201	2:5	125
1:11	13, 61, 119	3:1–6	89
1:13–14	116, 201	3:3–4	89
2:10	10, 14, 25, 68, 201	3:14	120
2:19–22	201	3:15–16	180
2:20	125	4:12	179
2:6	116	5:1–3	130
2:9	201	5:7	63, 201
3:16	13	2 Peter	
3:16–21	119	1:3–4	185
4	130, 131, 132, 133	1:5–10	186
4:11	132	1 John	
4:11–16	149	3:1	115, 116
4:14	163	3:16	178
4:22–24	10	4:8	25
5:22–33	95	2 John	
6:10–12	120	3 John	
6:10–18	119	Jude	
Philippians		Revelation	
1:6	119, 195, 201	2:17	160
1:21–26	31		
2:3–4	170		
4:13	201		
4:19	201		
Colossians			
1:13	201		

Confident Identity Bonuses

Go to http://www.confidentidentity.com/bonus to access your bonuses. Download worksheets found in this book. Eventually, you'll be able to take the self-assessments found in this book.

About Matt Pavlik

Matt Pavlik is a licensed professional clinical counselor who wants to see each individual restored to their true identity. He's written two books: one on identity (ConfidentIdentity.com) and the other on marriage (MarriageFromRootsToFruits.com). He has more than 15 years of experience counseling individuals and couples at his Christian counseling practice, New Reflections Counseling (NewReflectionsCounseling.com). He completed his Masters in Clinical Pastoral Counseling from Ashland Theological Seminary and his Bachelors in Computer Science from the University of Illinois. Matt and his wife Georgette have been married over 18 years and live with their four children in Centerville, Ohio.

Matt's mission is to use the wisdom he receives from God to help others understand God's design for life. Learn more at ChristianConcepts.com and MattPavlik.pro.

Also by Matt Pavlik

Will W Alejandro, MDiv, MA had this to say:

As I read through Matt's book, *Marriage From Roots to Fruits*, I felt hopeful. I thought of all the couples I have met along the way who looked at their relationship, present and future, with a sense of futility and hopelessness. The author gives details of God's design for a healthy relationship, with very practical tools, filled with real life examples to encourage them along the path of healing and living victoriously.

I have not read a book (manual) like it before. I believe it will help couples who are at the point of hopelessness and emotional pain to truly heal. I also feel it is very applicable for married couples who feel good about the relationship they have but want to have a stronger and deeper relationship with God and with themselves. Matt designed the book to be a tool for pastors and counselors, to use as a guide for premarital counseling, and to help hurting marriages. I feel that this book is a must-read for all caregivers.

www.ingramcontent.com/pod-product-compliance
Lightning Source LLC
Chambersburg PA
CBHW060511300426
44112CB00017B/2625